the **SOUND ON SOUND** book of

MIDI for the technophobe

Design: David Houghton

Printed by Thanet Press Ltd, Margate, Kent

Published by: Sanctuary Publishing Limited, The Colonnades, 82 Bishops Bridge Road, London W2 6BB

ISBN: 1-86074-193-2

the **SOUND ON SOUND** book of

MIDI for the technophobe

paul white

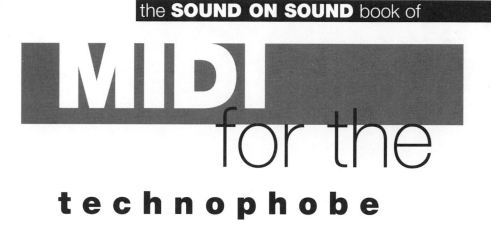

contents

introduction

It is probably no exaggeration to say that MIDI has had a greater effect on the way we create and record music than almost any other event since the introduction of written musical notation. Prior to MIDI, virtually the only way to hear a new musical composition was to have it performed by live musicians, but nowadays musical compositions can be created, recorded and replayed by a single musician using MIDI, sequencers and synthesizers.

The affordability of MIDI equipment has also empowered a vast number of musicians to be able to create and record their own music without the need to use traditional recording studios. Symphonies, pop songs, TV commercials, soundtracks and experimental music may be created by anyone prepared to turn their imagination to music. Indeed, a whole cottage industry has been built up by musicians providing music for TV, film, CDs, tapes, computer games and multimedia presentations.

Traditional keyboard playing skills are still immensely valuable, but because of the flexibility offered by MIDI sequencing, even musicians with very limited technique and no knowledge of traditional musical notation can still bring their ideas to fruition. Some music traditionalists see this as cheating, but this is to overlook the fact that a composer is primarily selling his or her musical ideas, not their musical virtuosity.

Musicians who work daily with MIDI must occasionally wonder how they ever managed without it, but a far greater number of musicians who could reap the benefits of this new technology are frightened off by the jargon, the apparent complexity and the change in working methods required to use it effectively. They're also unsure as to what MIDI can actually help them achieve.

My own first experiences with MIDI were far from comfortable, and ironically, the main problem seemed to be the books that purported to explain the subject! They'd invariably dive in with explanations of bits, bytes, data structure and so on, whereas all I wanted to know was how to use MIDI. You don't have to be able to understand the workings of the internal combustion engine to be able to drive a car, so why should you need to become a computer expert to use MIDI?

After buying my first MIDI system and playing about with it for a few days, I was surprised at how straightforward and logical everything was – but I was even more surprised by the fact that I hadn't needed to know more than a tiny fraction of what current books on MIDI implied I needed to know. The purpose of this book, therefore, is to explore the applications of MIDI in as straightforward and practical a manner as possible by using analogies with familiar everyday processes. In a very short time, you'll have a sound grasp of what goes on in a MIDI system, you'll know what you can expect to achieve, and you'll know how to go about achieving it.

chapter 1

introducing MIDI

Most musicians will be aware that you can use MIDI to help compose and record music, but what is MIDI, what can it help you achieve, and what do you need to buy to get started? While it's very tempting to jump straight in and start talking about MIDI synthesizers, soundcards, keyboards and interfaces, the first step is to try to create an overview of what MIDI is all about, and for that we have to wind the clock back to the early 80s, when in a rare moment of international co-operation, the major manufacturers of synthesizers got together and agreed on a standard system, by means of which, electronic instruments from different manufacturers could be connected together as part of the same system. Their initial aims were relatively modest, and they can hardly have known what an impact MIDI was going to have on music making in the future.

Rather than deluge you with information and then leave you to dig your way out, I'm going to try to explain the general concept of MIDI in terms with which you are already familiar, then, as soon as possible, get you trying things out for yourself. It's one thing reading about a process, but until you see it happen for yourself, it somehow isn't real!

During the many years in which I've been a technical writer, I've encountered hundreds of handbooks for musical instruments, studio equipment, computers, software and so on, and it still astounds me how badly some of them are put together. All too often they jump straight in by throwing facts at you before they've even given you an overview of the equipment in question. The information is all there, but you are often given no indication as to why you might need this information or how best to apply it. I find this approach as difficult as anyone else to deal with, which is why I've always been in favour of explaining the question properly before trying to provide an answer.

I must also confess at this stage that I intend to over-generalise where appropriate, and if there's anything technical which can be safely omitted, then I'm not going to put it in. We all create our own personal 'models' of the world that allow us to get on with life without actually understanding more than the tiniest fraction of what really makes the universe tick. My intent is to do the same for MIDI! There are many definitive works on MIDI, but this isn't one of them – my aim is to help you become a MIDI user, not a computer expert!

why?

Before even attempting to explain MIDI, let's instead see what sort of things we might want to be able to do with it. Indeed, why do we need it at all?

If you are an accomplished piano player who has no interest in recording or multi-part composition, then it's probably fairly safe to say that MIDI is unlikely to play a major part in your life, but even so, don't hang up just yet, because some MIDI sequencers have very advanced score writing facilities which you might find useful. On the other hand, if you play an electric keyboard and would like to put together multi-part compositions featuring the sounds of other instruments, complete with drums and percussion – all without having to hire or coerce other musicians – MIDI sequencing was made for you.

MIDI isn't only applicable to keyboard players, but as the keyboard is the best suited means of generating MIDI information, the majority of MIDI music is made using keyboards. However, there are practical alternatives for musicians who prefer to pluck, bow, blow or hit things, and these will be covered in the chapter on Non-keyboard MIDI Controllers.

a virtual orchestra

Imagine being able to record all the different musical parts of a score from your keyboard, one at a time, then hear them playing together in perfect synchronism, each part played back with the instrument sound of your choice. Furthermore, consider the benefits of being able to pick different sounds to play back the various parts, even after all the recording is complete. Even the simplest MIDI sequencing system will allow you to do this – you have your own virtual orchestra or band at your fingertips. You can also change the tempo of your finished recording without affecting the pitch, you can transpose the piece without affecting the tempo, and you can experiment with the musical arrangement by copying verses and choruses to new locations within the song.

The information that is communicated from a sequencer to a synthesizer via MIDI is exactly the same as that between a composer and a performer, except the medium is computer memory and floppy disks, not a written score, and the instruments are electronic rather than traditional.

the meaning of midi

To see how this is possible, we need to know a little about MIDI. The letters MIDI stand for Musical Instrument Digital Interface – a standard system by means of which, products from different manufacturers may be connected together as part of the same system. Prior to MIDI, there were some attempts at providing ways to connect instruments, but none were entirely standard and all were very limited.

At its simplest, MIDI means that a keyboard player can play several instruments from a single keyboard rather than having to dash around the stage whenever a change of instrument is required. However, shortly after the introduction of MIDI came the MIDI sequencer – a special type of multitrack recorder capable of recording not sound, but MIDI information. Before elaborating on this statement further, we have to take on board a few basic facts about what MIDI does and does not do. I'd also like to assure you that contrary to what some people would have you believe, MIDI is not something that 'takes over' your music or makes your work sound mechanical – it's simply a tool to do a job, and like any tool, it can be used well or it can be used badly.

the keyboard

Whatever type of MIDI system you decide on, you will need a MIDI keyboard, but these need not be expensive. Even if you decide to use an alternative controller, such as a MIDI guitar system, you'll probably still find a keyboard useful. If possible, choose a keyboard that has 'velocity sensitivity' because this will respond like a 'real' instrument in that the harder you hit the keys, the louder the notes will be. If you don't have velocity sensitivity, all the notes will be the same level, like an organ.

You can choose a 'dumb' master keyboard with no inbuilt sounds, or you may choose to use a conventional keyboard synthesizer with built-in sounds as your master. Either will work perfectly well, so the choice is entirely up to you. However, if you choose a keyboard synth for use with a sequencer, it's important that it has a MIDI Local Off facility. Why this should be will be answered later, but for now, don't rush out and buy a synth until you can be sure you can switch it to Local Off mode.

what is midi?

On the outside, MIDI is simply a neat cable connecting two pieces of MIDI equipment, but inside, it's a complicated digital data transmission system that requires quite a lot of specialised computer knowledge to understand fully. Thankfully, the inner workings of MIDI can be largely ignored by the musician using the system in the same way that the workings of an international telephone exchange can be safely ignored by someone trying to phone their grandmother in Australia. In other words, the knowledge required to make use of MIDI bears almost no relationship to the complexity of the underlying technology. Indeed, most of the confusion surrounding MIDI seems to have been engendered by books that try to explain its inner workings in far too much depth.

the midi link

Linking MIDI instruments is accomplished by means of standard MIDI cables – twin-cored, screened cables with five-pin DIN plugs on either end. And again, if you don't know what a DIN plug is, or if you have no desire to further explore the inner world of twin-cored screened cable, it doesn't matter – you just go to the music shop and ask for a MIDI cable. The only technical parameter you need to know is how long you'd like it!

MIDI, we now know, is a standard communication system that enables MIDI equipped electronic instruments to be linked together in a musically useful way, regardless of the model or manufacturer. Like computers, the data is in a digital form – a sort of ultra fast Morse code for machines. The method of MIDI connection, as we shall see shortly, is quite straightforward, but what is more important at this early stage is to appreciate precisely what 'musically useful' information can be passed from one MIDI instrument or device to another.

The following description covers the most important and basic aspects of MIDI but is by no means comprehensive. New concepts will be introduced only when they are needed, and for now, information will be handed out on a strictly 'need to know' basis. There are many excellent books which delve into the more frightening complexities of MIDI, and if having read this book you feel better prepared to tackle them, I will have done what I set out to do.

anatomy of a note

Electronic keyboard instruments are not like acoustic pianos where a physical hammer hits a string causing it to vibrate at whatever pitch it is tuned. Inside an electronic keyboard, the action of pressing a key simply generates electronic messages telling the internal circuitry what note to play and how loud to play it. When a key is depressed on a MIDI keyboard, a signal known as a Note On message is sent, along with a note number identifying the key, and when the key is released, a Note Off message is sent.

This is how the MIDI instrument knows what note to play, when to play, and when to stop playing it. Up to 128 different notes can be handled by MIDI, where each key on the keyboard has its own number.

The loudness of the note depends on how hard the key is hit, which is really the same thing as saying how fast the key is pushed down. This speed or 'velocity' is read by circuitry within the keyboard and used to control the volume of the sound being played. The term Velocity should be committed to memory as it is one piece of MIDI jargon that will crop up time and time again when we're referring to how loud a note is played or how hard a key is struck. The pitch of the note is determined by which key is pressed, though it is quite possible to transpose MIDI data before it reaches its destination – so pressing a middle C doesn't have to result in a C being played by the instrument at the receiving end if that isn't what you want. However, to keep things simple, let's assume that unless otherwise stated, pressing a key results in the corresponding musical note being played.

midi note data

If Pitch, Note On, Note Off and Velocity information all exist in the form of electronic signals, it should be possible to send them along wires to control a MIDI instrument some distance away from the keyboard, and at its most basic, this is exactly what MIDI allows us to do. A small computer inside the keyboard monitors the physical motion of the keys and converts these to MIDI messages, which appear at the MIDI Out socket of the keyboard. If we now plug the MIDI Out of the keyboard we are currently playing (which we call the Master keyboard), into the MIDI In socket of a second MIDI instrument (which we call the Slave), then the slave is able to play the notes as performed on the master keyboard. This simple MIDI connection is shown in Figure 1.1, but don't try it just yet as there are one or two more things to learn first.

MIDI Out: sends information from a controlling MIDI device (master) to other MIDI devices that it is controlling (slaves).

MIDI In: receives MIDI information which is then passed on to the MIDI Thru socket unchanged. However, if any of the incoming information is 'addressed' to the instrument in question, it will act on that MIDI data exactly as if it were being controlled directly from a keyboard.

MIDI Thru: sends a copy of the MIDI In signal allowing several MIDI instruments to be linked together.

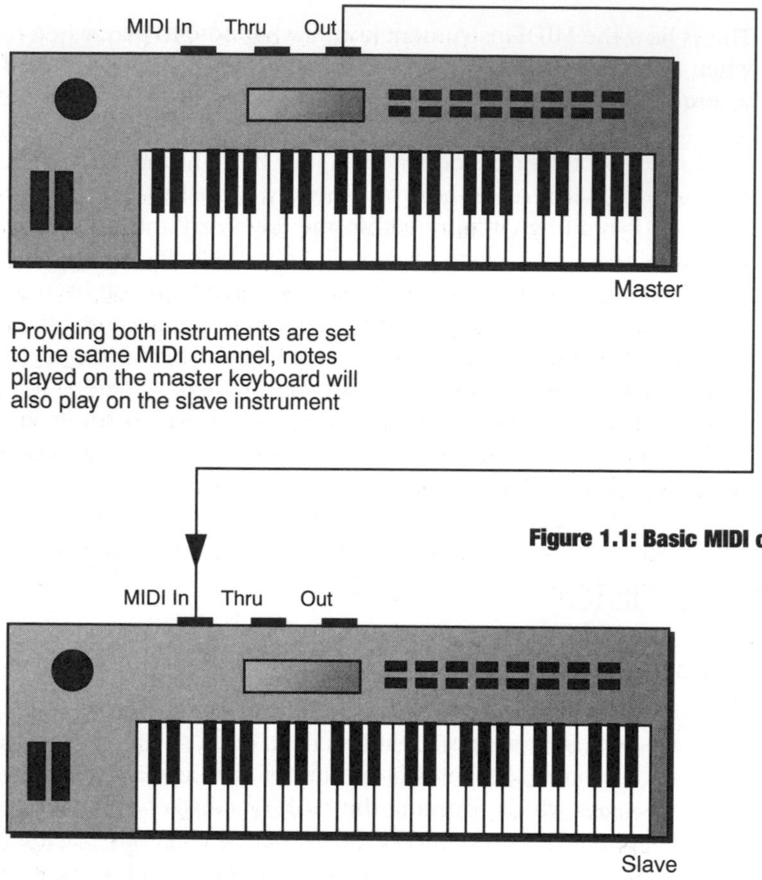

MIDI In
Thru
Out
Master
Providing both instruments are set to the same MIDI channel, notes played on the master keyboard will also play on the slave instrument
MIDI In
Thru
Out
Slave

Figure 1.1: Basic MIDI connection

instructions, not sounds

Before moving on, it's important to understand that MIDI isn't about transmitting sounds – it's about transmitting information that tells the instrument what your fingers were doing on the keyboard. Think of it like one of those paper roll 'player pianos', where the paper roll is the recorded sequence and the piano itself is the sound module. It's surprising how many people listen patiently to a description of MIDI sequencing and then ask if they can record their voice over MIDI as well! There are ways of recording conventional audio into certain computer-based MIDI sequencers, but that part of their operation has nothing at all to do with MIDI and would only serve to confuse the subject if introduced at this time.

the keyboardless synthesizer!

The ability to link a second instrument via MIDI means that the sounds of both instruments can be played from just one keyboard – convenient maybe, but hardly likely to revolutionise music as we know it! However, a little further thought reveals the second instrument doesn't actually need a keyboard at all, because everything is done from the master keyboard.

This leads nicely onto the so-called MIDI module, which is simply the sound generating and MIDI interfacing electronics of a keyboard instrument packaged in a rather more compact, and generally less expensive box. Doing this brings about two very real advantages – we save money because modules are much cheaper to build than full-size keyboard instruments, and we save a lot of space. For example, the electronics for a typical synthesizer module can be made to fit into a box little larger than a box of chocolates. There's also no reason not to control multiple modules from a single master keyboard – but to appreciate the full implications of this, the concept of MIDI channels must be introduced.

MIDI channels are the means by which we 'address' certain messages to be acted upon by specific instruments.

midi channels

In a typical master/slave MIDI system, the daisy chain way in which the instruments are linked means that they all receive the same MIDI information. In order to allow the master instrument to communicate with just one specific slave without all the others trying to play along, the MIDI channel system was devised. The idea is that MIDI note messages are tagged with an invisible address label carrying their MIDI channel number. That way, the messages are only acted upon when they are received by a MIDI instrument or device set to the same MIDI channel number – all other MIDI devices will politely ignore the message. The following explanation may make this clearer.

There are 16 MIDI channels which are, logically enough, numbered 1 to 16 and their concept isn't that different to that of television channels. After all, many different TV broadcasts arrive at the same aerial and reach the TV set down the same piece of wire, but we can only ever see one channel at a time.Which one we actually watch depends on which TV channel we select on the set. The key point here is that all the programmes are fed into the TV set simultaneously, but the channel system allows us to tune into them one at a time.

It's exactly the same with MIDI, where the information sent down the MIDI lead can be sent on any one of 16 channels as selected on the master keyboard. Likewise, the connected instruments may be set to receive on any of the 16 channels, so if we, for example, set the master keyboard to MIDI channel 1 and connect three different MIDI instruments set to receive on channels 1, 2 and 3, only the instrument set to channel 1 will respond. Figure 1.2 shows this arrangement. The others still receive the information, but the MIDI data tells them that the information is not on their channel so they simply ignore it. By switching channels at the master keyboard end, up to 16 different MIDI instruments set to 16 different channels can be addressed individually, even though they are all wired into the same system. The concept of MIDI channels becomes vitally important when we move onto MIDI sequencers. If you feel like trying the example in Figure 1.1 now, go ahead. Just make sure both devices are set to the same MIDI channel.

omni mode warning!

Though this next piece of information shouldn't really appear until much later, I'm introducing it now, because if a MIDI instrument is inadvertently set to Omni mode (an option usually buried in the MIDI setup menu), the system won't behave as you'd expect. As we've already said, most MIDI instruments can be set to receive on any of the 16 MIDI channels, but there is also a setting called Omni mode which allows a MIDI instrument to respond to all incoming data regardless of its channel. In other words, everything that comes along the MIDI cable is played – rather like having one member of an orchestra trying to play all parts of the score at the same time.

Some MIDI equipment, especially older models, tends to default to Omni mode whenever it is switched on, which means you have to set up the correct channel before you can do any work. Fortunately, the vast majority of instruments remember what mode they are in, even if they've been switched off. For normal 16-channel operation, instruments should be set to Poly mode. More about modes later.

more about modules

This book contains separate chapters describing the basic workings of MIDI synthesizers and other MIDI instruments, but there are some aspects of MIDI synthesizer modules that need to be dealt with now in order for everything else to make sense. So far I've described modules as being MIDI synthesizers in boxes but without any keyboard, and in so far as it goes, this definition is true enough. However, a great many modern modules actually contain several independent sound generating sections, each of which can be addressed on a different MIDI channel.

These sound generating sections are often known as Parts, because in a

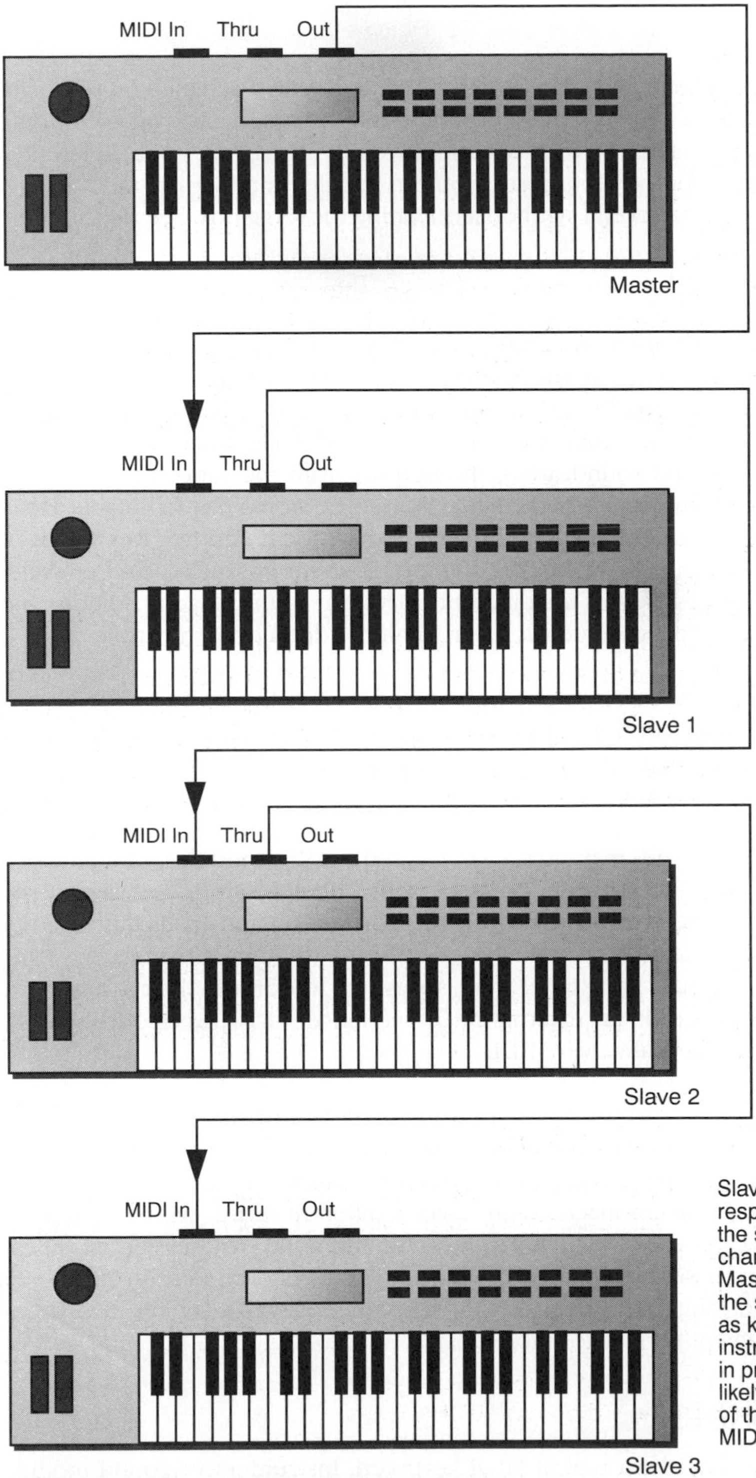

Slaves will only respond if they are on the same MIDI channel as the Master. Note that all the slaves are shown as keyboard instruments, whereas in practice, it is more likely that some or all of them would be MIDI modules

Figure 1.2: Multiple slaves on different MIDI channels

typical system, each section can be made to play a separate musical part. For example, a 16-part multitimbral module can play back up to 16 different musical sounds at the same time, each controlled via a different MIDI channel. For most purposes, you can visualise a multi-part module as being analogous to several synthesizers sharing the same box. See also Soundcards.

multitimbrality

Such multi-part modules are said to be Multitimbral, though the individual synthesizer sections they contain are rarely entirely independent of each other. For example, they all share the same set of front panel controls, and some parameters may affect all the voices globally. What's more, on low cost modules (and soundcards), the outputs from the various parts are usually mixed to stereo and then emerge via a single stereo pair of sockets. However, you'll invariably find that you have independent control over which of the available sounds (or Patches as they call them in synth-speak) are selected, the relative levels of the different voices, the left/right pan positions and the amount of effects (such as reverberation) added to each part.

Samplers also tend to be multitimbral, but at this point in the discussion, they can be considered as just a specialised type of synthesizer. Again, refer to the section on the MIDI instruments for an overview of samplers, sampling and the use of samplers.

Drum machines may also be considered as MIDI modules, though they have their own inbuilt sequencers allowing them to store and replay rhythm patterns and complex arrangements comprising numerous different rhythm patterns. Most drum machines are not multitimbral – that is, they can only play one part at a time. If it is desired to control their sounds from a keyboard or via an external MIDI sequencer, it is possible to access their sounds externally over MIDI.

The main difference between a standard synth patch and the way a drum machine organises its sounds is that a synthesizer tends to interpret incoming MIDI note data as different pitches of the same basic sound, whereas a drum machine produces a different drum, cymbal or percussion sound for each MIDI note. Most multitimbral synthesizer modules and computer soundcards tend to have one part dedicated to drum sounds, so it's no longer essential to buy a separate drum machine. See the MIDI instrument section for more details.

midi sockets

On the back of a typical MIDI keyboard, instrument or sound module are three MIDI sockets labelled MIDI In, MIDI Thru and MIDI Out, though some models may not have all three. It's now time to find out what these are for.

The master instrument in a simple MIDI chain sends information from its MIDI Out socket, which must be connected to the MIDI In socket of the first slave. The MIDI Thru of the first slave is then connected to the MIDI In of the second slave and its Thru connected to the MIDI In of the next one and so on. The result is a daisy chain, and while in theory this can be indefinitely long, this turns out to be untrue in practice. What actually happens is that the MIDI signal deteriorates slightly as it passes through each instrument, and after it has gone through three or four instruments, it starts to become unreliable and notes start getting stuck on, or refuse to play at all. It's rather like the old game of Chinese whispers where you try to pass a message along a line of people to see how much it has changed when it arrives at the other end!

A solution is to use a so-called MIDI Thru box that takes the Out from the master keyboard, then splits it into several Thru connections which feed the individual modules directly. Figure 1.2 shows the standard method of daisy chaining and Figure 1.3 shows the same system wired using a MIDI Thru box. A MIDI Thru Box is a relatively simple and inexpensive device which takes one MIDI input and provides two or more outputs carrying identical signals to the MIDI input data. In effect, it splits a single MIDI signal several ways. Thru boxes may also be used in combination with daisy chaining; if an instrument is fed from a Thru box, its Thru socket may be linked to another module to form a short daisy chain, the only proviso being that these individual chains are no more than one or two devices long.

Some people believe that chaining MIDI Thru connectors causes timing delays, but this is simply not true. Most MIDI delays can be attributed either to too much data being sent at the same time, or to delays within the instruments themselves. For example, some synthesizers take several milliseconds to respond once a MIDI note message has been received. For more on MIDI delays, see the chapter on sequencing.

programs and patches

We've established that MIDI operates on 16 channels and can be used to send note number, timing and velocity information from a MIDI compatible master instrument to a MIDI compatible slave, but what I haven't mentioned yet is that a lot more useful information goes down the wire too!

Modern synthesizers are, in the main, programmable, which means they have the ability to 'remember' many different sounds, each identified by its

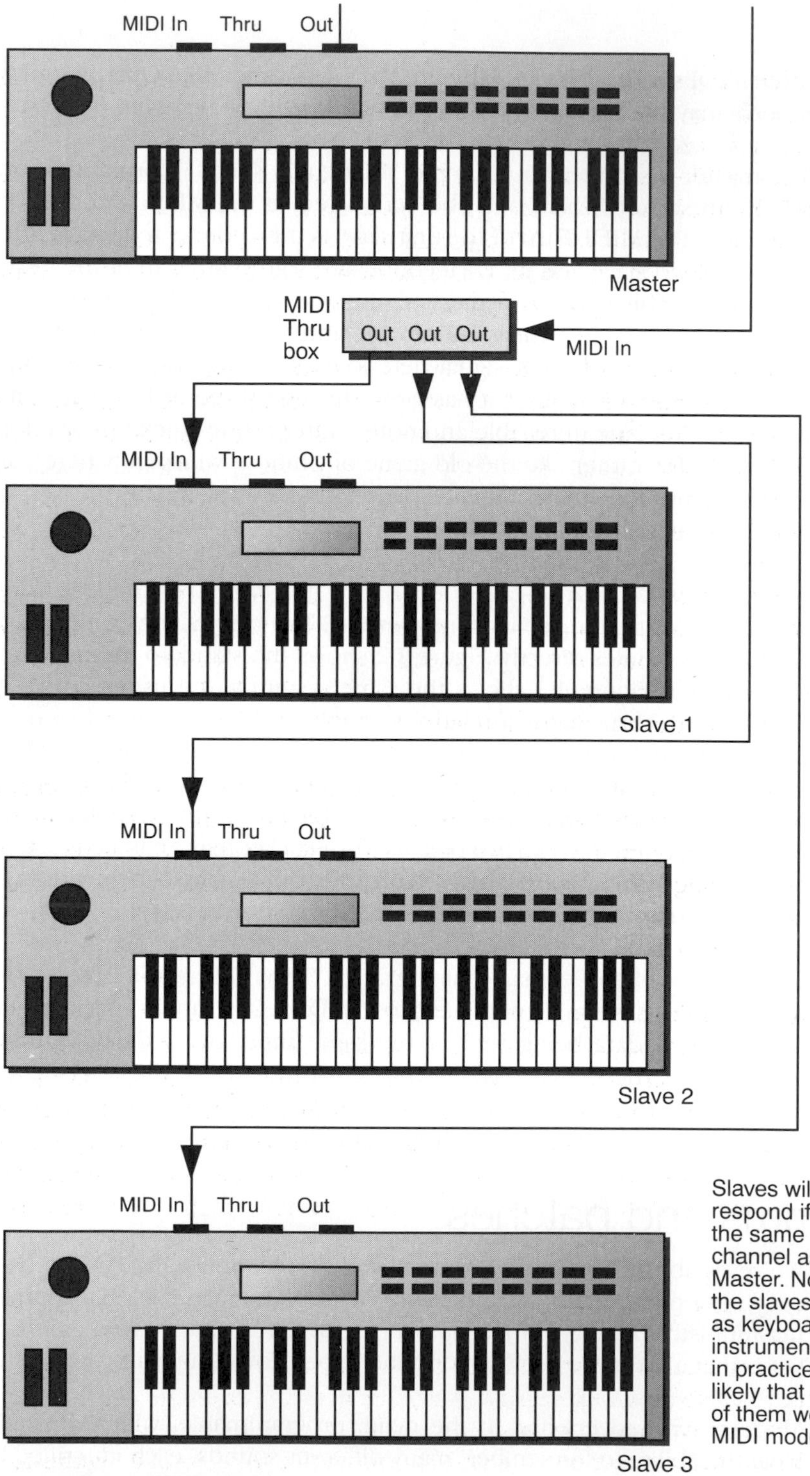

Slaves will only respond if they are on the same MIDI channel as the Master. Note that all the slaves are shown as keyboard instruments, whereas in practice, it is more likely that some or all of them would be MIDI modules

Figure 1.3: Using a MIDI Thru box

patch or program number. The terms Program and Patch tend to be interchangeable. New instruments inevitably come with some preset factory patches (which can't be changed), plus room for users to store their own patches. These user patches may be filled with sounds that you can edit at will, or they may be empty, depending on the model of instrument. The term patch is a throwback to very early electronic synthesizers, which used patch cables, rather like an old-fashioned telephone exchange, to connect the various sound generating building blocks.

MIDI can directly access up to 128 patches, sometimes numbered from 0 to 127 and sometimes from 1 to 128 – even standards aren't always all that standard! The buttons that are used to select the patches on the master keyboard also enable patch information to be transmitted to the slave synthesizer modules, so now, not only can we play the modules remotely, we can also select the sound or patch that they are set to. These patch change commands are known as Program Change messages, and their use isn't limited to MIDI instruments – they may also be used to call up effects patches on MIDI compatible effects units. If you have two MIDI instruments linked up so that you can play the slave from the master, try pressing the Program Change buttons on the master. You should find that the slave also changes to the new patch number.

Instruments containing more than 128 patches must have these organised into two or more banks containing a maximum of 128 patches per bank, because Program Change messages can only access 128 patches directly. Bank Change commands, comprising specific controller data, are used to switch from one bank to the next. See the section on MIDI Controllers for more information.

Some studio effects units are MIDI controllable, where MIDI Program Changes can be used to call up specific effects from within a library of different effects patches. But MIDI Program Change messages are just the start – an awful lot more useful information can travel down that deceptively simple MIDI cable. MIDI also serves a secondary purpose in allowing synchronisation signals to be sent between devices such as drum machines and sequencers, and there's a whole chapter devoted to this subject.

control and controllers

Real musical instruments aren't just about note pitches and loudness, they're also about expression. A violin player, for example, may add vibrato to a note or slide from one note to another. To help the keyboard player imitate the expression of a real instrument, a typical MIDI synthesizer or master keyboard has two or more performance wheels mounted to the left of the keyboard where at least one is invariably dedicated to pitch bend. The other wheel, or wheels, are sometimes reassignable to allow them to control various different effects, though the most common application is to control vibrato depth. Like the keys, these controllers work by generating electronic signals, which in turn, control the circuitry that creates the sound. And, like note information, control information may also be sent over MIDI – simply move the control wheel on the master, and the slave will respond.

Further control may be provided by means of footpedals inputs, that allow a conventional volume pedal to be used as a means of varying MIDI control functions.

Because pedals and wheels can be set to any position rather than simply being on or off, they are known as continuous controllers. In everyday terms, a car's steering wheel or accelerator position could be thought of as being continuous controllers, whereas the direction indicators are simple switched controllers that are either on or off. Continuous controllers aren't as continuous as they might seem however – MIDI deals with numbers, and because of the data structure used, the available range is from 0 to 127. That means that all continuous controllers really operate over a series of tiny steps, but as the steps are so small, the impression is of continuous change.

The different ways in which a musical instrument may be controlled include performance wheels, joysticks, levers, pedals, footswitches, breath controller, ribbon controllers and other less obvious but equally ingenious devices. All can be employed to exert their influence via MIDI controllers – which is why MIDI provides for so many different controllers to be used at the same time. You don't have to worry about MIDI channels or other technicalities when using controllers as the data automatically goes to the same destination (MIDI channel), as the notes you are playing on the keyboard.

Even though you only have two hands and two feet, MIDI provides the means to operate up to 128 controllers – though not all are used for expression control. The reason there are so many is so you can pick what aspect of the sound being played you control with your wheels, pedals and switches.

If more precision is required than can be afforded by 128 steps, two controllers must be used together, and the MIDI spec reserves a number of controllers for this purpose. Again, this is perfectly transparent to the user, but this degree of precision is rarely necessary or desirable – the more MIDI data is generated, the more chance there is of creating a MIDI data overload.

pitch bend scaling

By changing parameters in the MIDI Setup section, MIDI instruments can often be 'scaled' so that, for example, the maximum travel of the pitch bend wheel might cause a pitch shift of as little as one semitone or as much as a whole octave. As you can imagine, it is important to ensure that any instruments likely to play at the same time are set with the same scaling values, especially for pitch bend, otherwise when you try to bend a note on the master keyboard, the sound coming from the master instrument might go up by a third and the sound from the slave by a fourth – clearly not desirable unless you're inventing a new strain of modern jazz. For general use, most people set up a pitch bend range of two semitones so that a plus or minus one whole tone range is available from the centre position of the wheel. Pitch wheels are spring loaded so that they automatically return to their neutral position when released. Interestingly, though the pitch wheel is involved in expression control, it doesn't form a part of the MIDI Controllers group, but rather exists in a category of its own. This is almost certainly due to historical reasons.

more controllers

One other controller not mentioned so far is master volume – some instruments send and respond to it while others don't. On an instrument that does, turning up the master volume slider will send the appropriate control information (Controller 7) over MIDI and the receiving synth will respond to it. A multitimbral module receiving a master volume control message will vary the volume of whichever part is being addressed according to the MIDI channel of the message. Be warned though that some older instruments don't respond to controller 7, so any attempts to control the volume of these via MIDI will be fruitless.

Other commonly implemented MIDI controllers include the sustain pedal, which prevents the note envelopes from entering their release phase until the pedal is released. This operates rather like the sustain pedal on a piano.

The MIDI spec is constantly evolving, and not all 128 possible Controller numbers are used – yet! Controllers 0 to 63 are used for continuous controllers while 64 to 95 are used for switches. 96 to 121 are undefined and 122 to 127 are reserved for Channel Mode messages. A full listing of the Controller numbers and their functions follows, but don't panic if some of them don't make any sense at the moment.

controller listing

0	Bank Select
1	Modulation Wheel
2	Breath Controller
3	Undefined
4	Foot Controller
5	Portamento Time
6	Data Entry
7	Main Volume
8	Balance
9	Undefined
10	Pan
11	Expression
12	Effect Control 1
13	Effect Control 2
14	Undefined
15	Undefined
16 – 19	General Purpose 1 to 4
20 – 31	Undefined
32 – 63	LSB for Control Changes 0 to 31 (where greater resolution is required)
64	Damper/Sustain Pedal
65	Portamento
66	Sostenuto
67	Soft Pedal
68	Legato Footswitch
69	Hold 2
70	Sound Variation/Exciter
71	Harmonic Content/Compressor
72	Release Time/Distortion
73	Attack Time/Equaliser
74	Brightness/Expander-Gate
75	Undefined/Reverb
76	Undefined/Delay
77	Undefined/Pitch Transpose
78	Undefined/Flange-Chorus
79	Undefined/Special Effect
80 – 83	General Purpose 5 to 8
84	Portamento Control
85 – 90	Undefined
91	Effects Depth (Effect 1)
92	Tremolo Depth (Effect 2)
93	Chorus Depth (Effect 3)
94	Celeste Depth (Effect 4)
95	Phaser Depth (Effect 5)
96	Data Increment
97	Data Decrement
98	Non-Registered Parameter Number LSB
99	Non-Registered Parameter Number MSB
100	Registered Parameter Number LSB
101	Registered Parameter Number MSB
102 – 119	Undefined
120	All Sound Off
121	Reset All Controllers
122	Local Control
123	All Notes Off
124	Omni Mode Off
125	Omni Mode On
126	Mono Mode On
127	Poly Mode On

Note that not all controllers deal with performance control. In addition to the use of the last four controller numbers to change MIDI modes, there are also Bank Change messages, an All Notes Off message (to cut off all notes that may still be playing), Local On/Off and a Reset all Controllers message, so that all controller values can be reset to their default values. Most of these will have little impact on your day to day use of MIDI, though where they are important, they will be discussed further. Most of the time, at least while you're getting to know MIDI, you'll be concerned mainly with selecting and playing sounds, using the performance wheels on the master keyboard, and possibly a sustain pedal – also plugged into the master keyboard.

Where the initials MSB and LSB are shown, these stand for Most Significant Bit and Least Significant Bit – roughly speaking, computer speak for coarse and fine adjustments. Both MSBs and LSBs have a possible numerical range of 0 to 127, so no surprises there! In fact all variable controllers have values of between 0 and 127, while switched controllers are usually set at 0 for off and 127 for on. Most modern instruments will also accept any value of 64 and above as on and any below 64 as off, though some older instruments are more pedantic.

Pitch Bend can provide control in two directions, so its default position is midway between the two extremes – 64. Again, you don't need to get involved at this stage – your sequencer will take care of most of the obscure MIDI dialogue to and from your keyboard and modules for you, but when you come to edit MIDI sequence data, it is helpful to know what the more common controllers and their values mean.

non-registered parameters

Because not all synthesizers use the same type of synthesis, it would be impossible to provide a standard range of controllers able to access every parameter that had an influence over the sound being produced. Of course a few parameters are common to all instruments, and these are known as Registered Parameters, but to allow manufacturers to provide access to all the relevant parameters of different instruments, the Non-Registered Parameter (NRPN), system was added to the MIDI specification.

The Registered Parameters are: Pitch Bend Sensitivity, Fine Tuning, Coarse Tuning, Change Tuning Program and Change Tuning Bank. However, the vast majority of controls are non-registered, but for precisely that reason, it is usually necessary to have some form of customised hardware interface or editing software to access them. Because they are non-defined, the typical user has no means of knowing what they are unless they are detailed in the MIDI spec at the back of the instrument manual. However, NRPNs provide a convenient 'back door' for designers and software writers to access the invisible sound control elements inside synthesizers without having to get involved in the complexities of System Exclusive messages.

channel voice messages

Most MIDI messages are channel specific in that they are only accepted by the receiving device if it is on the same channel as the data is being sent.

MIDI Note Ons and Offs are Channel Messages, as are all other types of performance data relating to Velocity, Pitch Bend, Controller Data, Program Changes and so on.

A single musical note can be represented by a fairly concise MIDI message comprising only a channel number, a note-on event followed by a note-off event, plus a velocity value. Controller information, on the other hand, is rather more data intensive, because as long as you're moving a controller, it is sending out a continuous stream of MIDI data.

aftertouch

Another source of musical performance control information is Channel Aftertouch, produced by some keyboards when you press hard on the keys. This works via a pressure sensor under the keyboard and sends out lots of MIDI data, whether the receiving device responds to it or not, so if you're not using the Aftertouch on your master keyboard turn it off to prevent clogging up the system with unnecessary data. I tend to leave it off as a matter of course unless I specifically need it, because when you're working with a computer sequencer, unnecessary controller data takes up a lot of memory.

Aftertouch can be assigned to various functions, such as brightness, loudness, vibrato depth and so on. It is a useful way of adding expression to a performance, but you should keep in mind that channel aftertouch affects all the notes that are currently playing, not just the one you're pressing down on.

A few exotic instruments also feature polyphonic aftertouch, which means that when you press down on a key, the data sent applies only to that note, not to all the notes that are currently playing. Polyphonic aftertouch can generate a vast amount of MIDI data so must be used sparingly, but very few instruments support this facility.

Another very rare feature is release velocity. All touch velocity instruments generate MIDI note velocity depending on how quickly you push down the keys, but on an instrument with release velocity, additional information is generated depending on how quickly you release the keys.

sound banks

As discussed earlier, the maximum range of a conventional MIDI message is from 0 to 127, meaning MIDI can address a maximum of 128 different notes or send controller information with a maximum of 128 discrete values.

Similarly, you can only directly address 128 different patches, but to get around this limitation, some synths organise their sounds into multiple banks, with a maximum of 128 patches per bank. MIDI bank change messages (also forms of controller message involving controller numbers 0 and 32) are then used to access the different banks. Not all bank change messages are standard, but the relevant controller values will be supplied in the instrument handbook MIDI Implementation Table. Some of the more modern sequencers include a library of bank change commands for the more common instruments in circulation, so once you've told your sequencer what instrument is connected to it, it'll automatically send the right bank change command.

assignable controls

Often, instruments allow you to assign which Physical control device relates to a specific MIDI controller, so the Modulation wheel on your synth could be redirected to control something quite different, such as reverb amount, or the brightness of the sound being played.

How much you want to get involved with the various controllers is up to you. At first you'll probably be happy to use the pitch bend and mod wheels and the sustain pedal, but as you get more familiar with MIDI, you may be attracted by the possibilities of using a sequencer to automate your performance by controlling levels, creating automated panning, changing effects, patch changes and so on. The great thing about MIDI is that you can start off very simply, making music right from the outset, then as you get more comfortable with the concept, you can try out more ambitious things.

midi clock

Unlike channel specific messages, MIDI messages related to synchronisation and sequencer control have no channel address, so are received by all the instruments in the MIDI system. Perhaps the most important of all these messages is 'MIDI clock'.

MIDI clock is a tempo-related timing code and comprises 96 electronic 'clocks' or ticks for each four-beat bar of music. Think of it as the invisible conductor that keeps your drum machine and sequencer, or sequencer and tape recorder, playing together rather than going their own separate ways. You can't hear these ticks, but they are picked up by any drum machine or sequencer set to External MIDI Sync mode, enabling the slave machine to stay in sync with the master. A practical use of MIDI clock is to sync up a drum machine to a sequencer and either one can be master. Using a suitable interface box, it's also possible to use MIDI clock to keep a sequencer running in time with a recording on tape. The slave machine must be set to external MIDI sync, which means that it will follow exactly the tempo generated by the master device.

start, stop and continue

The slave device also needs to know when to start and stop, so MIDI also includes Start, Stop and Continue messages. Even so, these are only of any use if you start your master from the beginning of the song, otherwise, the slave won't know where it's supposed to start from. To get around this, the MIDI Song Position Pointer message was added to the MIDI specification. This is quite transparent to the user, but on starting the sequence, a message is sent which tells the receiving device where to start from. As a result, the slave device can lock up almost instantaneously. So-called Smart FSK (Frequency Shift Keying), tape to MIDI sync boxes using MIDI Song Position Pointers are often used to make a MIDI sequencer sync to a tape machine. A full chapter is dedicated to MIDI synchronisation issues later in the book.

serial killer

While I've promised to try to keep this book as non-technical as possible, it helps in understanding the limitations of MIDI to know that it is a serial system – in other words, information moves in single file. At this point, many books on MIDI present you with an in-depth description of the bits and bytes that make up a MIDI message, and if you're technically minded, this can be quite interesting. However, as this doesn't really help the typical user to make better use of MIDI, I make no apology for omitting it entirely.

The main point is that because MIDI is relatively fast, things may seem to happen all at once, but in reality, when you play a chord, the notes start to sound one after the other, not simultaneously. The times in question are far too short to be perceptible when only a few events are concerned, but if you were to try to play, say, 64 notes at once, you might just hear a delay between the first and the last.

In reality, the speed of MIDI is seldom a limitation when you're dealing only with notes, but if you're trying to replay a multi-part MIDI sequence that also contains lots of controller information, you could end up with the MIDI equivalent of a traffic jam, resulting in obvious timing errors. In practice, it's wise to use controllers only when necessary, and to switch off your master keyboard's aftertouch whenever you don't need it. The better sequencers give priority to MIDI note timing when traffic gets heavy so that timing problems are less likely to be audible.

midi modes

Instruments will generally be set to Poly mode for conventional operation, though some older instruments default to Omni mode every time they are switched on. Because the vast majority of work is done using Poly mode, most users rarely give MIDI modes a second thought, but there are actually four different MIDI modes defined as follows:

Mode 1: Omni On/Poly: The instrument will play polyphonically but MIDI channel data is ignored. Whatever you send it, on whatever channel, it will play it it. Some older instruments still default to Omni mode when they're powered up so you have to switch them back to Omni Off mode before use.

Mode 2: Omni On/Mono: The monophonic equivalent of Mode 1 and hardly ever used.

Mode 3: Omni Off/Poly: The 'normal' MIDI mode, especially for sequencing or multitimbral operation. In Mode 3, the instrument responds to messages on its own MIDI channel only and plays polyphonically.

Mode 4: Omni Off/Mono: The monophonic equivalent of Mode 3. Mode 4 is mainly for MIDI guitar players who need to have each string working on a separate MIDI channel in order to be able to bend notes or apply vibrato on independent strings. Because each string of a guitar is mono (it can only play one note at a time), it makes sense to use the receiving synth in mono mode to mimic the way a real guitar plays.

active sensing

MIDI also includes something called active sensing, (though it isn't always implemented), which is MIDI's way of checking that a connection exists between devices. In reality, it's the MIDI equivalent of the receiving device shouting "Are you still there?", and a short while later the transmitting device shouts back "Yes!". If a "Yes" is not forthcoming, the receiving device assumes the transmitting device has gone off in a sulk and, metaphorically speaking, takes its ball home!

What actually happens is that if the receiving device doesn't get back an 'all's well' message, it shuts off all notes that are playing. If it didn't do this and the MIDI cable was accidentally unplugged between a Note On being sent and a Note Off being sent, the receiving instrument would continue to play that note until it eventually rusted away! Happily, this too is completely hidden from the user, but it's nice to know it is there.

song select

Because MIDI sequencers can hold more than one song in memory, MIDI also includes a Song Select message. As you might expect, tunes can be requested by number in the range 0 to 127.

We're very used to MIDI instruments being perfectly in tune, but it is still possible for MIDI controlled analogue synths to drift in pitch over a period of time unless they have intelligent auto retuning systems. However, many of them do have an internal tuning routine which can be initiated manually or over MIDI using a Tune Request command. If a Tune Request command is sent, all the MIDI instruments in the system that have a tuning routine will give themselves a quick check over and retune to their own internal reference.

system exclusive messages

System Exclusive is a term that strikes terror into the hearts of those who know just enough about MIDI to know where the tricky bits are, but I mention it mainly so that if you decide to ignore it, at least you'll know what you're ignoring!

System Exclusive (or Sysex for short) messages are part of the MIDI System Message portfolio, but whereas the rest of MIDI is pretty precisely defined, Sysex is provided so that manufacturers can build instruments with different facilities yet still conform to the MIDI specification. Rather than use the MIDI channel system for locating their target, Sysex messages contain an ID code unique to the type of instrument for which they are intended. Where two or more identical instruments are being used in the same system, it is often possible to assign an additional ID number of between 1 and 16 to each one so that no two have exactly the same ID. If they did, they'd all respond to the same Sysex data.

In the main, Sysex allows those clever people who write sound editing software to gain access to all the sound generating parameters that might need adjusting. The programming parameters of analogue and digital synths tend to be quite different, so if you want to provide access to these parameters via MIDI, then manufacturers have got to be allowed to specify 'exclusive' codes to access their specific set of parameters, just as they provide NRPNs to access certain unique parameters using MIDI Controllers. This obviously couldn't be done using standardised codes as every different make and type of synth has different parameters, so a system such as Sysex is the only viable means of doing it.

Because Sysex messages are only recognised by the instrument type for which they are designed, there's no worry that your drum machine might try to interpret a message intended for one of your synths and blow a fuse. If the manufacturer's ID heading up the Sysex message code isn't recognised by the receiving instrument, the message is ignored.

patch dumping

Only very advanced MIDI users tend to have more than a passing association with MIDI Sysex data, but anyone can use it at a basic level for copying patches or banks of patches from a synth into a MIDI storage device such as a sequencer or MIDI data filter. How?

You'll find that most modern MIDI instruments have a Sysex dump facility tucked away in their MIDI configuration pages somewhere – all you have to do is connect the MIDI Out of the instrument to your sequencer's input, put the sequencer into record and then start the dump procedure. The Sysex data will be recorded in exactly the same way as MIDI notes – except if you look in the edit list to see what's there, it will look like nonsense. However, the synth knows what it means, and that's all that matters. Sysex Dump data usually takes a few seconds to record, after which it can be played back into the instrument at any time to restore the patches you saved. If you're in the habit of using lots of different patches in your songs and you don't have enough user memories to hold them all, you can store a Sysex dump right at the start of each song to set up the required patches for you. Depending on how long the dump takes, you may have to leave a few bars of count-in to allow it to finish before the music starts, and once you've loaded your new sounds, it might be a good idea to mute the Sysex track, otherwise the patches will get reloaded every time you start the song from the top. Also, don't quantise the Sysex dump after recording or it may not play back properly. If this last section doesn't make sense, read it again after you've read the chapter introducing sequencers. That's the trouble with MIDI, because of the way it evolved, it isn't always possible to keep everything in a perfectly logical order!

compatibility

If you expect every MIDI instrument to support every feature implemented in the MIDI specifications, you're destined to lead a sad and disappointed life. Most new instruments support most of the features, but few are actually compulsory and about the only thing you can take for granted is that a MIDI synth will send and receive MIDI note data, though virtually all will accept MIDI Program changes and velocity information. If a MIDI message is received by an instrument incapable of responding to that message, then the message is simply ignored, in much the way as you might ignore junk mail written in a foreign language.

However you should be aware that instruments can legitimately respond to the same MIDI message in different ways. To take an example mentioned earlier, the pitch bend range of an instrument is not tied to the data received but is set up in the MIDI menu of the instrument itself. Here full movement of the pitch bend wheel (the full range is 128 steps with 64 denoting the middle position), can be made to shift the pitch by as little as one semitone or by as much as an octave. Unless all your instruments are set to the same pitch bend range (two semitones is popular), you could end up with an horrendous discord.

As mentioned earlier, very few instruments incorporate polyphonic key pressure (aftertouch), or release velocity, but just about everything you can buy now (other than some really basic home keyboards) is velocity sensitive, and even relatively inexpensive keyboards have channel aftertouch. Some older instruments don't respond to MIDI Bank Change messages, even if they have banks of sounds accessible from the front panel, which can be rather frustrating, and you may also find some instruments which refuse to respond to Controller 7 (master volume) commands. If in doubt, the back of the relevant equipment manual should show a table of what MIDI facilities are supported where a 0 shows the facility is present, and an X shows that it is not supported. This is known as the MIDI Implementation Table, and once you know what to look for, it tells you a lot about the capabilities of your instrument in a very short space of time.

introducing general midi

Soundcards and general purpose synths and modules frequently include a set of General MIDI preset sounds that at least ensure nominal compatibility sound-wise between cards of different makes. Some GM synths sound noticeably better than others, but if you've created a composition for piano, at least you know it's going to play back with a piano sound, not a violin or a helicopter! General MIDI was a relatively late addition to the MIDI spec and is discussed in a later chapter. Its main use is in allowing MIDI sequencer files to be played back via a wide variety of different instruments in the knowledge that all the parts will be played by the correct type of instrument. GM is described in more detail in a later chapter.

midi merge

If there is a need to split the same MIDI signal to two or more destinations, you can either use the Thru connectors fitted to the various MIDI instruments or a MIDI Thru box, but merging two streams of MIDI data isn't quite so simple. MIDI data is quite complicated, so if you were try to join two MIDI cables with a Y lead, the result would be a jumble of meaningless data. Figure 1.4 shows how a MIDI Merge box might be used to merge the MIDI output from a keyboard and from a dedicated sound editing device enabling both to be fed into a sequencer at the same time.

To merge two or more MIDI data streams, a specialised Merge box is needed, inside which is a small computer designed to interleave the data in a coherent way. Merge facilities are needed when a sequencer needs to be controlled by a master keyboard at the same time as receiving MIDI sync

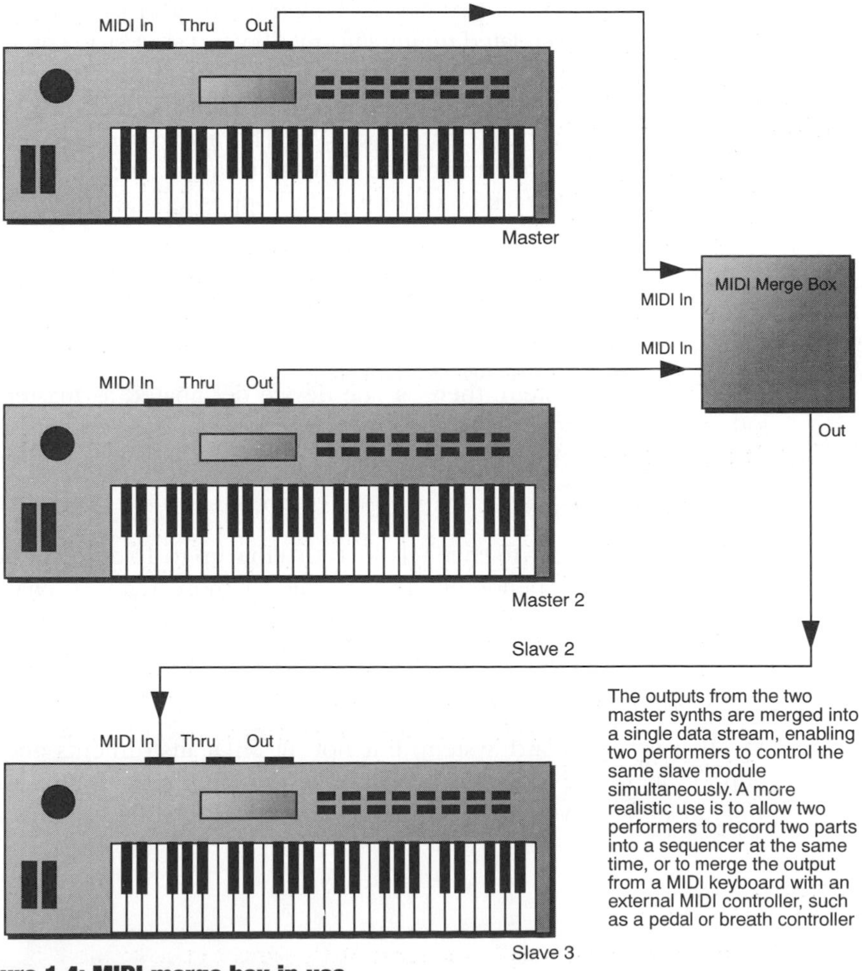
MIDI In
Thru
Out
Master
MIDI Merge Box
MIDI In
MIDI In
MIDI In
Thru
Out
Out
Master 2
Slave 2
MIDI In
Thru
Out
Slave 3
The outputs from the two master synths are merged into a single data stream, enabling two performers to control the same slave module simultaneously. A more realistic use is to allow two performers to record two parts into a sequencer at the same time, or to merge the output from a MIDI keyboard with an external MIDI controller, such as a pedal or breath controller

Figure 1.4: MIDI merge box in use

signals, or when you want to play two keyboards into your sequencer at the same time. There are other requirements for MIDI merge facilities which will be explained as they come up.

Although stand alone MIDI Merge boxes are available, some more sophisticated multi-port MIDI interfaces include two or more mergeable inputs. A merge facility can also enable two or more MIDI keyboards to be routed to the system at once – for example, when there are two players wishing to record different parts of a musical sequence at the same time.

crash course

● MIDI is used mainly to send note and performance controller information between instruments, though it can also carry patch change commands, tempo-related timing information and start/stop commands for the remote control of sequencers and drum machines. There is also a protocol for controlling compatible tape machines and hard disk recorders, known as MIDI Machine Control or MMC. This allows remote access to the main transport controls and record status buttons of a multitrack recorder – useful if your multitrack recorder is at the opposite side of the room from your sequencer.

● MIDI data describes keyboard (and expression controller) actions, not sounds.

● In any MIDI system, there is one device designated as master and the other devices function as slaves. In a basic system, the keyboard is usually the master, though when a sequence is played back from a sequencer, the sequencer is master.

● MIDI operates on 16 channels so as to allow up to 16 different devices to be controlled independently at one time. If more than 16 channels are required, a 'multi-port' MIDI interface is needed to provide two or more groups of 16 channels each. These will be covered in the sequencing section of this book.

● MIDI is a standard system, but not all MIDI instruments and devices support all of the functions described in the MIDI specification. However, the functions they do provide must conform to the MIDI specification.

chapter 2

general MIDI

In the introduction to synthesizers, General MIDI was given a brief mention, but it is a very important concept and deserves further explanation. General MIDI is simply another stage of standardisation which has been added to the existing MIDI protocol, but it doesn't have to be adopted by all MIDI instruments – only by those bearing the GM logo. Furthermore, a GM machine may also be able to function as a non-GM machine, in which case it will have a dedicated GM mode for when General MIDI operation is required.

The idea behind GM was to enable manufacturers to build synthesizers and synth modules that exhibit a specified degree of compatibility in terms of which sounds are located in which patches, to which keys the various drum sounds are mapped, and on the minimum performance capability of the machine in terms of multitimbrality and polyphony. Essentially, the aim is to allow a MIDI sequence recorded using one GM module to be played back on any other GM module without the need to remap patches, move drum note allocations or worry about running out of parts or polyphony. This doesn't mean that all GM synths have to sound exactly the same, but it does mean that, for example, a piano preset on one machine must be in the same patch location as a similar sounding piano preset on any other GM machine.

midi compatibility

Normally, whenever you record a piece of music using a sequencer, you insert the appropriate program change command at the start of each track so that whenever you play back the sequence through the same instruments and modules, the correct sounds will automatically be called up. However, if you play the sequence back on a friend's MIDI system, you may well find that all the sounds are completely wrong because the patches are not only completely different in sound, but any that are suitable are probably stored in different patch locations. In the case of programmable instruments, this kind of chaos is difficult to avoid because most users have their own system for storing their edited sounds. Furthermore, the factory presets provided with non-GM instruments tend to be arranged fairly arbitrarily.

drum mapping

Another potential stumbling block is the drum and percussion part. Even if your friend's drum sounds are on the same MIDI channel as you've used, the chances are that some or all of the drum sounds will be assigned to different keys. Roland have had their own more or less standard drum mapping system for some time now, but some other manufacturers have not been so well organised, so where you programmed a bass drum, your friend's setup might play a cowbell. Furthermore, you may have written the piece using drum sounds that don't have any close equivalent on your friend's drum machine.

midi too versatile?

Let's say you're lucky and you get all the sounds mapped out. There's still a good chance you'll come unstuck when it comes to controller information; perhaps one of your friend's modules doesn't respond to Controller 7 (master volume), or maybe his pitch bend ranges are all set to three semitones, when you do all your work with the range set to two semitones. MIDI is a wonderful system, but its very flexibility means that no two people's MIDI systems behave in exactly the same way.

General MIDI was devised to provide a solution for use in situations where a high degree of compatibility was essential, for example when replaying pre-recorded MIDI song files. Now, with the introduction of general MIDI, musicians working with GM synths can play each other's GM song files and be confident that they will sound more or less the way they should, even though there are subtle subjective differences between one manufacturer's GM machine and another. This has opened up the market for commercially available MIDI song files.

polyphony and multitimbrality

The problem with polyphony and multitimbrality is that you can never have enough of it! GM MIDI instruments provide the ability to play back 16 parts on 16 MIDI channels, with a total polyphony of at least 24 notes. In other words, there may be 16 different sounds running on 16 different MIDI channels, but the total number of notes playing at once can never exceed the maximum polyphony of the instrument.

If you try to play more notes than the instrument can handle, note robbing takes place and previously played notes start to drop out. What's more, where a synth layers two voices to make up a sound, the actual polyphony may be further reduced depending on how the manufacturer chooses to interpret the GM MIDI spec on polyphony. The whole idea of specifying a minimum level of polyphony is so that you don't run out of polyphony when trying to play a MIDI song file conforming to the GM format.

roland's enhanced gs format

Much of the present GM format owes its existence to Roland's own protocols, so it's hardly surprising that Roland have gone one step further and devised an enhanced version of General MIDI which they call GS. Realising that many users wouldn't be satisfied with 128 preset sounds, Roland have designed their GS machines to offer several alternative banks of sounds, the basic GM set (Capital Tones) being the first bank (Bank 0). There are up to seven 'Variation Tones' based on each of the Capital Tones and these are arranged so as to have the same program change numbers as the tones from which they are derived. In other words, all the variation tones of a Piano Capital Tone will still be pianos, though they will all be subtly different. Further banks are provided for sounds known as Sub-Capital Tones, which are less obviously related to the Capital Tones.

A Bank Change command allows the user to switch between the various banks. Conventional program change commands are then used to select the sounds within each bank – a neat way to get around MIDI's limitation of being able to directly address only 128 patches. Yamaha also introduced their own expanded General MIDI format which they call XG. Like Roland's GS mode, this enhances the basic General MIDI sound set with several banks of alternative sounds, but unfortunately, a different bank chance command is required to access these. At the time of writing, it seems that most Yamaha instruments also support Roland's GS format, so it looks as though GS will become the de facto standard for enhanced GM instruments.

editing

Because General MIDI is based on the concept of the same sounds always being in the same place, it stands to reason that any attempt at editing the sounds will risk negating any advantages the system has. Different instruments handle this dilemma in different ways, but as a rule, you can either switch between a GM mode based on preset sounds, or a non-GM mode where editing is permitted.

commercial midi song files

Commercial GM song files covering all musical styles from pop to classical are now available, and they have many applications, from general interest to song analysis. They are also used by solo performers to provide musical backings, within the conditions imposed by musical copyright law.

A huge advantage of MIDI song files over pre-recorded backing tapes is that the key can be changed at the touch of a button, making life rather less difficult for the solo entertainer. The overall sound quality is generally better too; with pre-recorded tapes, you either have to play the original night after night and risk wearing it out, or copy it onto another cassette with the consequent loss of quality.

the history of general midi

In 1991, General MIDI was ratified with the aim of defining a minimum set of MIDI capabilities to which all GM MIDI devices must adhere. The main points are as follows:

- A GM instrument must support all 16 MIDI channels simultaneously to provide 16-part multitimbrality.

- Percussion parts must be on MIDI channel 10, a minimum set of 47 standard sound types, including the most common drum and latin percussion sounds, must be provided and these must all be mapped in accordance with the GM standard. This mapping owes a lot to Roland's original mapping system.

- GM instruments must be capable of 24-note polyphony and notes must be allocated dynamically. However, the specification allows eight notes to be reserved for percussion, leaving 16 for the other instruments.

- All 128 preset sounds are defined as to their type and patch location. Though there is some variation in sound between one module and another, the instrument type (and even playing style in the case of basses, for example) for each patch location is quite rigidly defined, right down to the dog barks, helicopters and gun shots in the special effects section. Some of the more abstract pad sounds are a little more flexible, but they must still be of a roughly similar tone and character.

- All GM instruments must respond to the same set of MIDI Controllers, and the default ranges set for these controllers must be standard. The MIDI Controller implementation includes the ability to change the master tuning and Pitch Bend wheel range via MIDI, Reset All Controllers (which resets all MIDI Controllers to their default values), and All Notes Off, which silences any notes currently playing. All GM machines must also respond to Pitch Bend, Velocity and Aftertouch.

gm voice table

PROGRAM NO	INSTRUMENT
1	Acoustic Grand Piano
2	Bright Acoustic Piano
3	Electric Grand Piano
4	Honky-Tonk Piano
5	Electric Piano 1
6	Electric Piano 2
7	Harpsichord
8	Clavi
9	Celesta
10	Glockenspiel
11	Music Box
12	Vibraphone
13	Marimba
14	Xylophone
15	Tubular Bells
16	Dulcimer
17	Drawbar Organ
18	Percussive Organ
19	Rock Organ
20	Church Organ
21	Reed Organ
22	Accordion
23	Harmonica
24	Tango Accordion
25	Acoustic Guitar (Nylon)
26	Acoustic Guitar (Steel)
27	Electric Guitar (Jazz)
28	Electric Guitar (Clean)
29	Electric Guitar (Muted)
30	Overdriven Guitar
31	Distortion Guitar
32	Guitar Harmonics
33	Acoustic Bass
34	Electric Bass (Finger)
35	Electric Bass (Pick)
36	Fretless Bass
37	Slap Bass 1
38	Slap Bass 2
39	Synth Bass 1
40	Synth Bass 2
41	Violin
42	Viola
43	Cello

PROGRAM NO	INSTRUMENT
44	Contrabass
45	Tremolo Strings
46	Pizzicato Strings
47	Orchestral Harp
48	Timpani
49	String Ensemble 1
50	String Ensemble 2
51	SynthStrings 1
52	SynthStrings 2
53	Choir Aahs
54	Voice Oohs
55	Synth Voice
56	Orchestra Hit
57	Trumpet
58	Trombone
59	Tuba
60	Muted Trumpet
61	French Horn
62	Brass Section
63	SynthBrass 1
64	SynthBrass 2
65	Soprano Sax
66	Alto Sax
67	Tenor Sax
68	Baritone Sax
69	Oboe
70	English Horn
71	Bassoon
72	Clarinet
73	Piccolo
74	Flute
75	Recorder
76	Pan Flute
77	Blown Bottle
78	Shakuhachi
79	Whistle
80	Ocarina
81	Lead 1 (Square)
82	Lead 2 (Sawtooth)
83	Lead 3 (Calliope)
84	Lead 4 (Chiff)
85	Lead 5 (Charang)
86	Lead 6 (Voice)
87	Lead 7 (Fifths)
88	Lead 8 (Bass + Lead)
89	Pad 1 (New Age)
90	Pad 2 (Warm)

PROGRAM NO	INSTRUMENT
91	Pad 3 (Polysynth)
92	Pad 4 (Choir)
93	Pad 5 (Bowed)
94	Pad 6 (Metallic)
95	Pad 7 (Halo)
96	Pad 8 (Sweep)
97	FX 1 (Rain)
98	FX 2 (Soundtrack)
99	FX 3 (Crystal)
100	FX 4 (Atmosphere)
101	FX 5 (Brightness)
102	FX 6 (Goblins)
103	FX 7 (Echoes)
104	FX 8 (Sci-Fi)
105	Sitar
106	Banjo
107	Shamisen
108	Koto
109	Kalimba
110	Bagpipe
111	Fiddle
112	Shanai
113	Tinkle Bell
114	Agogo
115	Steel Drums
116	Woodblock
117	Taiko Drum
118	Melodic Tom
119	Synth Drum
120	Reverse Cymbal
121	Guitar Fret Noise
122	Breath Noise
123	Seashore
124	Bird Tweet
125	Telephone Ring
126	Helicopter
127	Applause
128	Gunshot

Note: some manufacturers number their patches from 0 to 127 rather than from 1 to 128

GM drum map

NOTE NO	DRUM SOUND
35	Acoustic Bass Drum
36	Bass Drum 1
37	Side Stick
38	Acoustic Snare
39	Hand Clap
40	Electric Snare
41	Low Floor Tom
42	Closed Hi-Hat
43	High Floor Tom
44	Pedal Hi-Hat
45	Low Tom
46	Open Hi-Hat
47	Low Mid Tom
48	High Mid Tom
49	Crash Cymbal
50	High Tom

NOTE NO	DRUM SOUND
51	Ride Cymbal 1
52	Chinese Cymbal
53	Ride Bell
54	Tambourine
55	Splash Cymbal
56	Cowbell
57	Crash Cymbal 2
58	Vibraslap
59	Ride Cymbal 2
60	High Bongo
61	Low Bongo
62	Mute Hi Conga
63	Open Hi Conga
64	Low Conga
65	High Timbale
66	Low Timbale

NOTE NO	DRUM SOUND
67	High Agogo
68	Low Agogo
69	Cabasa
70	Maracas
71	Short Whistle
72	Long Whistle
73	Short Guiro
74	Long Guiro
75	Claves
76	High Woodblock
77	Low Woodblock
78	Mute Cuica
79	Open Cuica
80	Mute Triangle
81	Open Triangle

chapter 3

introducing sequencers

So far, I've described how MIDI can be used to, in effect, remote control one or more instruments from a single master keyboard, but MIDI sequencing takes things a stage further, making it possible to record and play multi-part MIDI compositions, ranging from classical symphonies to rock and pop music. The term sequencer dates back to pre-MIDI days when synthesizers could be controlled from a sequencing device comprising a number of faders, each fader being used to tune one note in the sequence. When set to run, it would run around the sequence, typically of up to 16 notes, then it would repeat. The tempo could be set by the user, and while the effects that could be achieved were limited, a new genre of synthesizer bands and artistes emerged on the back of this technology.

the midi sequencer

A modern MIDI sequencer bears almost no resemblance to its crude predecessor and the term multitrack MIDI recorder would have been more accurate, but 'sequencer' stuck. In the context of recording, the term 'Track' refers to a means of recording a musical part in such a way that it may be edited, erased or re-recorded independently of the other parts. If you're familiar with the concept of multitrack tape, MIDI sequencing draws a close analogy with that way of working. Traditional musicians might prefer to visualise a sequencer track as being roughly equivalent to one stave of music in a multi-part score. A modern MIDI sequencer will provide a bare minimum of 16 tracks and often many more.

recording in layers

Using a MIDI sequencer, numerous separate musical parts can be recorded at different times, either by playing the parts one at a time on a MIDI keyboard, by entering note and timing data manually, or by a combination of 'live' playing and editing. The individual parts may be monophonic, or they may comprise chords – how much you want to record on each track is up to you. In fact a difficult part could be split over two or more tracks, then recorded in several takes. For example, a piano player with limited skills might first record the left hand part on one track, then record the right hand part later on a different track. Once recorded, these parts may be played back via any MIDI compatible synthesizer or collection of synthesizers.

Unless you have a sequencer with a built-in synthesizer, it can't play back any sounds on its own – it has to be used to control one or more synthesizers, and the number of different musical parts you can play back at once depends on the number and type of synthesizers you have. Fortunately, most modern synthesizers and PC soundcards are capable of playing back up to 16 different sounds at once, each controlled by a different MIDI channel. More on this later.

ethics

To those used to playing and recording using traditional methods and skills, the MIDI sequencer is sometimes viewed as little short of cheating, but to the sequencer user, MIDI and sequencing are seen as practical tools that make complex multi-part composition and performance a reality. Before MIDI, few people could compose a symphony, or even pop song for that matter, and ever expect to hear it performed, but now almost anyone can turn their musical ideas into a performance using affordable technology. Before getting onto the mechanics of sequencing however, I'd like to tackle the notion that sequencing is somehow cheating by looking at how things were done before the introduction of MIDI.

traditional composition

Having never written a symphony, I can't detail the exact stages, but I expect it goes something like this: the composer sits at his or her chosen instrument testing musical ideas, and the ones that are deemed viable are then written down on manuscript paper for the various sections of the orchestra to play. The composer imagines the parts already written down while adding new sections, harmonies and so on, then, when the score is nominally finished, it will be scrutinised and any required alterations made.

Once the score is complete, an orchestra will be engaged to play the composition, they'll be given copies of the score, and the music will be played back as written by the composer. Essentially, the composer, who may or may not be able to perform to an acceptable standard on a musical instrument, has conceived a piece of music and then written a list of instructions in the form of a musical score so that a musically proficient orchestra can perform it. The composer himself is not required to perform. Nobody has ever denounced the great classical composers for not being able to play all the instruments they wrote scores for, so why give the MIDI sequencer user a hard time for doing exactly the same thing.

the midi composer

By contrast, how does the MIDI composer write? As with the orchestral composer, the work usually starts at the keyboard, but this time the keyboard is a MIDI instrument connected to a MIDI sequencer, not a piano. Instead of writing down a score, the composer will record sections of the music into the sequencer against an electronic metronome set to the desired tempo, and instead of scanning a score to verify what's been done, it's a simple matter to play back the recording via a suitable synthesizer to hear exactly what has been recorded. Those composers who can't play well enough to record the parts in real time can enter notes directly into the sequencer in much the same way as a composer would write notes onto manuscript paper – it's tedious and time consuming, but it can be done.

Perhaps the best reason for using a MIDI sequencer is that you don't have to hire in an orchestra or a band of session musicians, because even a relatively inexpensive multitimbral synthesizer will provide all the sounds for you. A multitimbral synthesizer is one that can play several musical parts at once, and when used in conjunction with a sequencer, each 'part' of the multitimbral synth can be used to play back one musical part. For example, you might have a couple of sequencer tracks dedicated to strings, one to horns, one to percussion and one to woodwind.

the sequenced score

In some ways, the sequencer is better than the written score insomuch as it can play back a part exactly as you played it in the first place – it doesn't have to 'quantise' everything to equal subdivisions of a musical bar as the written score does – though it can if you want it to. And, just like the written score, if you're not happy with something you've done, you don't have to start from scratch, you can just erase the unwanted notes and 'write' in new ones.

When you summarise the way a musician composes using a sequencer, it isn't really too different from the way a traditional composer works. Both types of composer are likely to edit their compositions to some degree before they're entirely happy with them, and both bring in performers to play the finished composition. It doesn't really matter whether the finished piece is played by a bank of synths or by a hired orchestra whose role is simply to reproduce the composer's original work as faithfully as possible.

I'm a firm believer that electronic composition is as legitimate as any other form of composition, and if you have the talent to write a major symphonic work using a sequencer and a rack of synthesizers, you can always have a real orchestra play it for you later. Indeed, if you have access to a computer-based sequencer with score printing facilities, you can generate a written score directly from your recording. Having covered the philosophical groundwork, it's time to look more closely at the MIDI sequencer.

midi and sequencing

As mentioned earlier, it's often convenient to visualise a sequencer as being analogous to a multitrack tape recorder, but it is vitally important to keep in mind that what is being recorded is not the sound itself, but the electronic equivalent of a musical score. Just as a musical score is a series of instructions to the musicians, a MIDI sequence holds a series of instructions which tell your synths what to play and when to play it. It is, as I mentioned earlier, the electronic equivalent of the player piano or pianola, where a punched paper roll holds the instructions that make the piano play. The essential difference is that in the case of MIDI, the punched paper roll is replaced by computer memory and computer disks capable of controlling numerous different instruments at the same time.

sequencer setup

In a typical setup, a master MIDI controller (usually, but not invariably a keyboard), is connected to a sequencer via a MIDI cable, and when the sequencer is set to record, any notes played on the keyboard are recorded as MIDI data into whichever sequencer track has been selected for recording. In a simple system, you might have 16 MIDI tracks set up so that each is on a different MIDI channel, and if you feed the MIDI output of the sequencer to a 16-part multitimbral module, you can play back all 16 tracks at once. If you only have an 8-part multitimbral module, then you can only play back eight different sounds at once in the same way as a real-life eight-piece ensemble can only play a maximum of eight different lines of music at the same time. Figure 3.1 shows a typical computer-based sequencing system. If you have a keyboard that includes a synth (as shown in the diagram), simply select Local Off and connect it up like any other synth module. Local Off isolates the synth's keyboard from its sound generating circuitry so that, in effect, it behaves as if it were a separate dumb keyboard and MIDI synth module. This is necessary to prevent MIDI information being fed around the system in a continuous loop – which usually causes trouble, as is explained in the Troubleshooting section at the end of this chapter.

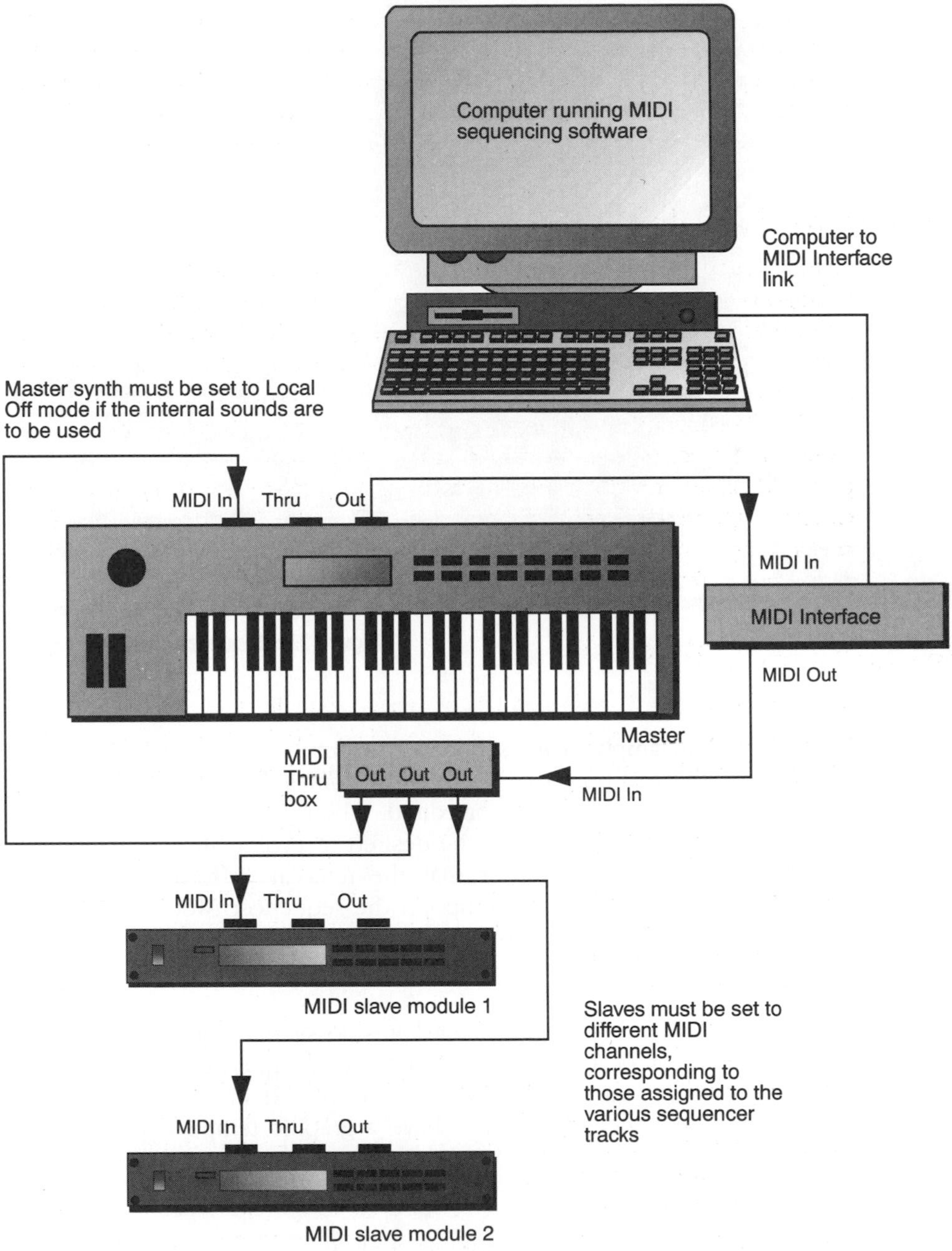
Computer running MIDI sequencing software
Computer to MIDI Interface link
Master synth must be set to Local Off mode if the internal sounds are to be used
MIDI In
Thru
Out
MIDI In
MIDI Interface
MIDI Out
Master
MIDI Thru box
Out
Out
Out
MIDI In
MIDI In
Thru
Out
MIDI slave module 1
Slaves must be set to different MIDI channels, corresponding to those assigned to the various sequencer tracks
MIDI In
Thru
Out
MIDI slave module 2

Figure 3.1: Basic sequencing setup

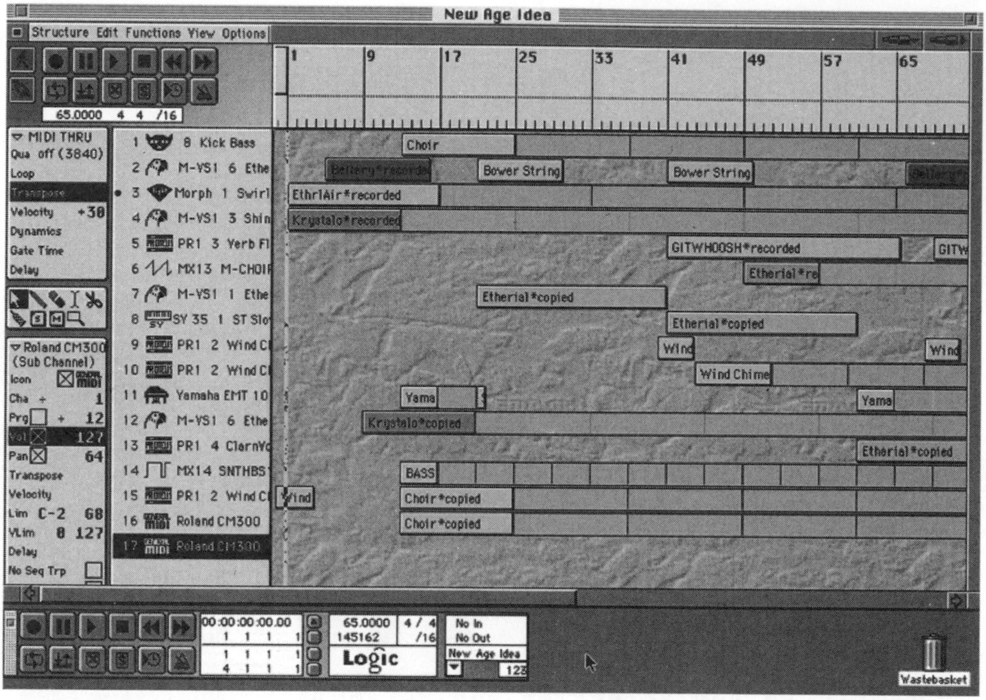

Figure 3.2: Sequencer Arrange pages

metronome

Though you can simply treat a sequencer as a multitrack recorder for MIDI information, the real power of a sequencer comes from the way in which recorded data may be modified or edited. When a recording is made, the sequencer is set to the tempo of the desired recording and a metronome click is made available in order that the musical performance can be synchronised with the internal tempo of the sequencer. Working this way, the MIDI data is arranged in musically meaningful bars, which makes editing note timing or copying and moving whole sections very easy and precise

For music incorporating tempo changes, it is possible to enter a new tempo at any bar and beat location, though some budget sequencers may impose a limit on how many tempo changes can be placed in each song. More sophisticated sequencers may even have a graphic tempo editing mode where you can draw curves or slopes to create smooth tempo increases or decreases.

If you don't want to be tied to tempo at all, you can simply turn off the metronome click and play as you would when using a tape recorder. The practical disadvantage of working this way is that you can't use the internal beat and bar structure to plan your edits, and you can't use the quantise function – the timing of your performance will be quite independent of the sequencer's internal tempo clock.

tracks and channels

At this point in the proceedings, it's very easy to get MIDI channels and sequencer tracks mixed up, but they're not the same thing. A sequencer track is simply somewhere to record one layer of your composition, but the MIDI information in that track can be on any MIDI channel you want it to be. A track can even contain MIDI information relating to two or more MIDI channels, though to save confusion, most of the time a single track records data on a single channel.

It's also possible to have several different tracks, all recording MIDI data set to the same channel. For example, if you're recording a complicated drum part, you might want to put the bass and snare drum on one track, the cymbals and hi-hats on another, and any tom fills on yet another. All the drum sounds may be on the same MIDI channel, but because they're on different tracks, they're effectively recorded as different layers. Not only does this make the parts easier to play, it also makes them less confusing to edit if you want to make any changes. Figure 3.2 shows the Arrange page of a popular computer-based sequencing package showing the layout of the tracks and the way recorded sequences are represented.

rechannelising

On early sequencers, every time you wanted to record a part on a different MIDI channel, you had to select a new MIDI channel on your master keyboard. This can be tedious when you're constantly wanting to hop from one music part to another, so to get around this, modern sequencers convert the incoming MIDI data to the appropriate channel for the track you're recording on. This is known as rechannelising. To use a postal analogy, the sequencer intercepts the MIDI messages as they come in, readdresses them by changing their MIDI channel, then it sends them on to their new destinations. This is another feat that's accomplished without any intervention on behalf of the user and it makes life very easy, because once you've completed recording one track, all you need do is select the next one and play.

cut, copy and paste

The remaining capabilities of a MIDI sequencer bear more resemblance to a word processor than anything else. Like a word processor, you can delete or replace wrong characters, in this case, musical notes, and if you want to use the same phrase more than once, you can copy it and paste copies into new locations to save having to do the same thing lots of times. For example, if a song has the same structure for each chorus, you only need play the chorus once, then copy it to any bar location where you'd like another chorus. What's more, you don't have to copy all the tracks – you could simply copy sections of the drum track, or perhaps the keyboard pad part.

We've already seen that MIDI information comprises not just note information but also controller data from mod wheels, pitch bend wheels, expression pedals and so forth. Unless you deliberately filter out certain types of MIDI data (some sequencers have the facility to do this), you'll find that your sequencer captures Note On/Off, Velocity, Pitch, Modulation, Aftertouch and other Controller information as well as MIDI Program Changes and Bank Change messages. A useful trick when recording a part that needs a lot of complicated pitch bending or vibrato adding is to record the part straight on one track, then record the vibrato and pitch bend wheel controller data on another track set to the same MIDI channel. As you record the controller data track, you'll hear it affecting the performance on the original track.

This may be a little early for a power user tip, but a MIDI Program Change recorded during the count-in period of a track will ensure that synth being used for that track switches to the correct patch before playing commences. However, you can also insert Program Changes part way through a track if you want the sound to change for, say, a solo. This is the orchestral equivalent of writing a note on the score at a certain bar number to tell a violin player to put down his violin and play the next part on a flute! This isn't something you'd usually do in real life, but a MIDI module is equally proficient on all instruments and, as yet, MIDI modules don't have trades unions!

A sequencer track must also be told what synthesizer sound it is expected to control, so in addition to the MIDI channel (which tells it which instrument, or part of a multitimbral instrument it is controlling), it is also necessary to enter the program number of the patch you want to hear and, if the synthesizer supports MIDI Bank Change messages, you also need to tell it which bank the sound is in. For this reason, it helps to photocopy the relevant patch lists from your synthesizer manuals and pin them to the wall close to your sequencer.

playback

When your MIDI sequence is played back, the sequencer transmits the MIDI information to the receiving synth in exactly the same order, and with the same timing, as you originally played it, though you can change the tempo after recording without affecting the pitch (unlike a tape recorder where you're dealing with sound rather than MIDI data). If you're still not sure why the pitch doesn't increase as the tempo goes up, think back to the orchestra and score analogy; if the conductor asks for a piece to be played faster, the orchestral instruments don't change in pitch. Similarly, if you pedal a pianola faster, the paper roll will be moving faster but the piano's tuning will remain the same.

In reality, MIDI does have a finite timing resolution because the computer has to work to an internal timing routine based on an electronic clock, but in practice, MIDI is far more accurate than a typical human performer and is capable of resolving a bar of music into at least 960 time divisions and frequently more.

editing

In the editing pages of a typical sequencer, you can change the value, start time, length and velocity of any of the notes you've played, or you can build up compositions by entering the notes manually by placing new notes onto the quantise grid in non-real-time, rather like writing out manuscript. If you have a package with a scoring facility, it's also possible to enter notes directly onto the score, almost as though you were scoring on manuscript paper. The non-real-time entry of note information is sometimes also referred to as step-time entry.

quantisation

One important feature common to both hardware and software sequencers is the ability to quantise data after recording and this is a useful feature for those users not possessed of a perfect sense of timing. Essentially, when you opt to quantise something, the timing is changed so as to push each note you've recorded to the nearest exact subdivision of a bar. For example, if you are working in 4/4 time and you select 16 as your quantise value, every note moves to the nearest point on an invisible grid dividing the bar into 16 equal time slots.

Quantise must be used carefully as it can strip all the feel from some types of music, but on the other hand, if you're doing dance music where precise timing is essential, the quantise feature is indispensable. Keep in mind that the quantise function will only produce meaningful results if your original recording was made in time with the metronome click of the sequencer. Furthermore, if your timing is really out, you may find that when you quantise, the occasional note snaps to a quantisation position one step away from where you originally intended it to go. Quantise pushes notes to the nearest quantise step, and if your badly timed note was more than half a step out, it will be quantised to the wrong step!

The more recent computer-based packages allow you to unquantise data as well as quantise it, but some less advanced software sequencers and a number of hardware sequencers perform what is known as destructive quantise, so if you think you might need to go back to the original version, it's vital that you keep a copy of the original.

On more sophisticated sequencers, you'll find a percentage quantise option that allows the notes you've played to be shifted towards the exact quantise division by a percentage. For example, if you set a 50% quantise value, the note will move to a position half way between where you actually played it and the position of the nearest quantise division. This is great for tightening up your playing without losing all the feel.

Yet another quantise-related function is 'swing' where the quantise grid is moved away from regularly spaced slots to alternating longer and shorter slots. This can be used subtly to add feel or used more aggressively to turn a 4/4 track into a 2/4 track.

destructive and non-destructive

Although quantising is irreversible on some budget sequencers and sequencing packages, all serious systems will allow you to unquantise something at a later time if required. In fact many reversible procedures are made possible because the original recorded data isn't actually changed – you only hear changes because the data is processed in real time as the sequence plays back. Such features are said to be non-destructive, because the original performance data is left intact. Though this makes the computer behind your sequencer work harder, it means that you don't burn your bridges behind you when you make changes.

A number of other related non-destructive editing options are often available, including the ability to transpose your music, either as you play or after recording, the ability to make the music louder or softer by adjusting the overall velocity, and the ability to use the same piece of data at different points within the same song. On some systems you can even 'compress' the dynamic range of your MIDI data to even out the difference between your louder notes and the softer ones.

It may also be possible to delay or advance tracks relative to each other to change the feel of a piece of music. For example, using a negative delay to pull a snare drum beat forward will help make the track 'drive' along, whereas delaying the snare will make the beat 'lay back'. Such operations are frequently achieved by recalculating the note data during playback, but the real data isn't changed, which means you can always revert to your original performance data if the edits don't work out as expected.

Of course some edits are destructive insomuch as the changes are permanent, though even then, there's usually an undo function that allows you to reverse the last procedure you did. For example, if you move a note to a new time or pitch, that's a destructive edit, or if you erase or add a note, that's a destructive edit.

midi drums

You can sequence the sounds from your drum machine just as you can any other type of MIDI sound module, but you'll have to turn off the drum-machine's external MIDI sync first, otherwise every time you turn on your sequencer, the drum machine's internal patterns will start to play. Unlike a conventional instrument where each note on the keyboard plays a different pitch of the same sound, drum machines place different sounds on different keys allowing access to many different drum sounds.

Because it's difficult to play a complete drum part in one go via a keyboard, it's common practice to spread the drum part over several sequencer tracks so you can record, say, your bass and snare first, your hi-hats next and finally your fills. This way of working makes it easy to edit your drum tracks without having to work out what note is what drum sounds, but once the drum part is completed, you can always merge the tracks into one for convenience. There's more on drum machines in the Synthesizers section of this book.

sequencer types

All MIDI sequencers are based on computer technology, but you have a choice of buying a sequencer system that runs on an existing computer (such as an Atari ST, Apple Mac, Apple Power Mac, IBM PC or Commodore Amiga) or opting for a piece of dedicated hardware where everything you need is built into one box. The two types work in a similar manner – what tends to vary is the way in which the recorded information is displayed and how easily it can be edited. Hardware sequencers also come built into workstation-type keyboard synthesizers, and some hardware sequencers have built-in synthesizer modules.

For relatively accomplished players, hardware sequencers offer the benefits of simplicity and convenience, but because they don't have the information display capability of a full-size computer screen, and because there's no computer mouse, editing is generally less comprehensive and more time consuming that it would be on a computer-based system. However, the recording process is usually just a matter of selecting a track, hitting Record and playing. Another significant benefit of hardware computers is that they are more practical in live performance situations; they are more compact and more rugged than a computer plus monitor and you don't have so many things to plug in.

midi data storage

It's one thing recording a MIDI sequence, but what do you do with it once it's finished? There's no manuscript paper to store your work on – instead, your song data is stored as a MIDI song file on a floppy disk or hard drive. Some MIDI sequencers (including all the computer-based ones) lose their stored information when they are switched off, so it is vital to save your work to disk at regular intervals. Computers occasionally crash when you're least expecting them to so don't wait until you've finished a day's work to save it – save your work every few minutes.

A single floppy disk will hold several average complexity songs, and most hardware sequencers have a built-in disk drive for this purpose. Some low cost models, however, use battery-backed-up memory instead of disks. Once the memory is full, you either have to save your work to a MIDI data filer (which has an inbuilt disk drive) or erase your old project before you can start a new one. Usually this kind of sequencer can only store a few songs at a time, so a model with a built-in disk drive is preferable.

computer complexity?

The computer-based sequencer is capable of more sophistication than most hardware models, which means there may be a steeper learning curve. You must also familiarise yourself with the general operation of the computer before trying to tackle a sequencer package. However, this is more than made up for, in my opinion, by the amount of visual feedback available, especially when it comes to creating new song arrangements or editing what you've recorded.

midi interface

With a hardware sequencer, you simply plug your master keyboard into the MIDI In socket, plug a synthesizer in to the MIDI out socket, and you're ready to go. Computers, on the other hand, don't usually have MIDI sockets – the obvious exception being the popular, but ageing Atari ST. This means that unless you're using an Atari ST, you'll need to buy an external MIDI interface or use one of the synth modules that comes with a MIDI interface built-in. To use a computer for MIDI therefore, you'll need a MIDI interface and suitable sequencing software. Typical systems will be covered later in the book.

MIDI interfaces for Apple Macintosh machines plug in to the modem or printer ports on the back of the computer while PC users need either an interface card that goes inside the computer or an external, plug-in interface. Most PC sound cards include a MIDI interface facility, though it may be necessary to buy a special adaptor cable to make use of it.

user interface

The majority of the leading software sequencing packages have adopted the style of interface pioneered by Steinberg in their Cubase software. The success of this interface is that it uses a multitrack tape analogy, where the sequencer tracks are depicted as individual 'strips' one above the other, with musical bars running from left to right. Once a section of a track has been recorded, it shows up as a 'building brick' running from the record start bar location to the record end bar location. This sequence may then be 'dragged' (using the computer mouse) to a new position in the same track, or it may even be moved to a completely different track so that it plays back with a different sound. Sequence building blocks may also be copied, split into shorter sections or deleted as required.

Most software sequencers comprise a main page to handle basic 'recording' and arranging plus a number of further pages addressing various aspects of editing and, where applicable, scoring. The record and playback controls are invariably designed to look something like a tape recorder's transport control buttons, and the edit pages usually allow you to examine (and change), the recorded data as a list of MIDI events, graphically as a 'piano roll' display, or in the case of 'score' versions, as a conventional musical score. Most sequencers also have graphical editing capabilities for controller information. Figure 3.3 shows some of the edit pages from a popular software sequencer.

Some computer software sequencing packages also include sophisticated score-writing facilities which enable you to print out sheet music for your compositions, in which case you'll need a printer which is compatible both with your computer and the software package. However, some musical literacy is useful, because the computer doesn't always interpret what you play in the same way that a trained score writer would.

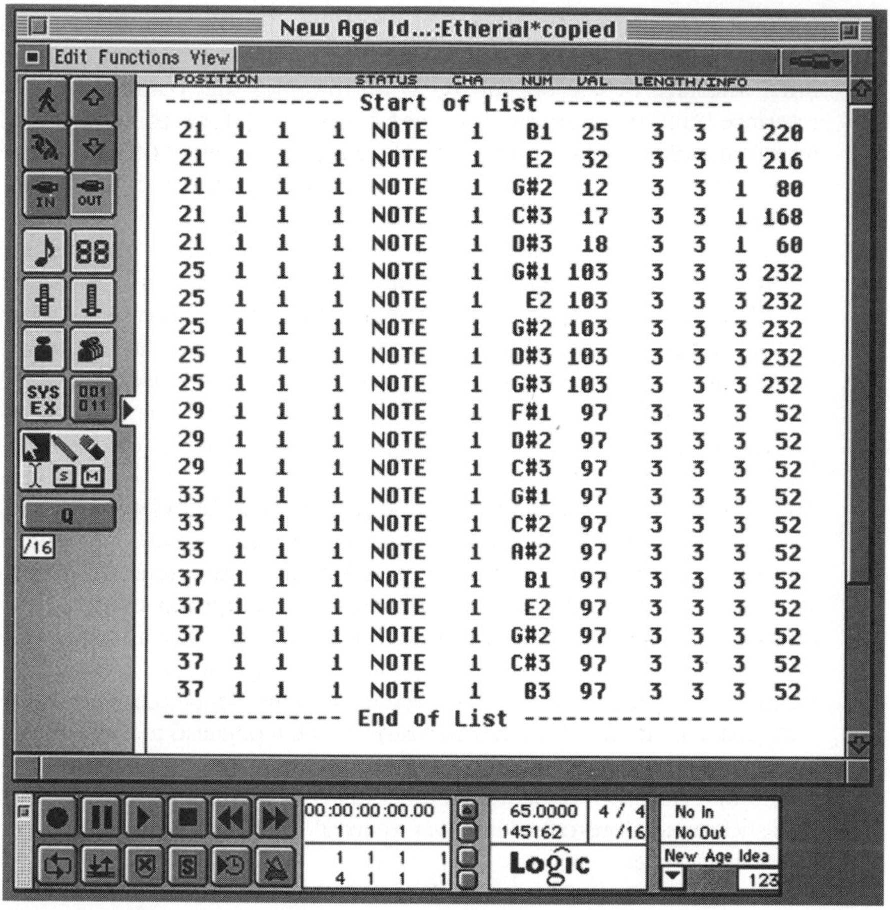

New Age Id...:Etherial*copied
Edit Functions View
POSITION STATUS CHA NUM VAL LENGTH/INFO
------------- Start of List -------------
21 1 1 1 NOTE 1 B1 25 3 3 1 220
21 1 1 1 NOTE 1 E2 32 3 3 1 216
21 1 1 1 NOTE 1 G#2 12 3 3 1 80
21 1 1 1 NOTE 1 C#3 17 3 3 1 168
21 1 1 1 NOTE 1 D#3 18 3 3 1 60
25 1 1 1 NOTE 1 G#1 103 3 3 3 232
25 1 1 1 NOTE 1 E2 103 3 3 3 232
25 1 1 1 NOTE 1 G#2 103 3 3 3 232
25 1 1 1 NOTE 1 D#3 103 3 3 3 232
25 1 1 1 NOTE 1 G#3 103 3 3 3 232
29 1 1 1 NOTE 1 F#1 97 3 3 3 52
29 1 1 1 NOTE 1 D#2 97 3 3 3 52
29 1 1 1 NOTE 1 C#3 97 3 3 3 52
33 1 1 1 NOTE 1 G#1 97 3 3 3 52
33 1 1 1 NOTE 1 C#2 97 3 3 3 52
33 1 1 1 NOTE 1 A#2 97 3 3 3 52
37 1 1 1 NOTE 1 B1 97 3 3 3 52
37 1 1 1 NOTE 1 E2 97 3 3 3 52
37 1 1 1 NOTE 1 G#2 97 3 3 3 52
37 1 1 1 NOTE 1 C#3 97 3 3 3 52
37 1 1 1 NOTE 1 B3 97 3 3 3 52
------------- End of List ---------------
IN OUT
SYS EX
Q
/16
00:00:00:00.00
1 1 1 1
1 1 1 1
4 1 1 1
65.0000 4 / 4
145162 /16
Logic
No In
No Out
New Age Idea
123

Figure 3.3: Sequencer Edit pages

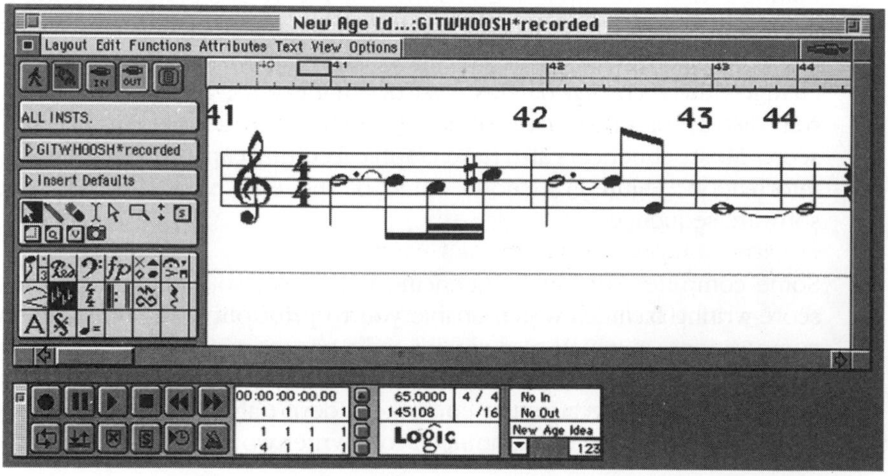

overview

MIDI sequencers are very powerful tools both for music composition and recording, and because they have become so sophisticated, there are still a great many things that I haven't discussed. For example, MIDI allows you to remotely control the volume of your synths – by recording MIDI volume information, you can create automated mixes. Wonderful though sequencers are though, they are still far from being perfect. Aside from the inevitable software bugs that creep in, they tend to force you to work in a way that you probably wouldn't work if you were playing and composing conventionally.

Most insidious is the metronome or tempo click that you have to play along to, and although you can turn this off and record 'free', regardless of bar positions, you won't be able to quantise your data and you won't be able to print out a meaningful score. This means that tempo changes have to be planned rather than being intuitive, and although software designers are now putting in features to help you in this area (such as re-barring), it takes a lot of determination to move away from the fixed tempo, four to the bar music that we've all become so accustomed to.

Despite the pitfalls mentioned, MIDI sequencing still offers far more advantages than disadvantages, and used creatively, it makes many things possible that would have been far too impractical or expensive in the pre-MIDI era. And finally, don't think that sequencing is difficult – once you've made a start and seen how easy it is to handle the basics, you'll wonder why the manuals ever needed to be so thick!

hardware versus software

Software sequencers have several obvious advantages over hardware sequencers, but that doesn't mean that they're better – it all depends on what facilities you need and whether you want your sequencer to be portable. The main pros of software sequencers are as follows:

- A good visual interface.
- More comprehensive editing facilities.
- You can still use the computer for other purposes.
- You're not tied to one manufacturer for software upgrades – if somebody comes out with a better program, you can always move over to it.

- Most computer sequencers support multiple MIDI output ports via a special multi-port MIDI interface (see MIDI Ports section). This means you are not restricted to 16 MIDI channels and a typical system will provide six output ports giving you up to 96 MIDI channels to work with. By contrast, the majority of hardware sequencers support only one or two MIDI output ports.

- The most popular sequencer software packages now allow you to transfer song data from one computer platform to another and, in some cases, even from one manufacturer's software sequencer to another's.

- Professional standard score printing is available from many sequencing packages using either an inexpensive ink-jet printer or a laser printer.

Hardware sequencers have their advantages too, the main ones being listed below:

- One-box solution to sequencing.

- Generally more reliable than computers in live situations or when being moved from studio to studio.

- Though they may have fewer editing options than a software sequencer, they also tend to be easier to learn.

- You don't have to learn to use a computer before you can begin to learn your sequencer software.

- No installation difficulties or hardware incompatibility problems.

midi ports

A basic MIDI interface provides a single MIDI output socket – which means you have a maximum of 16 MIDI channels available. However, you may want to use two or more multitimbral synthesizers to create a composition with more than 16 parts or, as is more often the case, you may have several synthesizer modules and want to change from one to the other without having to reconnect MIDI leads. The answer to this is to use a MIDI interface with multiple output ports.

You can never have more than 16 MIDI channels, but if you use a multi-port MIDI interface in conjunction with compatible sequencing software, you can have several different sets of 16 MIDI channels. Within the sequencer, the ports may be designated by number or letter, so that you have 16 channels on port A, another 16 on port B and a further 16 on port C. If a different 16-part multitimbral synth module is connected to each of these ports, you have 48 different sound sources, each of which can be addressed individually be specifying a MIDI channel plus port number A, B or C. Figure 3.4 shows how a multi-port system might be configured. It is important to realise that you must buy a multi-port interface that is supported by the sequencing software you choose, and a list of suitable interfaces should be listed in the sequencer manual. If in any doubt at all, consult your dealer.

Hardware-based sequencers tend to have only one or two output ports, and with no means for expansion, this constitutes one of their greatest limitations in a complex MIDI setup. Hopefully, future designers will realise this problem and build in the opportunity for port expansion, or at the very least, support for external MIDI multi-port interfaces.

main sequencer features

What basic features can you expect from a MIDI sequencer? Obviously every sequencer is different, but all should be capable of the following core functions.

● Real-Time Recording: a MIDI performance can be played in real-time from a keyboard and recorded in much the same way as a tape recorder. Unlike a tape recorder though, you can transpose, change tempo, pick a different synth sound and quantise your data after recording. If you want to use the quantise feature, you have to play to the internal metronome track.

● Step Time Recording: notes are played in one note at a time – it's rather like typing a letter with one finger! You decide where the notes go and how long they're going to be, after which you can play back your work at any tempo. Most people use mainly real-time recording with occasional recourse to step-time when the going gets tough. With a piano roll-type of editing screen, you can also 'draw' your notes directly onto the quantise grid and then use the mouse pointer to 'stretch' them to length. A package with scoring facilities will allow you to place conventional musical symbols onto a stave.

● Synchronisation facilities: though you can make music entirely by sequencer, it's sometimes useful to be able to use a drum machine or tape recorder at the same time. In order to make the tempo of a sequencer sync to that of another MIDI device of tape machine (equipped with suitable sync interface), it must be equipped with sync facilities, and these are sometimes omitted on very cheap budget sequencing software. There are several sync options, described in the chapter MIDI Sync.

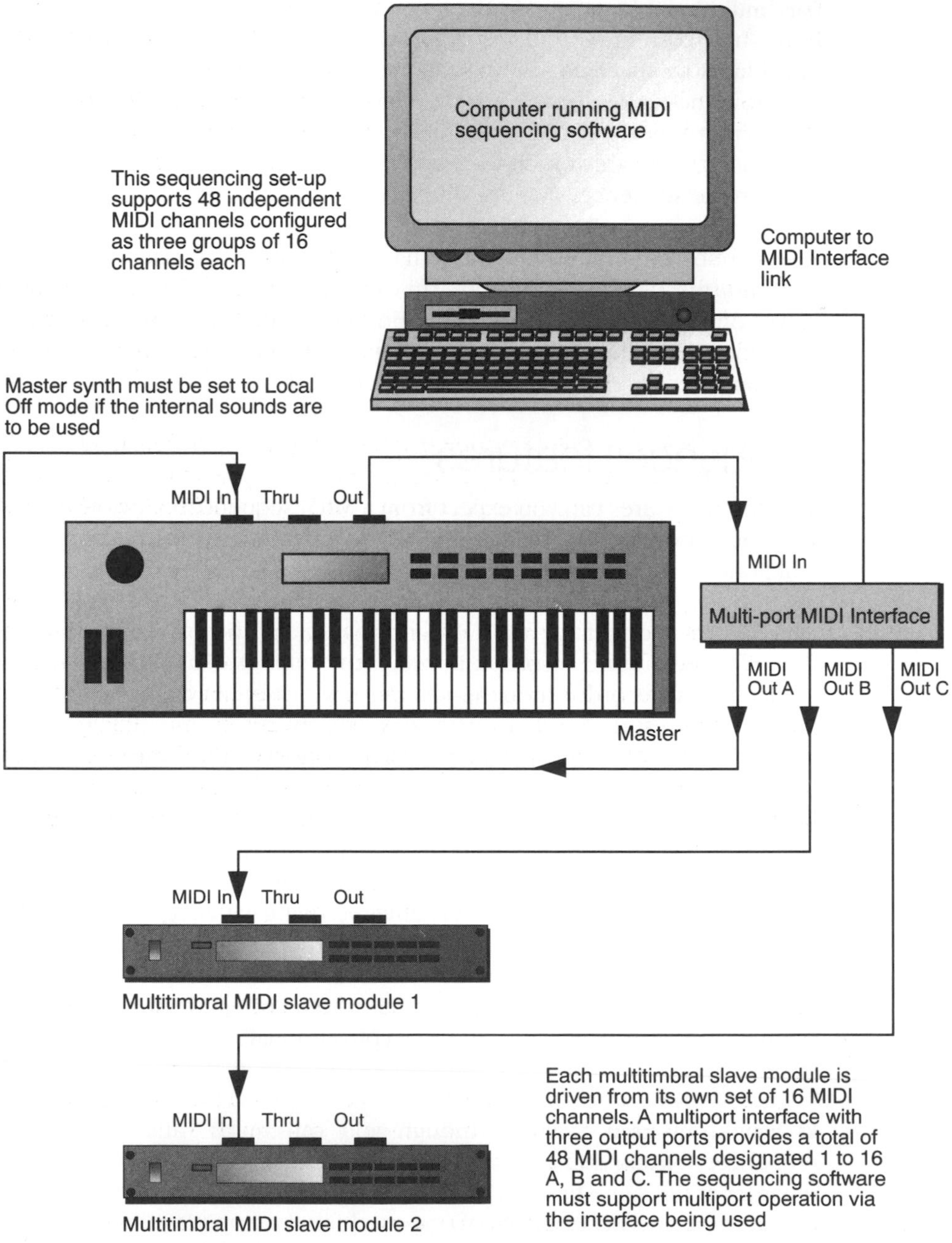
Computer running MIDI sequencing software
This sequencing set-up supports 48 independent MIDI channels configured as three groups of 16 channels each
Computer to MIDI Interface link
Master synth must be set to Local Off mode if the internal sounds are to be used
MIDI In
Thru
Out
MIDI In
Multi-port MIDI Interface
MIDI Out A
MIDI Out B
MIDI Out C
Master
MIDI In
Thru
Out
Multitimbral MIDI slave module 1
MIDI In
Thru
Out
Multitimbral MIDI slave module 2
Each multitimbral slave module is driven from its own set of 16 MIDI channels. A multiport interface with three output ports provides a total of 48 MIDI channels designated 1 to 16 A, B and C. The sequencing software must support multiport operation via the interface being used

Figure 3.4 shows how a multi-port system might be configured

● Multi-Port interface support: in a complex MIDI system, one set of 16 MIDI channels may not be enough. A multi-port MIDI interface, compatible with the sequencing software used, will provide up to eight separate MIDI outputs, each with its own set of 16 MIDI channels. This should not be confused with a simple multi-output interface where multiple output sockets carry duplicates of the same MIDI data. These are really just a combination of a single-port interface and a MIDI Thru box.

● File Import: MIDI sequencers tend to save song data in a proprietary format, which other sequencers may not be able to read. Some of the more advanced software systems include the ability to load and import song files from other sequencers, but a more common method of file transfer is to use the Standard MIDI File (SMF) format.

SMFs were devised to allow complete interchangeability between MIDI song files, and it also makes it possible for third-party companies to provide commercial sequencer files that can be read by any machine. SMFs can however, only handle the basic 16 MIDI channels, not multi-port data.

Note: Though the file format may be a standard, the floppy disk formats used by different computers aren't always interchangeable. For example, Atari STs and PCs can read the same format of disk (though the ST can't handle high density (HD) disks), and the Apple Mac can only read PC disks if it is running either System 7.5 software or upwards or, it is equipped with a PC to Mac file exchange program such as AccessPC. Hardware sequencers may have their own disk formats, in which case MIDI song files can only be loaded if they are stored on disks that have been formatted on the same type of machine.

● Edit: a typical sequencer will include a number of editing tools to enable you to change your composition after recording. These range from the ability to change individual notes to the ability to change entire arrangements and swap instruments. The main editing operations are listed below:

● Quantisation: this is the ability to move your notes to the nearest accurate subdivision of a bar (for example, 16ths of a bar). The user can set the number of quantise subdivisions in a bar prior to quantising.

● Transposition: notes can be transposed by any amount without altering their lengths while entire compositions or sections of compositions can easily be shifted to a different key.

- Copy/Cut/Paste: any section of music can be copied to different tracks or to different locations in the song. This is useful for duplicating repeated sections such as choruses, or for doubling up a line of music on two tracks by copying a part, then assigning the copy to a different instrument sound than the original. Cut allows unwanted material to be removed.

- Mute: most sequencers allow you to Mute tracks so that you can record a number of alternate tracks, then listen to only the ones you want. This is useful if you've just played three solos but you don't know which one was best.

- Solo: mutes all the other tracks so you can hear the soloed track in isolation.

- Cycle: simply allows you to continually loop around a specific section of music while you record or edit. This mode is also useful for rehearsing parts prior to recording

- Undo: if provided, the Undo function lets you reverse or undo the last operation. Usually, there is only one level of undo, though a few systems provide multiple levels of undo.

midi problems

A basic MIDI sequencing setup starts at your keyboard – it's here that the MIDI information to be recorded originates. The master keyboard is connected via its MIDI Out to the MIDI In of your MIDI interface or directly to the MIDI In of your hardware sequencer or Atari ST. As mentioned earlier, if your keyboard includes a synth section (in other words it makes sounds), then turn Local Off and patch a MIDI cable from the sequencer's MIDI Out to the keyboard's MIDI In. If you have other MIDI modules in the system, you can daisy chain them in any order by feeding the MIDI Thru of one piece of gear to the MIDI In, or use a Thru box.

If you have a master keyboard that doesn't have a Local Off facility, consult your sequencer manual to see if you can disable the MIDI Thru on the channel your master keyboard is set to. Most sequencers provide for this eventuality.

Up to three modules can normally be chained in this way without problems, but longer chains may suffer stuck or missed notes (due to corruption of the MIDI signal), in which case you should use a multiple output MIDI Thru box on the output of your sequencer, then feed each module (or short chain of two or three modules), from separate outputs on the Thru box.

midi timing

MIDI has a finite timing resolution because the computer's internal timing routine is based on an electronic clock. However, MIDI still is far more accurate than a human performer and is capable of resolving a 4/4 bar of music into at least 960 time divisions. Some software extends this to an even finer degree of timing resolution, but there are situations that can cause timing problems.

MIDI is a serial data protocol, which means all the data moves in single file. Because the data speed is reasonably high, this isn't usually a problem, but if you try to send too much data at once, such as all 16 channels trying to play a large musical chord at exactly the same time, you get a musical traffic jam causing the notes to be spread out slightly. Using lots of other MIDI control data can also slow things up, but the better sequencing software packages give priority to note timing which helps reduce the problem.

In most normal musical compositions, MIDI timing shouldn't be an issue, but if problems do arise, one tip is to put the most time-sensitive parts, such as drums, onto the first few tracks and less critical things, such as slow attack strings onto the later tracks. That's because the first track is usually dealt with first in terms of timing priority. Timing problems may also occur with older keyboards or instruments that take longer than they should to send out or respond to information. Some early MIDI keyboards took around 10mS to send a MIDI message after a key had been depressed, and a slow module or synthesizer could take the same time to respond to an incoming MIDI note message. Modern instruments are generally better, but some models are still noticeably faster than others.

check list

If you've connected up your system as described but no sound comes out, here are a few things to check.

- Verify that everything is switched on and that your synth modules are set to Multi or Sequencer mode (assuming you want to use them multitimbrally). Also make sure your synths are set to the same MIDI channels you're sending data on.

- Check your MIDI cable connections and don't rule out the possibility of a faulty MIDI lead. Some modules have a combined MIDI Out/Thru socket; if so, ensure MIDI Thru is enabled (see handbook for that piece of equipment). To help narrow the problem down, most sequencers have some form of indication that they're receiving MIDI data, and many modules have an LED or other indicator that blinks when data is being received.

- Check that Omni mode is switched off (Poly mode is most commonly used), on all modules. If two or more instruments try to play the same part, the chances are you've either got more than one module set to the same MIDI channel or something's been left set to Omni. If your master keyboard plays its own sounds whenever you try to record on any track or channel, check that Local Off is really set to Off. On some instruments, Local Off reverts to Local On every time you switch on the power.

- If playing a single note results in a burst of sound, rather like machine-gun fire, or if you get stuck notes, or apparently limited polyphony, the chances are you have a MIDI loop. In a MIDI loop, MIDI data generated by the master keyboard passes through the sequencer and somehow gets back to the input of the master keyboard where it starts its round trip all over again, rather like acoustic feedback. This usually happens when you have a keyboard synth as your master keyboard and you've forgotten to select Local Off.

If you have one of those rare instruments with no Local Off facility, you'll probably find that your sequencer allows you to disable the sequencer MIDI Thru on the channel your master keyboard is sending on (which most people leave set to channel 1).

If you are unfortunate enough to have neither facility, then all you can do is record with the MIDI In disconnected from your master keyboard and use the sounds from external modules. When you've finished recording, you can, if you wish, reconnect the master keyboard's MIDI In and use it to play back one of the recorded parts or to layer it with an existing synth voice.

chapter 4

MIDI and synchronisation

Sequencers with integral hard-disk audio recording systems offer a practical way of combining audio with MIDI, but they still tend to be expensive and there's also the problem of backing up very large audio data files. Because of this, many people still use multitrack tape, and though you can simply record your sequence onto multitrack tape, then add your vocals, guitars and whatever, this isn't the most effective way to work. Multitrack tape recorders are limited by the number of tracks they provide – and the more tracks you want, the more you have to pay. True, you can bounce or combine recorded tracks, then re-record the result onto a spare track, but every time you do this, the sound quality is degraded and you also lose the opportunity to rebalance, pan or add effects to those tracks that have been bounced.

In the early days of home recording, there was no alternative to recording everything on tape, but the introduction of MIDI sequencing changed all that. Obviously, you can't use a MIDI-controlled instrument to replace every instrument or sound that you'd normally want to record, but in the context of pop music, you can certainly use MIDI drums, bass and keyboard parts, as well as samples of instruments such as piano, brass, flute, and so on.

The ideal solution would be to find a way of making the sequencer and tape machine run in perfect sync with each other, that way the multitrack recorder could be filled up with real voices and instruments leaving the sequencer to look after the MIDI part of the performance. This way, the sequenced sounds can be fed into the final mix without ever having been recorded on multitrack at all. A major benefit of working in this way is that you can always change the sounds on your MIDI instruments, right up to the moment before you mix, whereas if you had mixed your MIDI sequence to tape, there would be no way to change it.

In the movie industry, cine film and magnetic audio tape are kept in sync by means of sprocket holes cut into the edges of the film and tape. These pass over toothed cogs fitted to the same shaft, so once the two are lined up, they always stay in sync. MIDI provides us with a simple means of doing this electronically.

time codes

The answer is to record some form of MIDI sync code onto tape – a series of pulses that do the same job as the sprocket holes in cine film. This means you use up one tape track to record the necessary sync code, but you gain as many 'virtual tracks' as your sequencer and synth/sound module collection can provide. For example, if you have a 4-track tape machine working on its own, the most you can get is four tracks, but if you sync a MIDI sequencer to run along with it, you have three tracks left on the tape after recording the time code, plus as many sequencer tracks as your sequencer and synth collection can provide. Figure 4.1 shows how this works in practice. The concept is simple, but to understand more about it, it's necessary to know a little more about 'MIDI clock'.

midi clock

MIDI sequencers (and drum machines) have an internal tempo clock – a kind of invisible timing grid on which all the notes are placed. Think of MIDI clock as being like a metronome, but instead of getting four ticks to each 4/4 bar, you get 386. This MIDI clock provides the electronic sprockets and gears that allow two or more pieces of MIDI equipment to be run in perfect synchronisation where one device acts as master (and thus dictates the tempo), and the others function as slaves. For example, using just MIDI clock, you can connect two drum machines so that they both run in sync, you can slave a sequencer to a drum machine or you can slave a drum machine to a sequencer. And with the aid of a suitable sync box, sequencers may also be synced to tape machines.

In physical terms, MIDI clock is a part of the data stream coming out of the master device's MIDI Out socket – no additional cables or connections are needed – just a regular MIDI lead. The MIDI Out of the master links to the MIDI In of the slave. The master machine constantly sends out MIDI clock at the currently set tempo, regardless of whether it is started or stopped so that any slave devices plugged into it will know exactly what tempo to start running at when a MIDI Start command is received.

MIDI Start, Stop and Continue messages are a part of the standard MIDI 'Real-Time messages' protocol and are automatically sent by the master device. Stopping the master sends a MIDI Stop command, so any slaves also stop. The Continue command forces the machines to continue playing from the point at which they were stopped so that you don't have to go right back

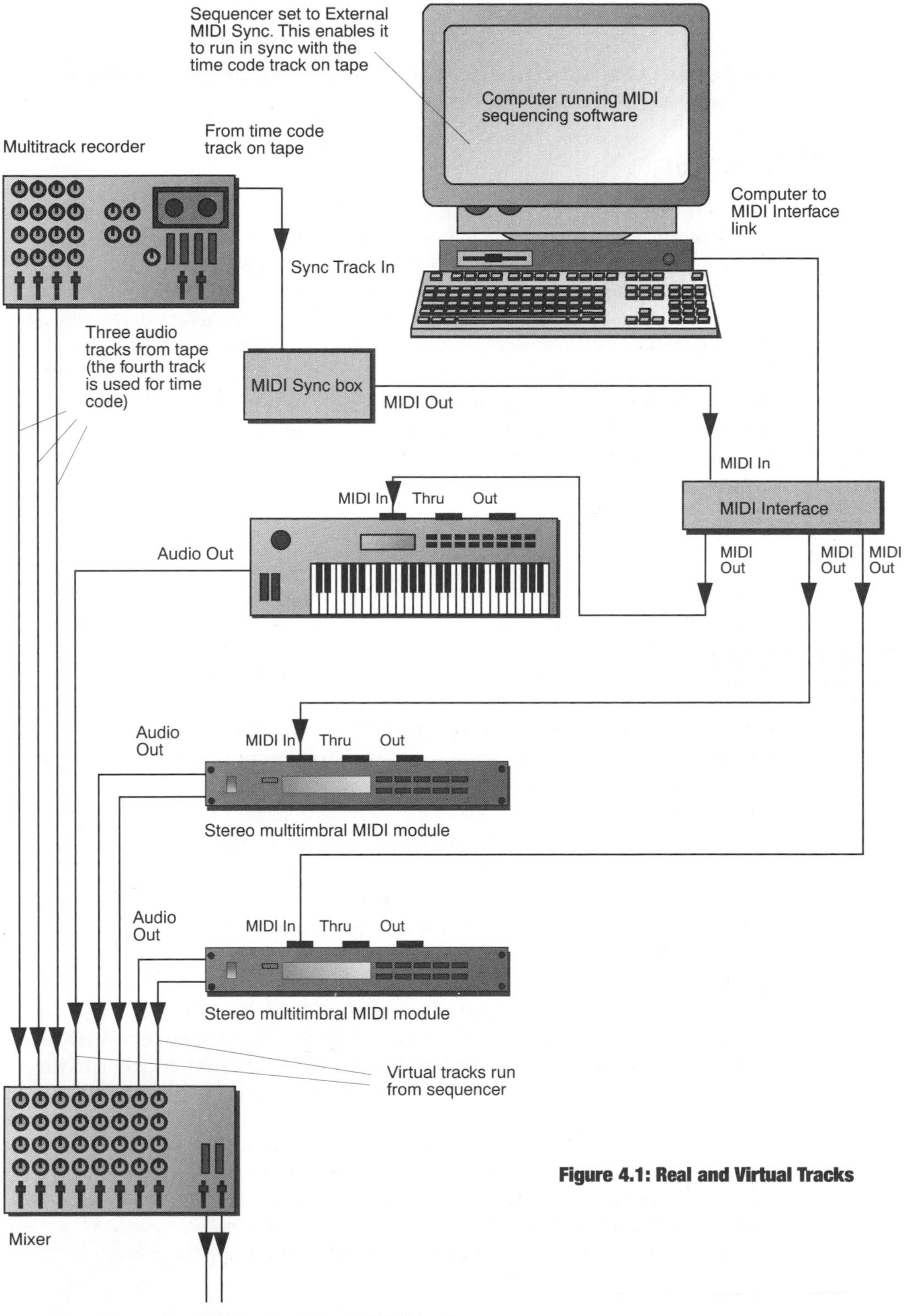

Figure 4.1: Real and Virtual Tracks

to the start. A MIDI Start message, on the other hand, always causes the song to start from the beginning.

external sync

To set up sync between two MIDI devices, the master unit is set to internal clock mode and the slave machine to external clock mode. Now, whenever you start the master machine, the slave will start automatically and run in perfect sync with it. This is all very well if you simply want to run a drum machine and a sequencer together, but how does it work with a tape recorder?

What's needed is a device that makes a sequencer set to external sync (slave mode) think it's hooked up to a MIDI master device when it's actually connected to a tape machine. Not surprisingly, such a device is called a MIDI-to-tape sync unit.

tape sync

Tape machines can't record MIDI signals directly, so the job of a MIDI-to-tape sync is to convert MIDI clock timing data into a form that can be recorded onto one track of the tape. In practice, there are several systems to choose from, though all convert the MIDI pulses into bursts of high pitched sound that can be recorded onto tape. The system works by switching between two different frequencies, and though this is quite transparent to the user and requires no knowledge to operate, it's interesting to note that this system is known as Frequency Shift Keying, or FSK for short.

The way a MIDI FSK sync box works is something like this: after writing your sequence, a MIDI-to-tape sync unit is connected between the sequencer and tape machine, then the sequence is played back while recording the time code on tape. The tempo of the song determines the speed of the MIDI clock and hence the tempo embedded in the time code.

To play back, you'd run the tape, play the time code track back through the MIDI-to-tape sync unit, and patch its MIDI Out to the sequencer's MIDI In with the sequencer set to external MIDI sync mode. As soon as you run the tape from the start of the song, the sequencer will start in sync with it. This system works fine – but only if you start at the beginning of the song every time. Figure 4.2 shows how a MIDI-to-tape sync unit is connected. This is clearly unsatisfactory if you want to work on a section a long way from the start.

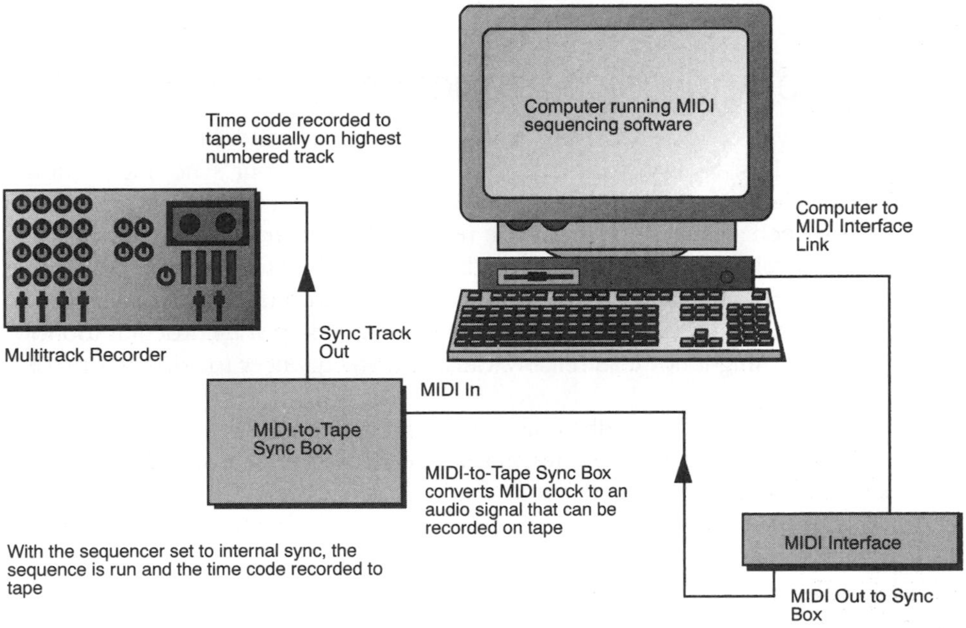
Time code recorded to tape, usually on highest numbered track
Computer running MIDI sequencing software
Computer to MIDI Interface Link
Multitrack Recorder
Sync Track Out
MIDI In
MIDI-to-Tape Sync Box
MIDI-to-Tape Sync Box converts MIDI clock to an audio signal that can be recorded on tape
MIDI Interface
With the sequencer set to internal sync, the sequence is run and the time code recorded to tape
MIDI Out to Sync Box

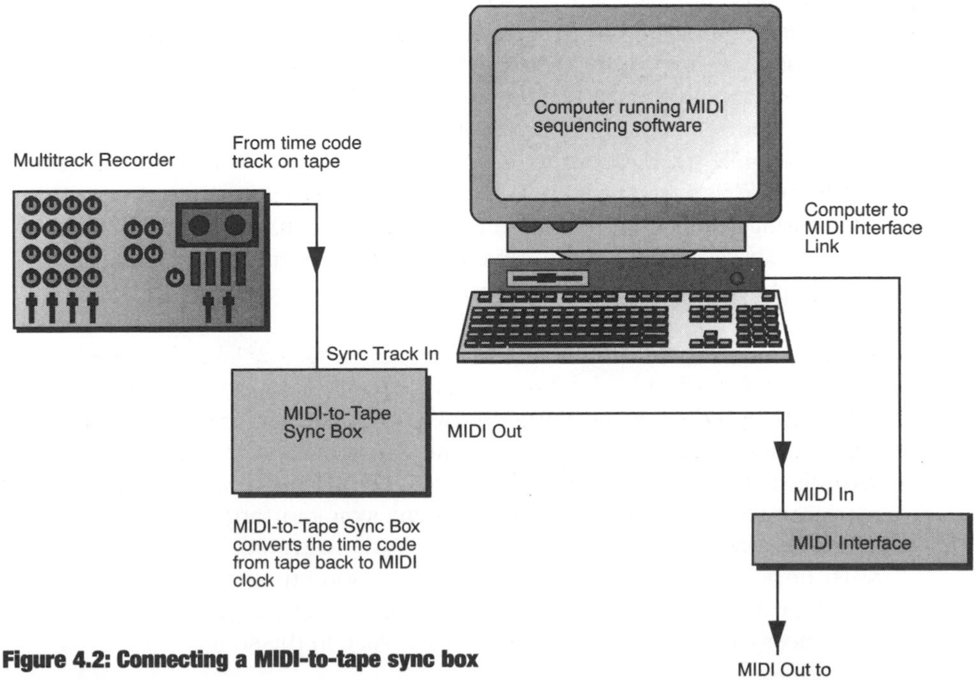
Computer running MIDI sequencing software
Multitrack Recorder
From time code track on tape
Computer to MIDI Interface Link
Sync Track In
MIDI-to-Tape Sync Box
MIDI Out
MIDI In
MIDI-to-Tape Sync Box converts the time code from tape back to MIDI clock
MIDI Interface
MIDI Out to connected modules

Figure 4.2: Connecting a MIDI-to-tape sync box

time code and noise reduction

Some types of tape noise reduction can affect the reliability of time codes, so it is best to switch off the noise reduction on your sync track if at all possible. If the multitrack has a dedicated sync input and output, these will have been arranged to bypass the noise reduction and any EQ controls, to allow a reliable recording to be made. You may need to experiment with the code level, since if recorded too high, it could 'bleed' over to the adjacent tracks, making it audible in the final mix. Conversely, if recorded at too low a level, it might not read reliably, causing the sequencer to 'hiccup' or stop.

As a very general rule, dbx noise reduction systems have the greatest effect on time code, whereas Dolby C doesn't seem to affect it at all. Unfortunately, some of the very early multitrackers only allow the noise reduction to be switched on or off globally for all four channels, which means that if you want to work with a sync code, you'll have to put up with more tape hiss.

multitrack sync facilities

In order to use a sync unit with a multitrack tape machine, it is vital that the machine either has a dedicated sync in and out or that you can access the output from your sync track directly without it having to be added into the stereo mix as might be the case with a budget cassette multitracker – time code is very unmusical! It is sometimes possible to work around the problem of not having a separate sync track output, but this usually involves some form of compromise. For example, with a tape machine that has only a single stereo output, you could pan the three audio tracks to the left and the sync code to the right. The left output would then contain all the audio in mono, while the right output contains only the sync code. Depending on the machine, it may also be possible to route the sync track to the outside world using one pre-fade (sometimes called Foldback) aux send and turning the channel fader right down. Of course, this prevents that particular aux send being used for any other purpose.

smart fsk

Smart FSK is a distinct improvement over simple dumb FSK systems, and it works using a piece of hidden MIDI information known as the MIDI Song Position Pointer or SPP. Again, SPPs are invisible to the user, and as most modern MIDI equipment recognises them, you can forget all about them and let the computer or drum machine do the worrying. In effect SPPs let MIDI devices know exactly whereabouts in a song they're supposed to be. Their great benefit is that you can start the tape anywhere and your slave sequencer will sync up at exactly the right place in the song.

A practical advantage of all MIDI Clock-based sync systems is that the tempo of the music is directly related to the clock rate of the sync code, and the sync code is created from the tempo of your original sequence. This means any tempo changes in the original sequence will be followed automatically when the tape is run, and if you speed up the tape, you speed up the code – which in turn speeds up the sequencer. Unless you need anything more sophisticated, Smart FSK is the most worry-free, and least costly way to achieve sequencer-to-tape sync. Of course it may also be used to sync a drum machine to tape if you don't have a sequencer.

Smart FSK MIDI-to-tape sync units are relatively inexpensive, and they're made by a number of manufacturers, but if you can afford a unit with built-in MIDI merge, it's worth paying the extra. The reason is that if you don't have MIDI merge facility, the MIDI In of your sequencer is occupied reading time code, so you can't record any new MIDI sequencer parts while the sequencer and tape machine are synced up. However, if your sync box has a MIDI merge input, you can plug your master keyboard into it and record new MIDI parts while the tape and sequencer are running in sync. This could be important if you're playing a part that relies on you hearing the vocals or an on-tape guitar solo to get the right feel.

smpte

There is another synchronisation system, originally developed for the film industry, but now it is also used in many musical applications. If you need to sync a sequencer to a video tape or film, then some knowledge of SMPTE time code is essential, and like MIDI clock, a hardware interface box of some kind is required. Many of the modern multi-port interfaces have inbuilt support for SMPTE and MTC (which will be covered shortly).

SMPTE (pronounced Simptee), is not directly related to MIDI in any way, but is instead a sophisticated time code system based on elapsed time rather than, as in the case of MIDI clock, bars and beats. SMPTE is unnecessarily sophisticated for syncing MIDI sequencers to tape machines, but if your model of sequencer has a dedicated, low cost SMPTE sync unit available for it, all the complications will be taken care of for you.

Why is SMPTE more complicated than MIDI clock? Because SMPTE time code is related to absolute time, not to tempo; it's rather like having an invisible ruler printed on your tape marking out hours, minutes, seconds, and film frames. For example, the SMPTE readout for 1 hour, 10 minutes, 30 seconds and 11 frames would look like – 01:10:30:11. Because there is no tempo information inherent in the time code itself, a conversion has to be done somewhere along the line, either by the computer used to run the sequencing software, or by the microprocessor inside the SMPTE-to-MIDI sync box. To convert the SMPTE frame rate to tempo requires a bit of basic maths, but if you're lucky, your sequencer software will handle this for you quite automatically. If it doesn't, you have to key in a 'tempo map' telling the sync box or sequencer when the song starts, what tempo it runs at, and where any tempo changes are. This is obviously tedious, especially if you compose music with lots of tempo changes. Fortunately, most modern software-based sequencers handle SMPTE sync without you having to decide anything other than when the song starts, though it is important to note that some low cost sequencer software leaves out synchronisation facilities to save on cost.

smpte frames

Because of the different film and TV frame rates used around the world, SMPTE comes in several frame formats, the most common being 30fps for US TV, 25fps for European TV and 24fps for film. Strictly speaking, we should use the term SMPTE/EBU to cover all the US and European formats, but most users abbreviate it to plain old SMPTE anyway. There's also a format called drop-frame which is used when converting one picture format to another, but this is rarely used for musical work and will not be discussed further here.

mtc

MIDI Time Code follows the same format as SMPTE in that it is independent of musical tempo and expresses elapsed time in hours, minutes, seconds and frames, and all the common SMPTE variants have an MTC equivalent. Standard MIDI clock sync doesn't include any position information – it's rather like the sprocket holes in cine film – so if a sync pulse gets lost, the sequencer will happily follow along one pulse late. SMPTE, on the other hand, comprises a continuous stream of positional data, so if a short section of code gets lost or corrupted, the system knows exactly where it's supposed to be the next time a piece of valid code is read.

MTC also includes positional information but, because it has to share the MIDI data highway with other information, its data is sent in short bursts – four to each SMPTE frame. It takes eight of these 'quarter frame' messages to carry enough data to make up one complete set of location data, which means that the receiving MIDI device must read two frames of code before it knows where it's supposed to be. Technically, MTC can't pass on positional information as quickly or as accurately as SMPTE, but for practical tape-to-MIDI sync applications, a little clever software writing on behalf of the sequencer designers ensures that there's no practical difference.

mtc and timing

If MTC has a weakness, it's that its position in the MIDI data stream can get jostled about when a lot of data is being sent, and if you have a multi-port MIDI interface, it's usually best to make sure the port carrying the MTC isn't clogged with other MIDI data. If the MIDI data stream is running close to capacity, the MTC data may arrive a little behind schedule which has the effect of introducing a small amount of timing jitter, and in really adverse situations, this may be serious enough to be noticeable.

Fortunately, the major packages support MTC very effectively and do all the hard work for you, so don't be frightened off before checking how your sequencing package handles MTC. All the current major sequencing packages handle MTC sync quite transparently, producing and storing a tempo map as part of the song file.

To make use of MTC sync with a traditional tape recorder, a hardware sync box is required to convert the MTC MIDI signal into an FSK signal that can be recorded onto tape. Such devices are available separately, but it is more normal to use a multi-port MIDI interface with MTC sync capability built-in. Some tapeless recording systems (and ADAT digital tape recorders running with a BRC remote control) have the ability to generate MTC directly, in which case all that is needed to sync up a sequencer is a MIDI cable.

striping tape

Unlike working with MIDI clock, when using MTC or SMPTE, you don't have to create your sequence before recording the code onto tape. FSK, on the other hand, requires that you have programmed your sequence, at least as far as its length and tempo goes, before you start work. Furthermore, if you do decide a tempo change is in order, you have to re-stripe with a new FSK code, whereas with SMPTE or MTC you simply have to create a new tempo map.

Before you can do any work with SMPTE or MTC, the code must be recorded onto tape – a process known as striping. However, ensure that the correct frame rate is selected before you do this. Once the tape is striped, a start time must be entered into your sequencing software so that it knows where to start playing relative to the code on tape. Many SMPTE and MTC systems don't work reliably when crossing the 00:00:00:00 'midnight hour', so it's quite common to enter a time offset when striping the tape (one hour is an easy amount to deal with), so that when you start the tape a few seconds before the song begins, you don't go back across the midnight hour. Failure to observe this can result in a loss of sync or even a total 'freezing' of the system. With most sequencer packages, once you've set up a SMPTE start time, the tempo map is created automatically and stored along with the song data when you save to disk. If the tempo is modified at any stage, the tempo map will be modified next time you save your song.

key points

● The master machine in a sync system must be set to internal sync mode, while any slaves should be set to external sync.

● When a MIDI clock-based code is being recorded to tape, the sequencer is the master, but when it comes to playing back the code, the sequencer becomes the slave and so should be set to external sync.

● With any MIDI clock-based sync system, it is not possible to vary the sequencer tempo once the code has been recorded to tape – once the sequencer is synced up, it will always play at the tempo of the code on tape, regardless of any new changes.

● With SMPTE and MTC, the time code is 'striped' onto the tape before the session starts. You can even stripe the entire tape with code in one go, then enter the appropriate start times for the various songs into the sequencer software.

● Because SMPTE/MTC carries only real absolute information, a tempo map must be created in order for the sequencer's tempo to be calculated. Most contemporary sequencing software packages manage this task automatically and save the tempo map as part of the song file.

● Be warned that tape noise reduction systems can cause sync codes to work unreliably. Many cassette multitrackers have a dedicated sync option which defeats the noise reduction on the track the code is being recorded onto (usually the highest numbered track). If no such facility is available, set the EQ to its flat position and experiment with different record levels to see which provides the most reliable operation. Most Dolby noise reduction systems can be used with sync codes, though dbx often gives trouble.

chapter 5

the basics of synthesis

Synthesizers are fascinating instruments, though they still fall far short of their original ideal, which was to be able to produce any conceivable sound. Having a keyboard instrument that could emulate any known instrument, produce an infinite range of new sounds and respond to the player's touch like a 'real' musical instrument is an admirable goal, but the more you learn about the mechanics of sound, the further away this goal seems. Nevertheless, electronic designers have spawned a varied range of complex and fascinating instruments, all of which come under the generic heading of synthesizers.

The forerunner to the synthesizer was the electronic organ, but unlike true acoustic instruments, the organ can only produce fixed level sounds which are tonally constant throughout their duration. What's more, the note produced by an organ starts abruptly when a key is pressed and stops abruptly when that key is released again. By contrast, real life instruments are far more complex – their sound may start abruptly, or it may increase gradually as in the case of a gently bowed violin or cello. Furthermore, the level of the note may decay as in the case of a plucked string, and the harmonic structure may also change as the note evolves.

Before we can approach synthesis in a meaningful way, we need to know something about the fundamental principles of sound and how those principles apply to traditional musical instruments.

sound

Sound is produced by airborne vibrations which impinge on the human ear and are translated by the human brain into the sensation we know as hearing. The textbook analogy of sound has us observing the ripples when a stone is thrown into a pond – the ripples spread outwards in a circular fashion, and their level decreases as the distance from the source increases. Sound is simply ripples in the air, and a human hearing system in good condition can register frequencies of between 50 ripples per

Figure 5.1: A pure tone sine wave

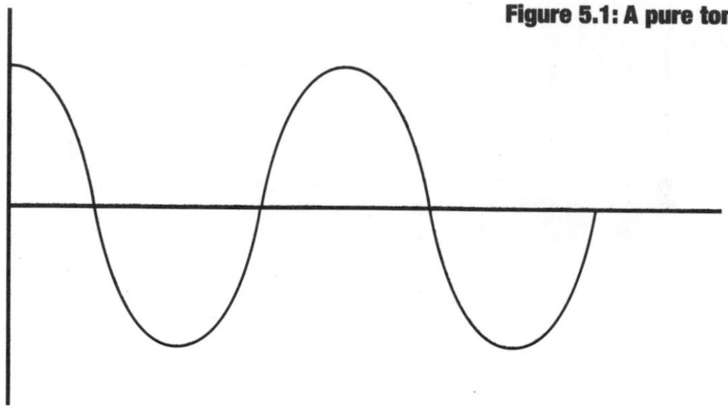

A sine wave generates a pure tone at a single frequency

second and 20,000 ripples per second. The time it takes for each ripple is known as a cycle, and the official measurement for cycles per second is Hertz, or Hz for short. Multiples of 1,000 cycles are known as kiloHertz or kHz.

The higher the frequency of vibration that causes the sound, the higher the perceived musical pitch, and a doubling in pitch produces a rise in musical terms of one octave. But there's a lot more to sound than mere pitch – what is it that gives each instrument its unique tonal character? Why does a flute playing middle C sound totally different to a piano playing the same note?

waves

The simplest sound is a pure tone, by which is meant that only a single frequency is present. If we were to plot out the changes in air pressure caused by a pure tone on a piece of graph paper, the result would be a sine wave, as shown in Figure 5.1. The electrical output of a microphone 'listening' to this signal would also be a sine wave, but this time the air vibrations would be represented by a sinusoidal modulation of voltage.

A continuous sine wave sounds like a whistle or test tone – every cycle of the waveform is identical, there's no variation in level, and as a sound, it's musically uninspiring. A continuous, pure tone possesses a fundamental pitch, a level, and nothing else. By contrast, real life sounds are infinitely more complex – instead of being made up of single tones, they are made up of a whole series of tones known as harmonics and overtones.

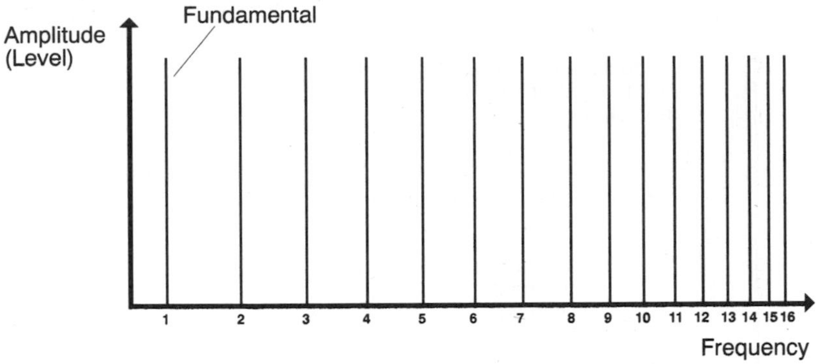

Harmonic series for the note A 110Hz as far as the tenth harmonic. Note that all the harmonics are shown as being of equal amplitude. This would not be the case for naturally generated sounds

Harmonic	Frequency
Fundamental (A)	110Hz
Second	220Hz
Third	330Hz
Fourth	440Hz
Fifth	550Hz
Sixth	660Hz
Seventh	770Hz
Eighth	880Hz
Ninth	990Hz
Tenth	1100Hz

Each harmonic in the series is a whole number multiple of the fundamental

Figure 5.2: Harmonic series (odd and even)

Harmonics are simply other frequencies that are exact multiples of the basic or fundamental pitch.

Most musically meaningful sounds generally exhibit a strong fundamental frequency, which determines the musical pitch or note, and this is accompanied by a series of harmonics that are higher in frequency (pitch), but generally lower in level, than the fundamental. As stated, harmonics occur at exact multiples of the fundamental frequency; if they are even multiples they are called even harmonics, whereas if they are odd

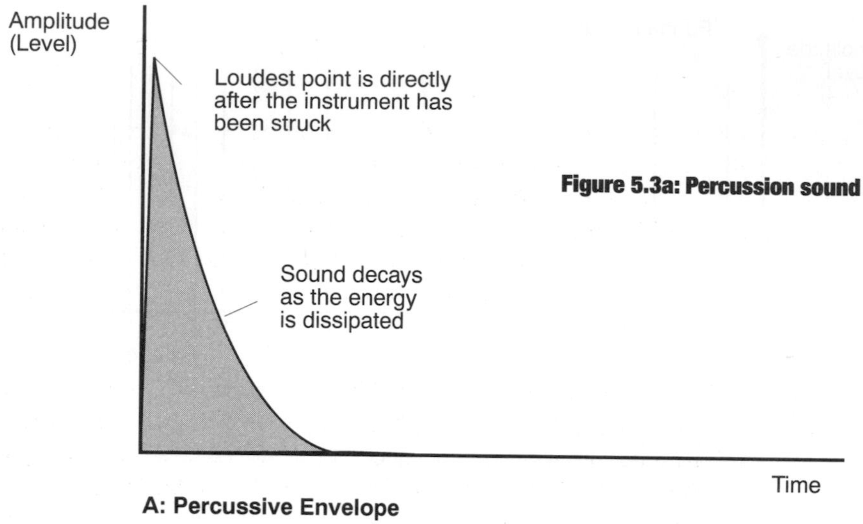
Amplitude
(Level)
Loudest point is directly after the instrument has been struck
Sound decays as the energy is dissipated
Time
A: Percussive Envelope

Figure 5.3a: Percussion sound envelope

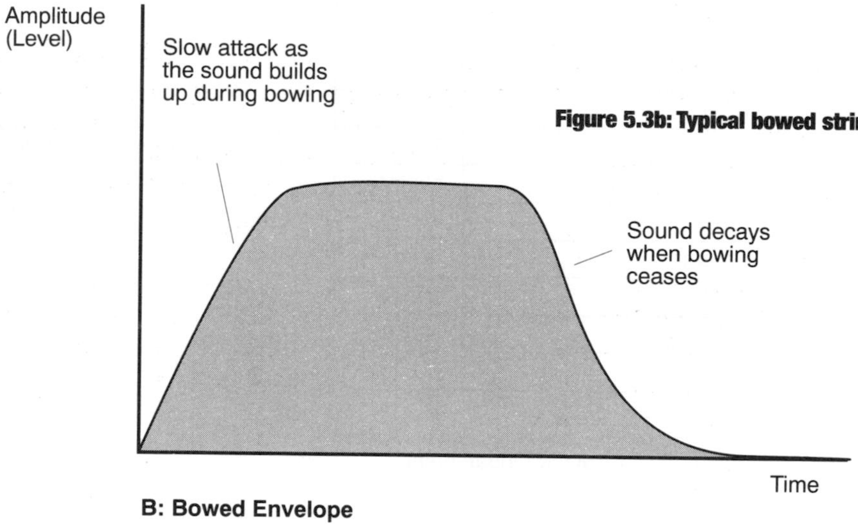
Amplitude
(Level)
Slow attack as the sound builds up during bowing
Sound decays when bowing ceases
Time
B: Bowed Envelope

Figure 5.3b: Typical bowed string envelope

multiples, they are called odd harmonics. Figure 5.2 shows how the harmonic series is constructed.

Sounds may also contain frequencies that aren't directly related to the fundamental frequency and these are known as non-harmonic overtones. Sounds such as bells contain many such complex overtones, but even instruments that are perceived to have a single pitch often contain some overtones.

timbre

The character or timbre of a sound is determined by two key factors: the harmonics (and non-harmonic overtones) that make up that sound, and the way that these components change in both level and pitch as the sound evolves. In other words, most sounds can be viewed as dynamic events, not as continuous or constant. This is in direct contrast to the electric organ, which tends to produce notes with the same harmonic structure from start to finish.

The way in which the levels of the different harmonics and overtones change with time determines the so-called envelope of the sound, and this has a profound bearing on how we interpret what we hear. For example, a percussive sound starts very suddenly, then the vibrational energy dies away because no new energy is being applied to sustain the sound. It follows, then, that a typical percussive sound will start suddenly and then decay, as shown in Figure 5.3a.

A bowed sound, on the other hand, may build up relatively slowly as the energy driving the sound is being applied over a period of time, not in one hit. When the driving energy – the bow – is removed, the string vibrations will decay in much the same way as a percussive sound due to the string energy being gradually absorbed by the instrument and the surrounding air. Figure 5.3b shows a typical bowed string envelope.

When most natural sounds, including acoustic instrument sounds, decay, the higher frequency harmonics decay faster than the low frequency components because high frequency energy is dissipated more rapidly than low frequency energy. This knowledge can be useful when it comes to synthesizing natural sounds.

additive synthesis

To accurately synthesize a 'real' sound, it would be necessary to recreate all the harmonics and overtones of the sound in question, set their relative levels, apply a separate envelope to each harmonic, then vary the frequency of each of them to emulate the way they behave in real life. What's more, there would need to be some way of controlling the sound so that it changed depending on playing technique, exactly as a 'real' instrument does.

Building a sound from scratch in this way is known as additive synthesis, and it is technically possible, but in practice, it is extremely difficult and expensive to implement. Modern resynthesis techniques can build up sound from its constituent frequencies, but this is a rather specialised subject and not very relevant to the way most affordable synthesizers work. Of course all this can change overnight as technology breakthroughs are frequently followed by dramatic price reductions.

Despite the apparent impracticality of additive synthesis, there are ways of approximating the behaviour of a real instrument, and though early attempts didn't produce a particularly accurate caricature of the original sounds, they did have a certain musicality. No one instrument yet built satisfies all needs, and it can be argued that the relative strengths and weaknesses of modern instruments is also what makes them interesting.

analogue synthesis

Mainstream synthesis started with the analogue synthesizer, so called because it relies entirely on analogue circuitry, where oscillators, filters and envelope shapers are controlled by electrical waveforms and voltages. It isn't necessary to know how any of this works in detail, but it is helpful to be able to visualise the process of synthesis as a series of simple building blocks.

Analogue circuitry doesn't possess the inherent stability of modern digital designs so parameters such as tuning tend to 'drift' a little, especially if the room temperature changed significantly, but the subtle detuning effects this causes are thought to contribute to the warm, 'organic' sound of analogue instruments. Though few modern instruments are based on analogue circuitry, many attempt to emulate it by digital means, and it is valuable to look at the basic building blocks of a typical analogue synthesizer as they're almost identical in concept to what goes on inside a modern digital instrument.

To the musician brought up on modern polyphonic instruments – instruments that can play multiple notes simultaneously – it might seem curious that the original analogue synths were all monophonic and had no velocity sensitivity. In other words, the note produced was always at the same level, no matter how hard the key was struck, and you could only ever produce one note at a time.

subtractive synthesis

Analogue synthesis is a form of subtractive synthesis because the process starts out with a harmonically rich sound, after which filters are used to reduce the level of unwanted harmonics. Subtractive synthesis is, therefore very much like sculpture – you take a large block of material, then trim away anything that isn't needed for the block to become the final statue.

Unfortunately, the original tools available for sonic sculpting were far less precise than the chisels and scrapers used by the sculptor. Indeed, analogue synthesis is akin to trying to create a sculpture using a clumsily wielded shovel! In other words, the available tools are not sufficiently refined to enable us to produce a sculpture that captures anything like the detail of real life. At best, analogue synthesis rather produces a caricature of the sound being imitated, though in the case of some types of sounds, the simulation can sometimes be more attractive than the real thing.

Modern S&S (Sample and Synthesis) instruments also work on the subtractive principle, but instead of starting out with electronically generated waveforms, they use electronic samples (short recordings stored in microchips), of real instrumental sounds that are then further modified by filters and envelope shapers.

building blocks

Any subtractive synthesizer can be thought of as a number of quite separate building blocks which can be wired together in a variety of ways, depending on the desired result. Indeed, the early modular analogue systems were precisely that – electronic circuitry in separate sections that could be linked together using short patch cables. The result often looked like a mad woman's knitting, but the sonic results could be wonderfully abstract. The term 'patch' as applied to synthesizer sounds originated from these early patch cord systems.

The basis of any subtractive synthesizer is the oscillator that produces the raw sound – the block from which the end result will be sculpted. In the case of an analogue synthesizer, the raw materials are simple repeating waveforms, whereas a modern synthesizer might use a recording of a real sound as its starting point.

A very basic analogue synthesizer might comprise one oscillator followed by one filter and one envelope shaper, as shown in Figure 5.4. The oscillator generates the starting waveform that gives the sound its pitch and harmonic structure, and this harmonic structure is further shaped by means of a circuit known as a filter. The filtered sound is then controlled in level by means of an envelope shaper to determine how fast the level builds up after a key is pressed, and how fast it decays to silence once the key is released. The filter and envelope shaper are the main tools used to trim away unwanted elements of the sound.

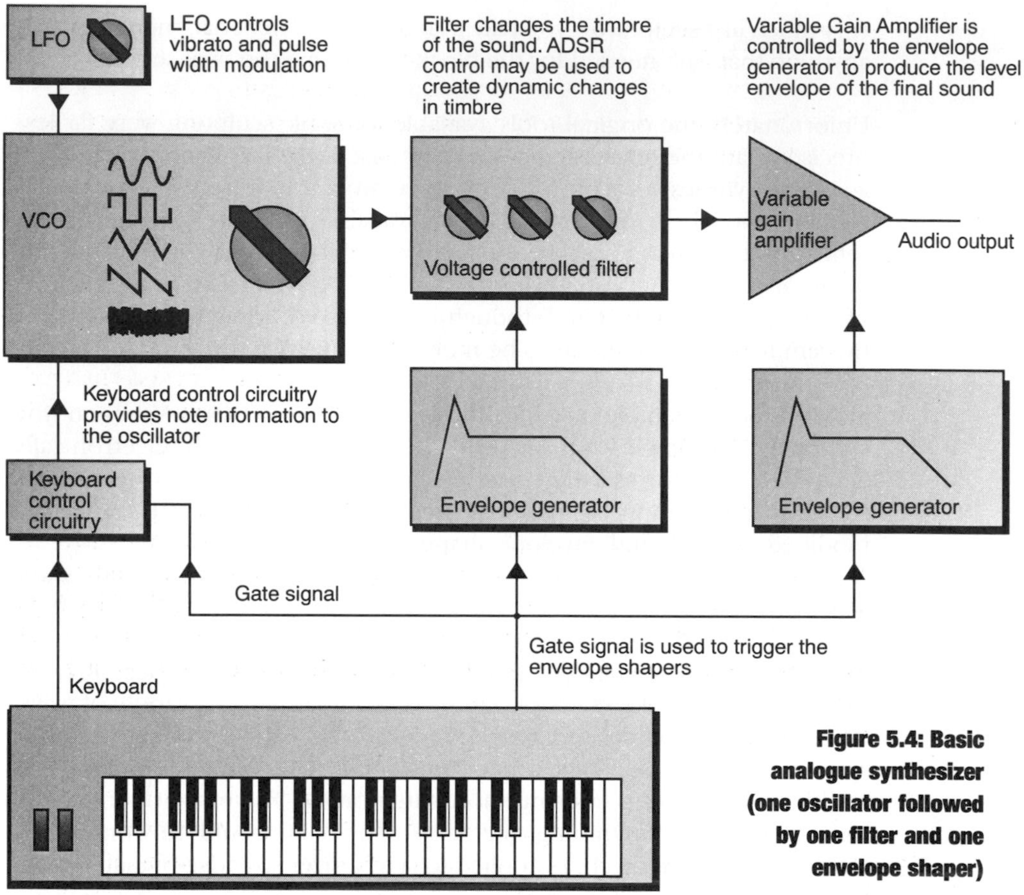
LFO
LFO controls vibrato and pulse width modulation
Filter changes the timbre of the sound. ADSR control may be used to create dynamic changes in timbre
Variable Gain Amplifier is controlled by the envelope generator to produce the level envelope of the final sound
VCO
Voltage controlled filter
Variable gain amplifier
Audio output
Keyboard control circuitry provides note information to the oscillator
Keyboard control circuitry
Envelope generator
Envelope generator
Gate signal
Gate signal is used to trigger the envelope shapers
Keyboard

Figure 5.4: Basic analogue synthesizer (one oscillator followed by one filter and one envelope shaper)

oscillators

In the original analogue synthesizers, there was usually a choice of just three or four basic waveform types, but in the modern S&S synth, there's usually a choice of basic waveforms plus samples recorded from acoustic instruments and other sources. Noise generators produce broadband hiss – a random electrical waveform containing all audio frequencies at all times. By filtering noise, it's possible to simulate the sound of breath noise, wind, surf, steam engines, helicopter, percussion, and even rudimentary cymbals. There are four main oscillator waveforms used in analogue synthesis: sine wave, square/pulse wave, triangle wave and sawtooth wave.

sine and square waves

The sine wave comprises a fundamental frequency with no harmonics, so no further modification can be made other than to control its pitch and level. However, it makes an ideal LFO control waveform for adding vibrato or tremolo because of its smooth, natural characteristics.

Square waves and triangle waves, on the other hand, contain the fundamental frequency plus a series of odd harmonics, the triangle wave having a lower harmonic content than the square wave. Both produce a characteristically hollow, reedy tone, but the square wave sounds brighter than the triangle wave. If the mark/space ratio of a square wave is changed, the resulting pulse waveform produces a different harmonic series and is useful for creating reed-like tones.

Though the square wave is one of the basic waveforms used in analogue synthesis, its close relative, the pulse waveform is arguably just as important, because many acoustic instruments generate an asymmetrical waveform. The square wave is so called because the 'period' of its high state is exactly the same as the period of the low state; it has a 1:1 mark/space ratio where the mark is the time the voltage is high and the space is the time the voltage is low.

If the mark/space ratio is altered, the sound becomes thinner and more buzzy as the mark/space ratio is increased. The harmonic content changes, and instead of having a square wave, we now have a pulse wave, which is particularly useful for creating buzzy reed tones. Many synths allow the mark/space ratio to be modulated using the output from a low frequency oscillator (LFO) running at just a few cycles per second, which produces a very interesting result called Pulse Width Modulation.

If you were to use two square wave oscillators running at exactly the same frequency, then modulate the pitch of just one of them using an LFO to produce vibrato, the result would be a simple but effective chorus, and if you were to examine the waveform, it would look exactly the same as a single square wave having its mark/space ratio modulated. Consequently, pulse/width modulating a single oscillator provides a useful way to fatten up the sound of an unsophisticated synth as the result sounds just like two slightly detuned oscillators playing at the same time.

sawtooth

The sawtooth wave comprises the fundamental plus a series of both odd and even harmonics and is used to create string, brass and many synth pad

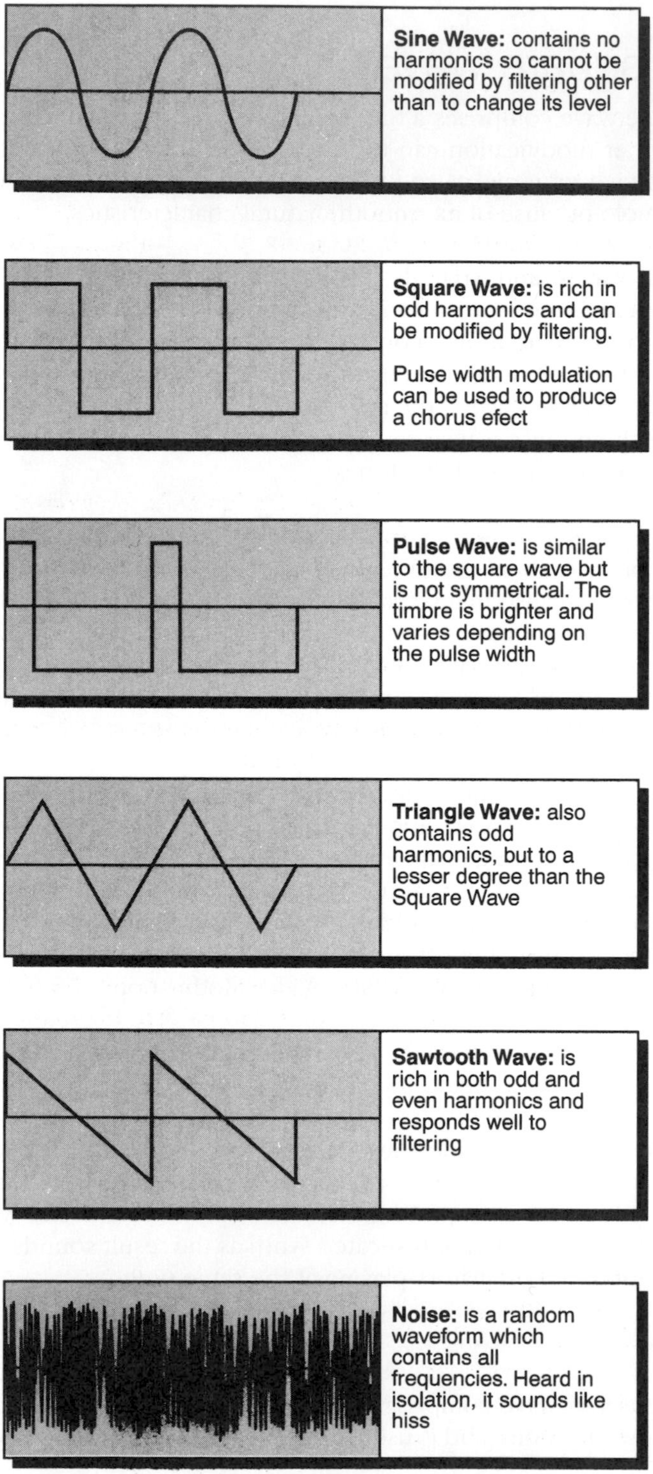

Sine Wave: contains no harmonics so cannot be modified by filtering other than to change its level
Square Wave: is rich in odd harmonics and can be modified by filtering.
Pulse width modulation can be used to produce a chorus efect
Pulse Wave: is similar to the square wave but is not symmetrical. The timbre is brighter and varies depending on the pulse width
Triangle Wave: also contains odd harmonics, but to a lesser degree than the Square Wave
Sawtooth Wave: is rich in both odd and even harmonics and responds well to filtering
Noise: is a random waveform which contains all frequencies. Heard in isolation, it sounds like hiss

Figure 5.5: Main synth waveforms

sounds. To produce a different mix of harmonics, the oscillator waveforms may be added in different proportions. Figure 5.5 shows the main waveform types available.

Though it's educational to examine the harmonic structure of both real and electronically generated sound, it's arguable whether a knowledge of the subject is of much practical benefit to the synthesist. Most synthesists work by ear, and even though it can be shown mathematically that a square wave has a very similar harmonic series to a clarinet, the reason you ultimately choose to use the square wave as the basis for your clarinet patch is because it sounds right.

key gate

In a synthesizer, the action of pressing a key tells the circuitry what pitch to produce, but it also produces a gate signal to let other elements of the synthesizer, such as envelope generators know when a key has been pressed and when it has been released. In MIDI terms, this corresponds to a Note On and a Note Off message. If we were to set up a synth so that the oscillator sound appeared at the output as soon as a key was pressed, and stopped again when a key was released, the result wouldn't be unlike that produced by a simple organ. It's only when the sound is filtered and given a new envelope that things get interesting.

portamento

Not all acoustic instruments produce neat chromatic pitches – some can slide from one note to another, for example, the trombone or violin. This effect is emulated in synthesizers by the Portamento control – whenever a new key is pressed, the oscillator pitch will glide from the old note to the new note over a finite period of time rather than changing abruptly. In most instruments, the portamento time is adjustable from instantaneous to several seconds per octave of glide. A fairly fast glide is useful in simulating brass sounds, especially trombone, while slow rates are useful in creating special effects.

lfos

I've already mentioned LFOs once or twice, so I guess now is as good a time as any to introduce them formally. The simplest LFO is a sine wave oscillator running at just a few cycles per second, and the mod wheel on a modern synth usually defaults to using the LFO to create vibrato. It does this by allowing the LFO to modulate the pitch of the oscillator. An LFO may also be routed to the filter envelope generators to modulate the timbre or output level. Modulating the output level of a patch using an LFO produces a tremolo effect. By using the LFO amount control, the modulation depth applied to the pitch or level of the sound can be set to a musically suitable value so as to emulate the vibrato applied by a violin or flute player.

more about oscillators

Running two oscillators together at nominally the same pitch produces a rich, dynamic sound; a slight degree of detuning allows the phase of one oscillator to drift relative to the other to produce a natural chorus effect. It's also possible to tune one oscillator higher or lower than the other by, for example, an octave or a perfect fifth. This can produce very fat sounds, especially when combined with suitable filtering.

oscillator sync

Many analogue synths using two or more oscillators have the ability to sync one of the oscillators to the other, which can be used to create a dynamic, aggressive sound that's quite distinctive once you've heard it. In phase sync mode, one oscillator is designated the master and the other the slave – they may be tuned to the same frequency or to any interval, but the slave oscillator waveform will always 'restart' whenever a cycle of the master oscillator's waveform is complete. Though originally developed for analogue instruments, some digital instruments also have phase sync capabilities.

If the slave's oscillator's tuning is manually increased while the master remains constant, the slave can be heard jumping from one harmonic to the next, accompanied by an interesting change in timbre. A popular way of using this effect is to control the slave oscillator from the pitch-bend wheel of the synth but leave the master unmodulated. As the bend wheel is turned, the output signal runs through a series of harmonics, resulting in a sound far more complex than can be achieved simply by adding the oscillator outputs together as normal. Phase sync is popular for creating searing lead solo sounds.

digital synthesis

Though analogue synthesizers eventually evolved to become polyphonic, and later to become MIDI controlled, the basic waveforms remained the same until sample-based synthesizers were developed in the early 80s. The main conceptual difference is that instead of a simple electronic waveform, the starting point for a modern S&S synth is a sampled sound such as a

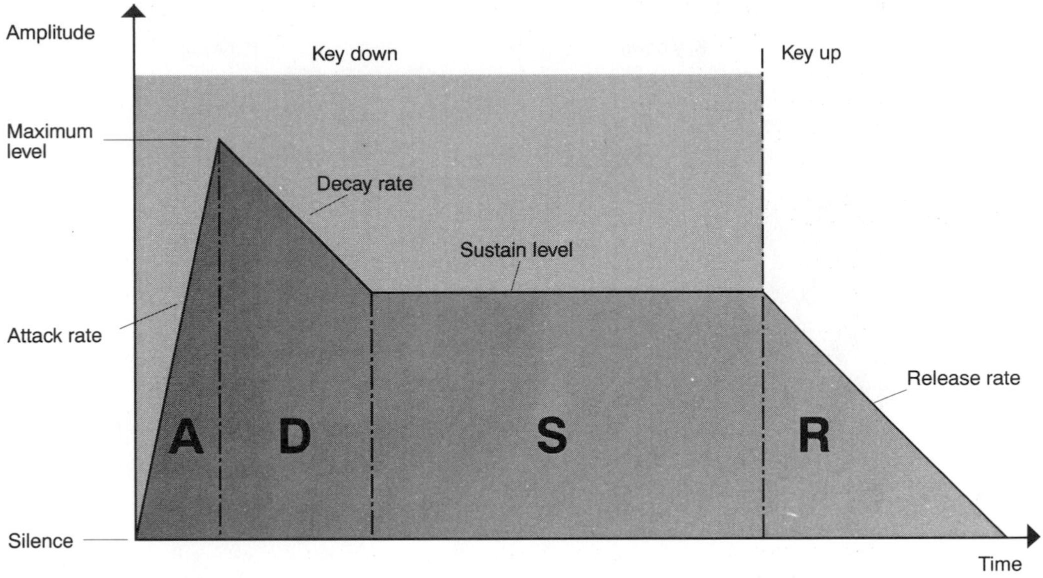

Figure 5.6: ADSR envelope shaper

sustained violin note, a flute or even a human voice. This may still be thought of as an oscillator, because in most cases, the sound continues as long as the key is held. The exception is percussive sounds where the sound may be allowed to decay naturally.

filters and envelopes

Regardless of what type of oscillator is being used, the resulting signal is usually passed through a filter and invariably through a level envelope shaper. On current digital instruments, the filters and envelope shapers are all implemented using microcomputer technology, but the block diagram remains the same as for an analogue instrument.

The character of a natural sound is largely determined by its harmonic content and its envelope, the envelope being the way in which the level of the sound changes with time. As we've seen, percussive sounds start suddenly and then die away whereas a bowed sound might start quite slowly and then sustain at a more or less fixed level. The envelopes of real sounds can be very complex, but in the early days of synthesis, it was felt that an adequate approximation could be achieved using a basic, four-stage ADSR (Attack, Decay, Sustain, Release) envelope generator controlling a VCA (Voltage Controlled Amplifier). An ADRS envelope is shown in Figure 5.6. The envelope shaper is triggered by the action of pressing a key.

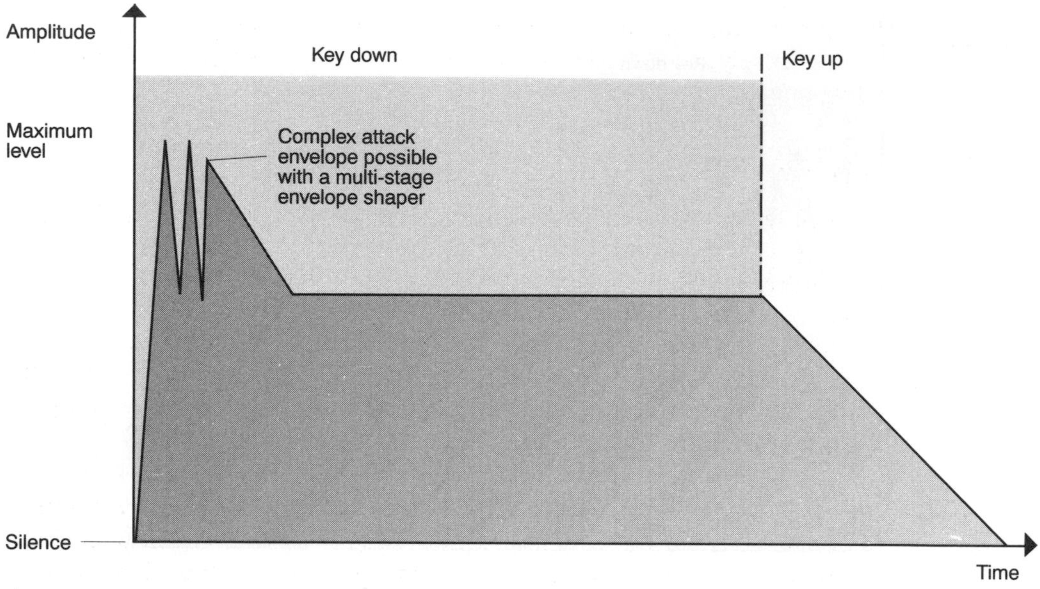

Figure 5.7: Multi stage envelope (showing multiple attack spikes)

The Attack portion of the envelope is simply the time taken for the amplitude to reach maximum, so for percussive sounds, the attack time should be as short as possible. Once the sound has reached its maximum level, it starts to decay at a rate set by the Decay time setting. The sound then continues to decay until it reaches a level known as the Sustain level, (another user variable parameter), and it remains at this level as long as the key is held down. Once the key is released, the sound resumes its decay, this time at a new rate determined by the Release setting. If a new key is depressed before the envelope generator has completed its Release phase, the old Release is abandoned and a new envelope initiated. This type of envelope generator, and more complex variations of it, are regularly found in modern digital synthesizers. It is important to note that while Attack, Decay and Release control the rate at which the envelope settings change, the Sustain parameter is a level, not a rate.

complex envelopes

Modern synths often have envelope shapers with far more than four stages, the reason being that many sounds cannot be accurately synthesised using a simple four-stage envelope. For example, a brass ensemble sound may contain several staggered attack transients which correspond to several performers starting to play at slightly different times.

Using a multi-stage envelope shaper, an envelope could be created with several closely spaced spikes at the start of the note as shown in Figure 5.7, a feat quite impossible using a single ADSR generator.

filter envelope control

We nearly always associate envelope generators with level (amplitude) control, but they have a far wider range of creative uses, the most common alternative being the control of filter frequency. Filters will be covered in more detail later in this chapter, but for the moment, imagine the filter to be just a remote-controlled tone control. If we control the filter's frequency from an envelope generator, we can create a huge range of tonal sweep sounds that range from a slow, lazy change in timbre to a resonant twang.

It is also possible to invert the output of the envelope generator so that the filter sweeps from low to high instead of high to low. Even fairly modest analogue synths tend to have a switch for inverting the filter sweep direction, though on the very basic models, you may find that the same envelope generator is used to control both the amplitude envelope and the filter sweep restricting the range of sounds that can be produced. Even so, the filter invert option helps squeeze the most sonic variation out of what is available.

delay vibrato

When an acoustic instrument is played naturally, it's quite common for vibrato to be added after the note has started sounding. This can be duplicated on a synth by using the vibrato depth controller wheel, but it is also possible to use a delayed LFO to achieve a similar effect. When a key is pressed, the LFO level will build up gradually so the sound starts off unmodulated, and then the vibrato depth increases as the LFO envelope moves towards its maximum level.

envelope control of tone oscillators

An envelope may also be used to modify the oscillator pitch. This has an obvious application in creating sci-fi oscillator sweeps, but used subtly, it may also be used to put the finishing touches to a patch simulating a natural instrument. For example, some wind instruments tend to go slightly sharp when they are first blown, and this characteristic can be imitated by setting up an envelope with a fairly fast attack and decay, and then feeding just a small amount of this signal into the oscillator's pitch control input. As the envelope rises at the start of a note, the pitch will be forced slightly sharp, then it will return to normal as the envelope finishes its decay phase.

A more drastic level of envelope pitch control can be useful when setting up oscillator sync effects. In this example, two oscillators are used, one set to track the keyboard pitch normally, and the other with a generous helping of added envelope control to produce a long pitch bend of several semitones. When the second oscillator is synced to the first, the envelope shape will control the way the harmonic structure changes whenever a key is pressed. A long envelope will produce a harmonic sweep effect whereas a very short envelope could be used to create a harmonically rich attack to the sound.

filtering

Though some very basic modern synths dispense with the filter altogether and instead include ready filtered sounds within their menu of basic waveforms, a filter is very useful: firstly, simply mixing the basic sine, square (pulse) and triangle waveforms doesn't provide a broad enough range of timbres, and secondly, real sounds very often change their timbre as the sound develops. For example, a picked string produces a sound that is, initially, rich in high frequency harmonics, but as the sound decays, these harmonics die away faster than the fundamental.

To simulate this effect using a filter, we need a filter that can be made to vary its characteristics in a controllable way, and the answer is to use an envelope generator to control the rate at which the filter frequency increases and decreases.

Like oscillators, filters may be controlled from a keyboard (the higher the note you play, the higher the filter frequency), from an envelope generator, or from an LFO, resulting in a filter characteristic that varies rather than remaining static. Cheaper synths tend to share the same envelope generator for the filter and for the output level, while more sophisticated models have separate envelope generators for each function. Obviously there's more flexibility in being able to set up one envelope for the filter and a different one for the amplitude.

filter types

Most synthesizer filter circuits operate as high-pass, band-pass or low-pass filter types based on those used in the original analogue instruments, though more complex filter types are possible. If an instrument has only one filter type, it's invariably low-pass, which means that it passes only

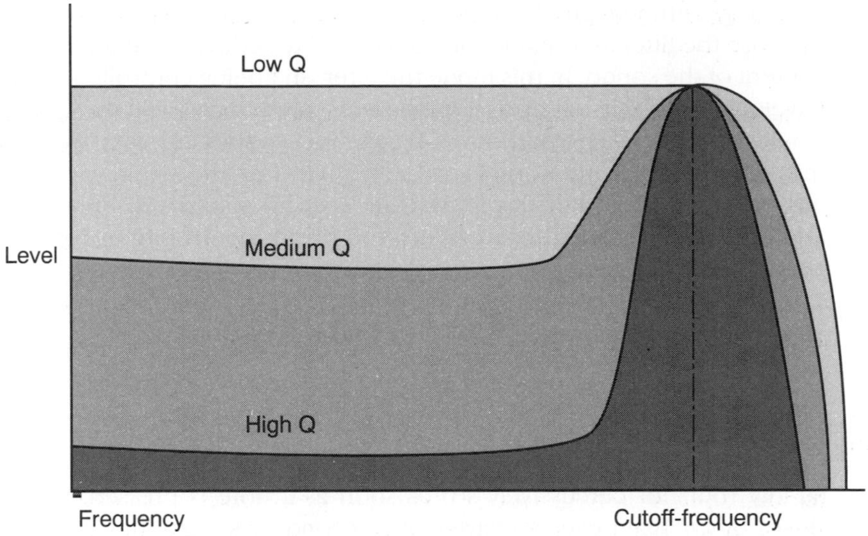

Figure 5.8: Effect of varying the Resonance of a low-pass filter

frequencies below the frequency at which the filter is set. The slope or sharpness of the filter is usually 12dB per octave or, in some cases, 24dB per octave depending on the make. The more dBs per octave, the sharper the sound of the filter. The two types produce a subtly different sound which is one reason why two synths offering apparently identical facilities might sound quite different.

A filter as described, with no other controls, would sound much like any other form of EQ enabling the user only to soften bright sounds, but the addition of a Q or Resonance control greatly increases the creative potential. Essentially, increasing the Q or Resonance of a filter makes it emphasise harmonics at the filter's cutoff frequency, rather like a wah wah pedal or the mute of a trumpet. If the filter frequency is then varied by some means or other, the familiar filter sweep sound is produced. The graph in Figure 5.8 shows the effect of varying the Resonance of a low-pass filter. By juggling the starting frequency of the filter with the rate, depth and direction of sweep, a wide range of dynamically changing timbres can be created.

filter applications

Just because a filter has variable frequency and Q parameters, it doesn't mean that every patch you set up has to be based on a fierce filter sweep. For example, to produce a mellow string pad, you might choose a couple of slightly detuned, gently modulated sawtooth oscillators as your source, then use the filter as a simple top-cut control to reduce the high frequency content of the sound. In this mode the filter isn't being controlled from the envelope at all – it is set up as a purely static filter. Increasing the Q slightly would produce a sharper, more tightly focused sound that would cut through a mix well, but if you increase the Q too far, the sound will become obviously resonant and the illusion of a string sound will break down. Adding a little keyboard control into the filter's control input makes the filter frequency dependent on the note you're playing. This can be useful if you're trying to simulate an instrument that sounds brighter on the higher notes and more mellow on the lower notes.

brass sounds

Brass sounds tend to make use of filter sweeps where the filter opens fairly rapidly (but not percussively so) as soon as a note is pressed, but then closes down again over a quarter of a second or so resulting in a bright attack followed by a more mellow sustain period. The attack time of the filter envelope needs to be adjusted by ear so that it matches the time it takes for a typical brass instrument to 'speak'. Convincing brass patches are easiest to achieve using a synth that provides separate envelope generators for both filter and level, but quite passable imitations can be still achieved using a single envelope generator.

Most classic synth bass sounds are set up in a similar way to the brass patch but require the oscillators to be set to a lower octave. Fashionable techno bass sounds tend to make use of fast attack times and fairly high Q settings, and if the direction of filter sweep can be inverted, this produces interesting alternatives. A fast release time on both the filter and VCA envelopes helps create a tight, well-defined bass sound whereas longer release times are better suited to more atmospheric music or deep bass sounds.

Classic filter sweep sounds tend to use a Q setting that is so high the filter is almost (but not quite) oscillating and either a long attack or release is used so as to create a dramatic sweep effect. In all cases involving envelope control, the manual tuning control on the filter sets the starting state of the filter and the envelope level sets the range of the sweep.

s&h filter

The filter can be controlled from a number of sources, limited only by the patching arrangements of the particular synth you're using. One very popular effects is achieved by feeding a random stepped waveform into the control input of the filter. If the filter is adjusted to a high Q setting, the result is a kind of wah wah which jumps instantaneously from one random position to the next at whatever rate you care to set.

polyphony

Polyphony really signalled the end for analogue instruments, because although it is possible to build polyphonic analogue instruments, every oscillator, filter and envelope shaper has to be duplicated for every note that is to play simultaneously. In practical terms, few analogue synths were built that provided more than eight-note polyphony, and ultimately it became clear that going completely digital was the only feasible solution. Similarly, the patching systems that worked so well on the old modular synths would be completely unmanageable if the same patch had to be duplicated eight times to obtain eight-note polyphony.

The modern digital equivalent of the old analogue patching system is usually a button and menu-driven system, and though this isn't as convenient as a panel full of knobs to which you have permanent and full access, it does make very powerful instruments cheap to build. Digital control systems also made programmable synthesizers possible for the first time, enabling the user to save patches for instant recall rather than having to write all the settings down in a book.

modern synthesizers

Now MIDI is fitted as standard to virtually every serious electronic keyboard, and instruments tend to come with a wide variety of factory preset sounds built in, and further user memory where newly created sounds can be stored. A typical instrument will have a four or five octave keyboard that responds to velocity, pitch bend and mod wheels will be provided for performance control, and there will be provision to plug in a sustain pedal. As with the majority of MIDI instruments, the notes that can be played are not limited to the physical size of the keyboard – notes above and below the keyboard range can be played via MIDI or by using any on-board octave transpose facilities.

on board effects

It is now common practice for synthesizers to come complete with built-in digital effects such as reverb, chorus and echo/delay to add life and realism to a performance. Usually, there is a choice of effects types or effect combinations, and users with the inclination to do so can edit the effect to change things like reverb decay time, echo delay time and so on. Because the majority of effects produce a stereo output, most synthesizers are fitted with stereo outputs, though some top end models may have multiple outputs so as to allow the various sounds to be mixed via a studio mixing console. Multiple outputs are only really applicable to multitimbral modules – see the chapter on Multitimbrality.

At the time of writing, the majority of synthesizers work on the 'Sample and Synthesis' methods where digitally stored waveforms similar to those used in analogue machines, plus digitally stored samples of real instruments, voices and sound effects are used as the basic building blocks of sound. Several sound sources can be layered together and processed via filters, envelope shapers and so on, and the results that can be obtained from such instruments are initially very impressive. The range of available sounds ranges from imitations of vintage analogue synthesizers and acoustic instruments to abstract sounds, sound effects and choirs. Piano sounds based on samples can be very convincing as can ensemble strings and brass.

However, S&S synths don't do a great job at creating certain solo sounds, such as violin or saxophone, because the real instrument can be played in so many different ways, yet the synthesizer creates each note from the same basic sound. Skilled use of the performance controls and inventive sound programming can help overcome this problem, but there is no completely satisfactory solution.

All General MIDI instruments are based on S&S synthesis, and the chips used in computer soundcards also tend to use S&S synthesis. Despite its limitations, this is a very flexible, easy to use and cost effective method of synthesis, but as mentioned earlier, nothing stands still in this business – it will eventually be superseded by something better.

physical modelling

The latest wave of synthesizers employ a brand new method of sound generation known as physical modelling. Instead of creating the sound using oscillators and filters, the instrument uses sophisticated models to emulate the behaviour of a real acoustic instrument. If this seems rather abstract, it's not dissimilar to the way a flight simulator is used to 'model' the way a real aircraft behaves.

A clarinet simulation would involve simulating the vibration of the reed, the resonance of the tubular body of the instrument, and the effect of the flared end of the tube. This is a very complicated technology, but the advantage is that the modelled instrument can be made to behave much

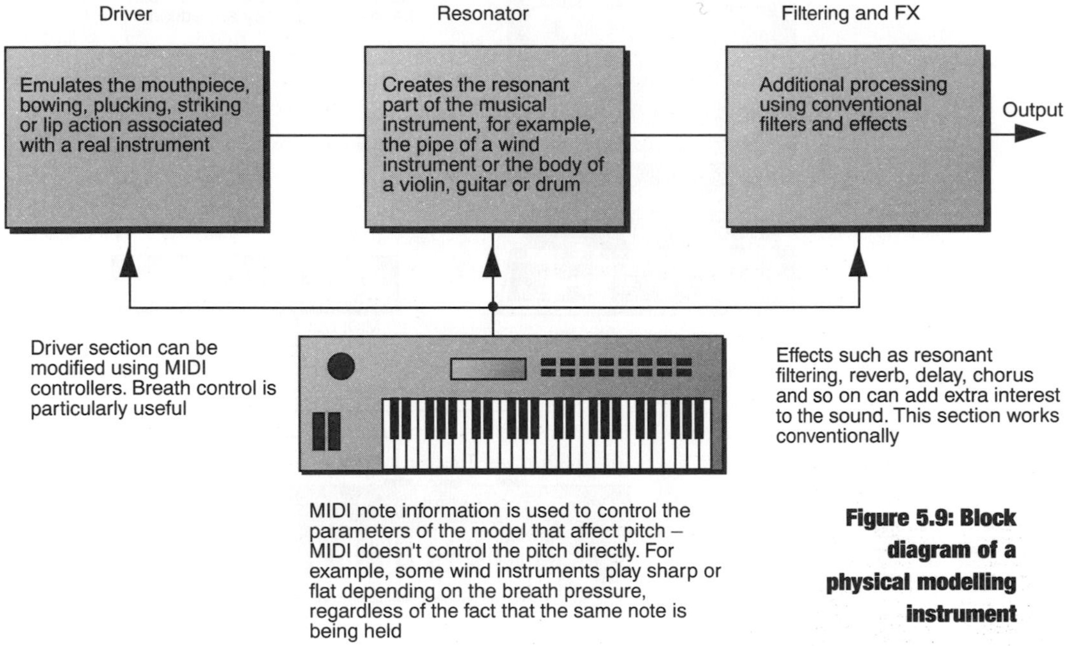

Figure 5.9: Block diagram of a physical modelling instrument

more like the real thing. For example, a physical model of a flute might change its harmonic structure when played hard to make it sound like a real flute being 'overblown', whereas playing very quietly will result in more wind noise resonating in the tubular body.

Different mathematical models are required for different instruments, but it is possible to convincingly model many acoustic instruments by this method. A violin emulation would need to model the behaviour of a bowed string, the resonance of the violin body, and the decay of the sound once bowing ceases. A drum, on the other hand, requires the modelling of a tensioned membrane and a resonant shell. The quality of the final sound depends on the accuracy of the mathematical model and the skill of the sound designer. Figure 5.9 shows a conceptual block diagram of a physical modelling instrument.

Furthermore, various aspects of different instruments can be combined to produce the sounds of instruments that don't exist in real life, yet they still respond like true instruments. For example, you could have the reed of a clarinet, the body of a flute and the bell of a trumpet, or you could create a double size sax. You can even build a bowed flute or a blown violin with a reed! Because of the complexity of physical modelling, the number of user parameters is usually limited, though some instruments have software editing packages available for those people with the expertise and patience

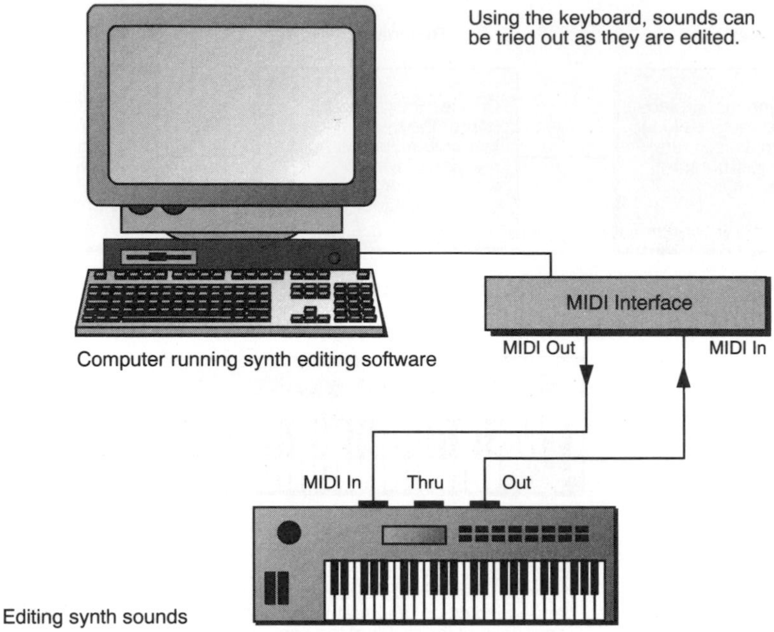
Using the keyboard, sounds can be tried out as they are edited.
MIDI Interface
Computer running synth editing software
MIDI Out
MIDI In
MIDI In
Thru
Out
Editing synth sounds

Figure 5.10: MIDI connections for a software editor/librarian

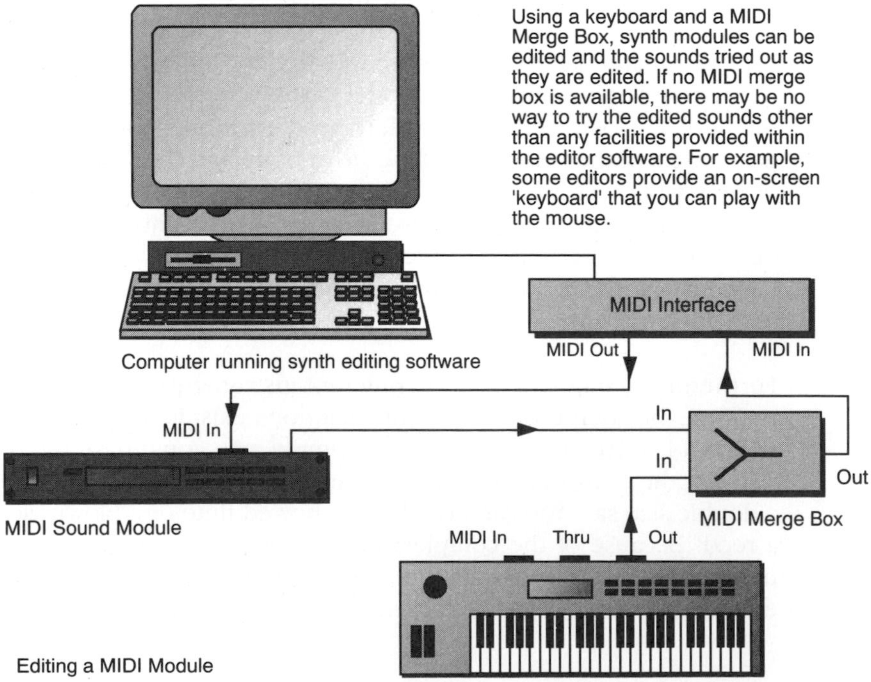
Using a keyboard and a MIDI Merge Box, synth modules can be edited and the sounds tried out as they are edited. If no MIDI merge box is available, there may be no way to try the edited sounds other than any facilities provided within the editor software. For example, some editors provide an on-screen 'keyboard' that you can play with the mouse.
MIDI Interface
Computer running synth editing software
MIDI Out
MIDI In
MIDI In
In
In
Out
MIDI Sound Module
MIDI Merge Box
MIDI In
Thru
Out
Editing a MIDI Module

to do their own sound design. Furthermore, the most powerful physical modelling instruments tend to be monophonic – but that makes perfect sense if you're modelling a monophonic wind instrument, such as a flute or saxophone.

performance control

The secret of a convincing performance when using any synthesizer is to make full use of real-time control, but in the case of a physical modelling instrument, you can use several real-time controllers to vary the aspects of the sound that would change if the real instrument were being played. For example, if you are playing a flute patch, a breath controller might be used to control the level of the sound, aftertouch could be used to change the harmonics of the sound or to add 'growl', the modulation wheel could be used to add both vibrato and tremolo, and the pitch wheel could be set up not only to change pitch, but also to cause the same timbral change that the real instrument would undergo if it were pulled off pitch. Saxes can be made to squeal or growl, violins can be played with varying bowing pressure, flutes can be made breathy or they can be overblown, and so on.

user interface

The original analogue synthesizers had discrete knobs and switches for every function, so although they looked daunting, at least you could go straight to any parameter and adjust it. By contrast, modern digital instruments look far simpler, but behind the scenes, there are still lots of parameters that can be adjusted if you've the patience to try to create new sounds of your own. Though some current instruments are built with knobs on the front panel, only the simplest can offer a dedicated knob for every parameter, and what is more common is that a small number of multifunction knobs can be used to access a small number of parameters at a time. Indeed, many instruments provide access only to one parameter at a time – the parameter itself is selected using buttons and a visual display window, usually via a menu system, then the selected parameter is changed in value either using Up/Down buttons or a single rotary control.

Most keyboard synthesizers provide a number of buttons for the direct accessing of sound patches and to change between banks of patches. Patches are often named, the name being shown in the display window, and if new sounds are created by the user, they can be given new names.

By using a limited number of controls and a menu access system, very powerful instruments can be built at relatively low costs – the tradeoff is that sound editing is time consuming and not always intuitive. Software editing systems are available for many synthesizer types providing more comprehensive parameter display and access using a computer screen and mouse, though users who don't have the time or patience to create sounds from scratch may find it easier to make minor modifications to existing 'factory' sounds, or even buy new sounds from third-part sound design companies. Depending on the model of synthesizer, new sounds may be available on memory cards or floppy disks.

software editors

Because most modern synths employ a menu and button driven user interface, it is often easier to edit them from a computer screen where several parameters can be seen and adjusted at once using a mouse. Level and filter envelopes may also be presented graphically with facilities for using the mouse to 'drag' them into new shapes. This makes for more intuitive editing, but buying a software editor for each instrument you own can be expensive.

Universal synth editors adopt a modular approach where software modules relating the various synths in circulation can be loaded in and used. Such a software system may initially be more expensive than a single synth editor, but the benefit is that you gain the ability to edit dozens of different models and makes of instrument.

Editor systems tend to include librarian facilities, so that if you fill up your synth memory with new sounds, you can store them on disk, via the librarian software. This way you can build up a vast library of different sounds for your various instruments, then transfer these to your synthesizers as they're needed.

To use an editor/librarian system, it is necessary for the MIDI Out of the instrument being edited to be connected to the MIDI In of the interface serving the computer, and the MIDI Out of the interface must be connected back to the MIDI In of the instrument. This provides for two-way communication between the instrument and the computer so that patch data and instructions can be sent both ways. (See Figure 5.10.)

more performance control

I've already mentioned mod wheels, bend wheels, and sustain pedals as means of performance control, but there are numerous other options, some more popular than others. Pedals are practical as they require no hands, but not all keyboards are designed to accept a pedal input. Add on boxes that convert volume pedals to MIDI pedals are available commercially as are MIDI pedals themselves.

Aftertouch is a useful performance control that comes built into many keyboards, though it tends to act on all the notes currently playing – only very few high end keyboards have note independent aftertouch. Essentially, aftertouch works via a pressure sensor beneath the keyboard that converts downward pressure into MIDI data that can be used to control parameters such as level, brightness, pitch, modulation depth and so on, but as mentioned earlier, it also generates a lot of data, so it's best to switch it off at the keyboard if you're not using it.

The pressure response of most keyboards tends to be a little uneven, and you'll often find that you have to press quite hard to get any response at all, but there are occasions when aftertouch really can add life to a performance so try it if you have it just to see what it can do. What parameter the aftertouch affects is programmed as part of a synthesizer patch or program.

Joysticks are fitted to some instruments, and these are useful devices insomuch as they can control two parameters at a time – one vertically and one horizontally. Often these can be assigned to any of the regular MIDI controllers, which means you can decide what parameters they will affect.

Ribbon controllers are rarely fitted to modern instruments, but they seem to be making a bit of a comeback in some circles. A ribbon controller is a flat ribbon beneath which is a conductive strip, so that when you press down on the ribbon, it makes an electrical contact. As you slide your finger from one end of the ribbon to the other, the electrical resistance of the contact changes, just as though you were using a normal slider, so you can control any function dynamically. Unlike a slider however, as soon as you remove your finger from the ribbon, the contact is broken and the original condition is restored. Ribbons are useful for controlling such things as level, pitch, vibrato, filter brightness and so on.

Breath controllers are relatively inexpensive and have been around for a long time, but they never became really popular – possibly because they look rather foolish and tend to cause you to dribble! In fact most modern keyboards don't even have a breath controller input, so if you want to use one, you'll either need to buy a third-part breath control interface box or use a synth module that has its own breath control input.

The breath controller itself is a simple mouthpiece attached to a headset into which the performer blows. A pressure sensor converts breath pressure to electrical information where it is subsequently used to generate MIDI controller data. Anything that can be controlled via a MIDI controller can be controlled via a breath control unit, though most people have them set to Controller 7 so as to provide overall volume control. This is uncannily effective for articulating wind sounds, but it is also useful for adding feel to other instruments, such as bowed strings. The new generation of physical modelling synthesizers responds exceptionally well to breath control, and this alone could be sufficient incentive for more people to experiment.

chapter 6

multitimbrality

Today virtually every synthesizer or expander module has some multitimbral capability – the ability to play several different sounds at the same time, where each different sound or musical 'part' is controlled by a different MIDI channel. If you wanted to create a mind's-eye model of an eight-part multitimbral synth module, you'd probably be thinking along the lines of eight separate synthesizer modules built into one box. Up to a point, this is an excellent analogy, but what you do have to remember is that these 'virtual' modules are not really separate, and in many ways, their operation is linked. At the simplest level, they all operate from the same power supply, so you can't turn them on or off individually. Also, even though the sounds may appear to be generated separately, on the more affordable models, these sounds will probably be mixed to stereo inside the machine so there is no way of accessing them separately. Some machines have four or even eight outputs to which different voices can be assigned, but to date, I've never seen a 16-part multitimbral module with 16 separate outputs.

level and pan

To help overcome the limitations imposed by having all the sounds pre-mixed inside the module, the user invariably has control over the sound level and pan position of the individual parts, though on some of the cheaper modules, these parameters may only be accessible via MIDI from a sequencer or a suitable editing software package. In addition, simple effects such as chorus and reverb are often included, even in very inexpensive modules, and though the same effect setting applies to each part, the effect level can be set by the user, allowing some creative freedom. More advanced synths and expanders may incorporate effects processing sections to rival those of stand-alone multi-effects units.

polyphony

A more important consideration is that of polyphony, and this is one area where the 'virtual' modules really are linked. Polyphony is a term used to describe how many music notes may be played at the same time, and in the

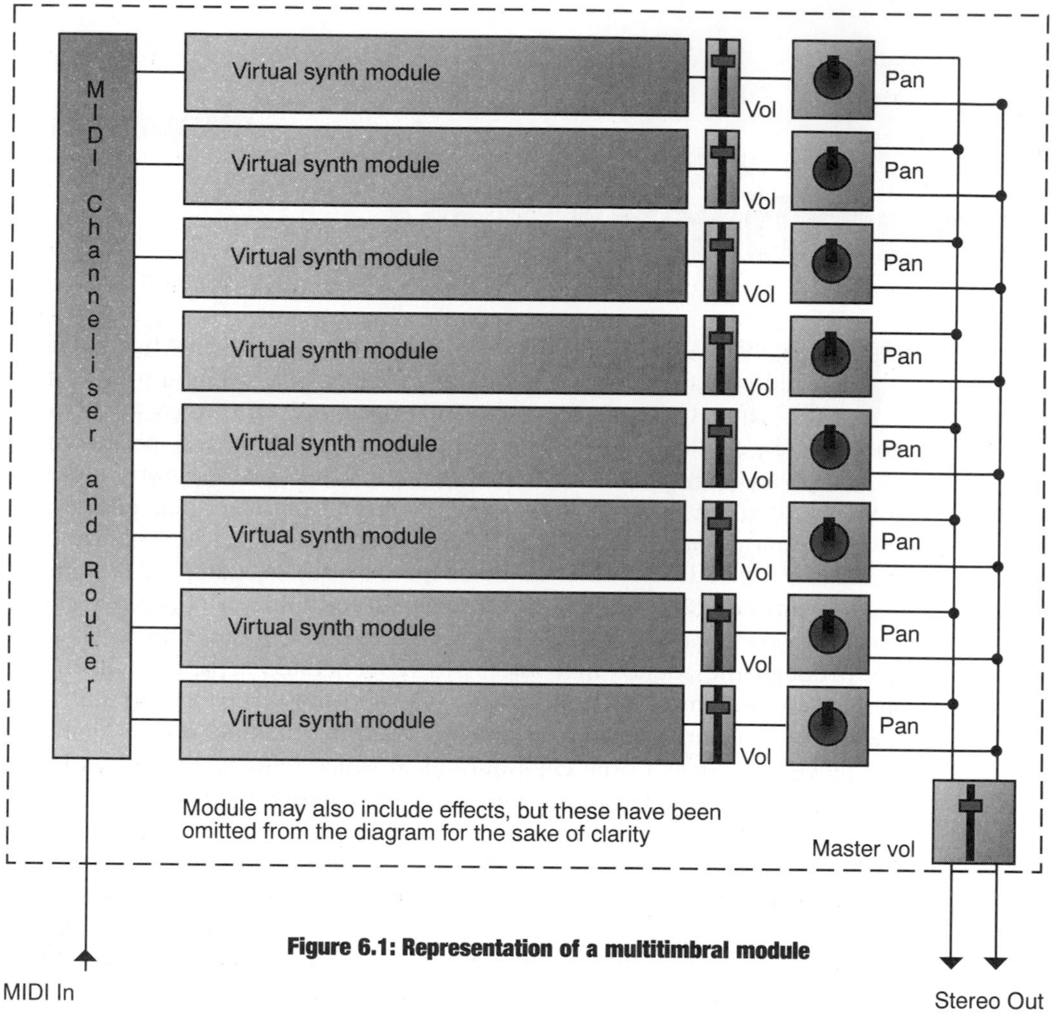

Figure 6.1: Representation of a multitimbral module

case of a multitimbral module, a mental picture helps clarify the situation. Imagine that the musical notes the unit can produce are marbles stored in a single box. If the unit has 24-note polyphony, then there are 24 marbles in the box. When one of the parts is required to play a note, it borrows one of the marbles when the note starts, and it keeps it until the note has ended, at which point, it returns it to the box. Clearly, this is fine until all 24 notes are playing at once, because now there are no more marbles left in the box.

If a 25th note is played while the other 24 notes are still being used, you might expect nothing at all to happen because the marble box is empty, but that would be musically unacceptable, so another system is used. Instead, the usual solution is to 'steal' a note from one of the already playing parts and, to help disguise the theft, it's normal for the voice allocation system to steal whichever of the notes was played earliest.

Even this apparently fair system can cause problems, especially if your song starts with a long drone note, because in a note robbing situation, this is the one most likely to be taken – and that would leave an obvious hole in the music. For this reason, most modules use a system whereby a minimum number of notes are reserved for use by each of the parts, so that if robbing does take place, it is less likely to be noticeable. For example, if one part is playing a pad chord, and one of the notes in the chord is robbed just as it's dying away, that's less likely to be a problem than if the whole chord went. It is often possible for the user to change the number of 'sounds' reserved for each part so that important parts have more notes at their disposal. Figure 6.1 shows a representation of an eight-part multitimbral sound module.

effects

Because the sounds from the various parts are often mixed together internally to produce a stereo output, some means is required for adding different amounts of effects, such as chorus or reverb, to each part. Virtually all multitimbral synthesizers have inbuilt digital effects, though very often, the same effect or effect combination is applied to all the 'parts' of the instrument. For example, a General MIDI instrument will provide reverb and chorus for all 16 parts, but the same chorus settings and reverb setting will be used throughout. However, to make this more flexible, each part provides control over the effects level, and in the case of GM instruments, the minimum requirement is for independent control over chorus amount and reverb level. These are adjusted using MIDI Controller information, and the relevant controllers will be shown in the MIDI instrumentation chart for the instrument. More experienced sequencer users will find it a simple matter to insert controller information at the start of a song, usually during the count-in bars, so that the effects levels are set up automatically. As a rule, the higher the controller value, the greater the level of effect.

Many of the better sequencers now allow on-screen faders (which are moved using the mouse), to be set up, that can vary the values of any kind of MIDI data, and in my own system, I've created a page of 32 faders to control my GM module, 16 for the various reverb levels and 16 for the chorus level. If your sequencer handbook mentions this facility, check it out as it's much easier to do than you might imagine. The same types of faders can be used to perform just about any function that can be accessed over MIDI, but manipulating MIDI controller data is probably the easiest thing to try first.

reverberation

The most useful effect is reverberation, or reverb for short. Reverberation describes the pattern of complicated echoes and sound reflections that occur when a sound is heard in a real space, for example a concert hall or a cathedral. Different types of space have different characters, so most reverb units provide room, hall and chamber simulations as well as emulations of the studio reverb plate – often used on drum sounds. The main adjustable parameter is decay time – the time the reverb takes to die away to inaudibility, but you may also find you have control over the brightness of the reverb. More sophisticated units may offer control over many more parameters, such as the reflection density of the reverb, or the pre-delay time between the sound and the reverb that follows it – one of my studio units has 99 different reverb parameters to adjust. However, you'll be pleased to know that in most instances, control over the reverb type, its decay time and its brightness is quite enough to get the job done.

delay

Delay is simply another term for echo, and if you feed some of the echo back to the input of an echo device, it recirculates causing many repeat echoes before it finally dies away. The number of repeats and how rapidly they die away are set using the Feedback control while the time between repeats is set using the Delay Time parameter. You may find that preset effects are good enough to use as they are, without any editing, but a useful musical trick is to set a delay time to a multiple of the tempo of the song. That way, all the repeats are perfectly in time and help reinforce the rhythm.

Stereo delays are sometimes provided where the repeats alternate between the left and right speakers. This is sometimes known as ping-pong delay.

chorus

Chorus is a simple effect that takes a signal and mixes it with a version of itself that it delayed slightly and subject to a slow modulation of pitch. The result sounds much like two performers playing the same part, and chorus is most effective in thickening pad parts or string ensemble sounds. The two important parameters are Depth and Rate.

flange

Flange is a similar effect to chorus except that the delay times used are very short and some of the output is fed back to the input. The result is a psychedelic 'whooshing' sound that you'll recognise as soon as you hear it.

The relevant controls here are Speed, Depth and Feedback, where feedback sets the strength of the effect. Because flanging is such a dramatic effect, it should be used sparingly. It works best on harmonically rich sounds such as bright string pads, though it can also be used on drums and cymbals.

phaser

The phaser was originally a guitar effect and it produces an effect that is similar to, but rather more subtle than flanging. Slow sweep rates are most effective, and the effect works well on sustained pad sounds, electric pianos or 'plucked parts'. The main controls are Speed, Depth, and Intensity.

rotary speaker

The electric organ sound is inexorably linked with the rotary speaker cabinet, the most famous being the Leslie speaker/Hammond organ combination. A series or rotating horns and baffles is used to create a complex tremolo effect which contains elements of both pitch and level modulation. A two-speed motor drives the baffles and is controlled by a knee switch or footswitch. Because of the mechanical inertia of the baffles, changing speed takes a second or two, and this 'run up and down' time is an important part of the effect.

Most effects units include an electronic simulation of the rotary speaker effect, some more successful than others. Some are little more than a chorus effect while others are very authentic, and most include the speed change 'run up/down' characteristic of the original. Though designed for use with organ, this effect works well on a whole range of sounds.

advantages of multitimbrality

Multitimbral synth modules have many advantages, though they need to be used with a sequencer to make the most of their considerable features. The main advantage is cost; it's obviously cheaper to buy a single multitimbral module than eight or 16 separate MIDI instruments. There's also a convenience advantage in that a single unit is compact and easy to wire up, and if it has a mixed stereo output, as most have, you can still get by with a relatively small mixer.

A further advantage is that most modules (including all GM modules), have on-board drum and percussion sounds, which means you don't have to spend extra on a drum machine or drum sound module. In the case of GM modules, the drum part is set to MIDI channel 10, but this cannot be relied upon for non-GM machines. These tend to handle their drum sounds in a number of different ways, so it's important to read your instrument handbooks.

The newer breed of GM/GS compatible modules enable users to be able to exchange MIDI song files in the knowledge that the song will play back on any GM module with appropriate sounds, regardless of the manufacturer, and equally important, the drum mapping will be consistent so you won't find that a snare drum on one machine plays back as a cow bell on another. See the chapter on General MIDI for more details.

using modules

On a practical level, just because a machine is eight-part multitimbral, it doesn't mean you have to use all eight parts. Indeed, it may be better to use just two or three parts from each of a number of different modules in a composition to avoid the possibility of note robbing and to provide a wider variety of available tone colours. This is particularly true of earlier machines, some of which had very limited polyphony.

voices and tones

One of the problems facing anyone coming to terms with multitimbral synths is the manufacturer's jargon – and different manufacturers tend to use different jargon. It's fairly logical to call the various virtual synth modules Parts, because these equate fairly well to the different musical parts they may be called upon to play. But what do we call the sounds of the notes that these Parts play? Indeed, 'Sounds' seems like a good word to me, but Roland, for example, call them 'Tones' – and life still isn't simple, because a Tone may be built up from more than one basic sound. Roland call their basic building blocks of sound 'Voices', and their quoted polyphony relates to Voices, not Tones. In other words, if you play a sound or Tone which is made up from two Voices layered together, that counts as two marbles out of the box, not one.

facilities

The most basic multitimbral sound module or soundcard will provide between eight and 16 parts, though GM modules must provide a minimum of 16 parts as standard. See the separate chapter on soundcards for more information on what facilities to expect. Some modules aimed at the computer music market also include an inbuilt MIDI interface, which represents a cost saving and makes setting up easier. All GM and most non-GM modules include digital effects, and apart from some modules designed to be used exclusively with computers, front panel control should be provided for selecting sounds, plus setting part level, pan and effect settings. It's also usual for the front panel controls to provide access to sound editing on programmable machines.

chapter 7

samplers & sampling

At its most basic, a sampler is a tapeless recording device, and once a sound has been recorded (into RAM memory), it can be played back at varying pitches under the control of a MIDI keyboard or sequencer. To play a sample back at a higher pitch than it was first recorded, the sampler has to speed up the sound with the result that the sample also plays back faster. Exactly the same thing happens with tape – if you double the tape speed, everything happens twice as quickly and the pitch goes up by one octave. Conversely, if you drop the pitch by slowing down the sample, the sound will go on for longer. Because RAM memory only works when power is supplied, most samplers forget everything when you switch them off which means that some form of permanent sound storage is required. Most samplers use floppy disks with the more serious models also offering the option of hard disk storage.

sampler uses

Before proceeding further with exactly what goes on inside the box, it is helpful to look at the two main ways people use samplers. If you sample single musical notes such as strings or organ sounds, you can play the sampler much like any other synthesizer, the beauty being that you're not restricted to the manufacturer's own internal sounds. The other great thing is that absolutely any sound can be sampled and used as a musical instrument – one of the first things everyone does when they get their first sampler is to go around the house hitting and scraping things to see what sounds good.

To make the sampled sound musically useful, a sampler needs to work polyphonically so you can play chords. As with synths, there is a limit on the available polyphony and most modern machines are also multitimbral in the same way that conventional synths are.

The other popular way of using samplers is to record not just individual notes but whole musical or rhythmic phrases, and this way of working forms the cornerstone of modern dance music construction. A typical application might be to sample a four-bar drum rhythm and then trigger this on the first beat of every bar to provide a continuous rhythmic backing.

sample memory

One thing that you soon discover after having bought a sampler is that you could always use more sample memory. Because sampled sounds are held in RAM, the maximum sampling time is always limited by the amount of memory you have, and on a basic sampler you may only get a maximum of ten seconds or so of sampling time. Ten seconds may seem like quite a lot, but if you're using your sampler multitimbrally, the available sample memory is divided up between the various sounds you have loaded at any one time. A fully expanded, top-of-the-range sampler may hold several minutes of samples, and now that RAM prices are much more reasonable than they were in the mid 90s, it's worth fitting as much as you can afford.

Because RAM memory is finite, various strategies are routinely adopted to make the most of it. At a full audio bandwidth of 20kHz using a 44.1kHz sampling rate, one minute of stereo sound takes up around 10Mbytes of RAM. If you can make do with mono, this immediately doubles the amount of sampling time available, and if you can tolerate a lower audio bandwidth by setting a lower sampling rate, this time can be extended again by a factor of two or more.

looping

The other time saving strategy used when sampling sustained musical sounds such as strings or flutes is to loop the sample (not to be confused with sampling the loop which I'll come onto later). Most sustained sounds have a distinctive attack portion, but as they start to decay, the sound becomes more consistent. Listen to something like a flute or a string section playing a sustained note and you'll notice that very little changes after the initial attack. This being the case, there's no reason to sample the whole sound being played – you simply sample the first few seconds, then use the sampler's editing facilities to create a loop so that the middle part of the sample repeats itself continually until you release the key. Obviously there's little point in trying to loop short or percussive sounds – they probably wouldn't sound right anyway, but you can loop long percussive sounds such as the decay of a cymbal.

There's another good reason for looping sounds, and that's to get around the way the sample length changes as you play higher or lower on the keyboard. What's more, the length of the original sound will probably be too short if you want to hold a string pad down for the next 24 bars. Once

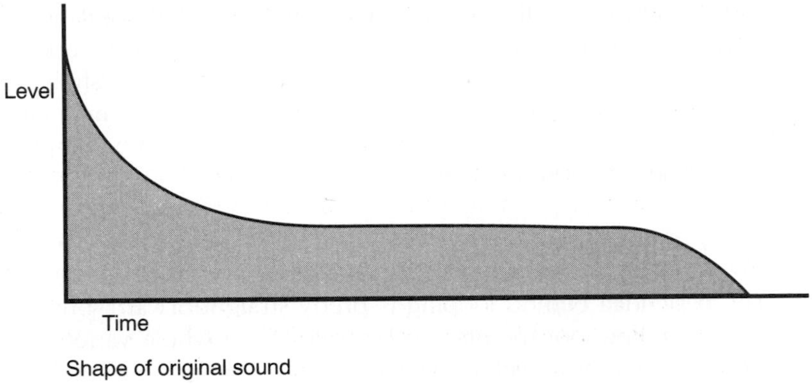

Figure 7.1: Looping a sustained sound

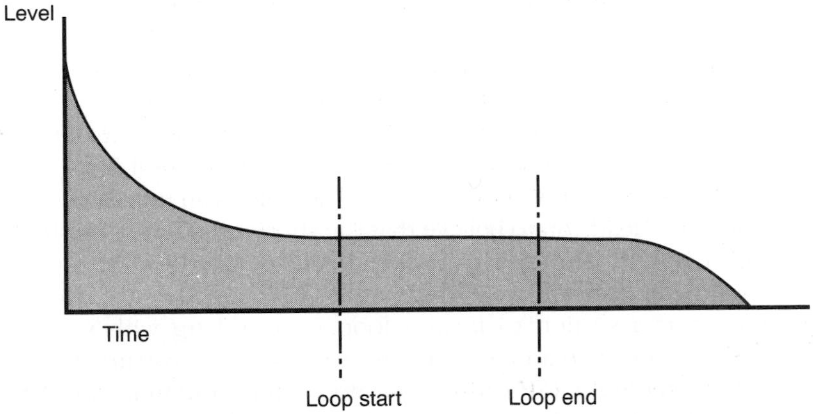

a sound is looped, its level never has to decay to zero because you're always looping around the same section of sound as shown in Figure 7.1.

crossfade looping

Sometimes, no matter how careful you are, you'll find that the point at which you've looped a sample remains audible as a change in tone, a change in level or even a click. When this happens, crossfade looping can help. Most serious samplers have this facility, and what happens is that instead of your loop point being a sudden transition between beginning and end, the sampler's internal editing software can overlap the start and end of the loop for you, then smoothly fade one into the other. The trick is to make the crossfade as short as possible, otherwise the sound may appear unnatural, but at the same time, you need to make it long enough to hide any unpleasant artifacts. If the start and end of the loop are too badly matched, you'll hear a change in timbre at the crossfade point, and if the loop is short, this will take on an irritating, cyclic quality. Slowly decaying sounds can sometimes be looped more successfully if they are compressed in level before being sampled as this will maintain a more consistent level, but unless you have access to a studio compressor, this may be beyond your control.

looping problems

The basic idea behind looping is pretty straightforward, but finding the best sounding loop points can be tricky for a whole variety of reasons. Firstly, unless the waveform shapes at the beginning and end of the loop match up in level, shape and phase, you're quite likely to end up with a click. Clicks can be minimised by looping at zero-crossing points (the point where the electrical signal crosses over from being positive to negative or vice versa), but if the waveform levels and shapes don't match pretty closely, you may still hear a glitch.

If you take too long a section to form your loop, you may find that the sound's own natural decay means you have a different level between the loop start and loop end which will be audible as an unnatural modulation. This might lead you to believe that the shorter the loop, the smoother the result will be. The reality of the situation is that even apparently steady sounds are constantly evolving in their harmonic texture, and if you take too short a section to form a loop, you end up with something that sounds more like an electronic tone than a real instrument. Part of the skill in getting good loops is to choose the optimum loop length, and that's something that really needs practise and experience.

Sounds should always be sampled without vibrato or other forms of modulation because the modulation rate will change depending on what note you play. Not only that, it's harder to loop a sample with vibrato because not only do you have to match up the basic waveforms, you also have to ensure that you've looped a whole number of complete modulation cycles, otherwise you end up with a repeating hiccup in the vibrato.

Finally, stereo sounds can be very difficult to loop because a good waveform match on one channel may not correspond to a good match on the other channel. Where stereo looping is essential, crossfade looping may be necessary to hide the join, so where you can, keep looped samples in mono and reserve stereo for longer musical sections such as drum loops.

envelopes

To recreate the effect of the sound's own natural decay, samplers include envelope shapers just like those found in synths to allow you to modify the envelope of your sampled sounds. In most cases, the attack of the original sound can be left as it was, but a new decay has to be created to prevent the sound stopping abruptly when you release the key. If you've sampled an organ sound, then an abrupt stop is okay, but most instruments have a slower decay time which can easily be duplicated by using the Release phase of the envelope shaper. At its simplest, this will mean that the sound will remain constant in level while you're holding down a key and then fade out at your chosen release rate when the key is released. Of course you can use the envelope generator more creatively to set up any envelope you like, just as you can in a conventional synth. Similarly, some samplers offer complex, multi-section envelope generators and they may be able to generate two or more different loops within the same sample, but for the sake of simplicity, I'll stick to the basic features.

triggering

If you have a sound that plays through from start to finish without looping, you'll find that there are different ways of triggering it. For example, if you hit the same key twice, and you want the original sample to carry on to its natural conclusion while the newly triggered one plays over the top, then you need to select the 'one-shot' trigger mode. On the other hand, if you want the original sound to stop and then trigger again from the beginning for that cliched 'n n n n nineteen' effect, then you need the 'retrigger' mode. Again, most samplers support these basic triggering modes, but there may be slight differences in the terminology used.

multisampling

So far, I've covered the rudimentary principles of sampling, but what I haven't touched upon is the way in which sounds become very unnatural when transposed far from their original pitch. Sometimes you can use this unnatural quality very creatively, but when you're trying to capture a real instrument such as a piano, you only have to move a few semitones either side of the note's original position and it starts to sound quite alien. This is where the concept of multisampling makes an entrance.

If a sampled piano sounds natural for, say, only a couple of semitones either side of its original pitch, the only way to maintain a natural sound

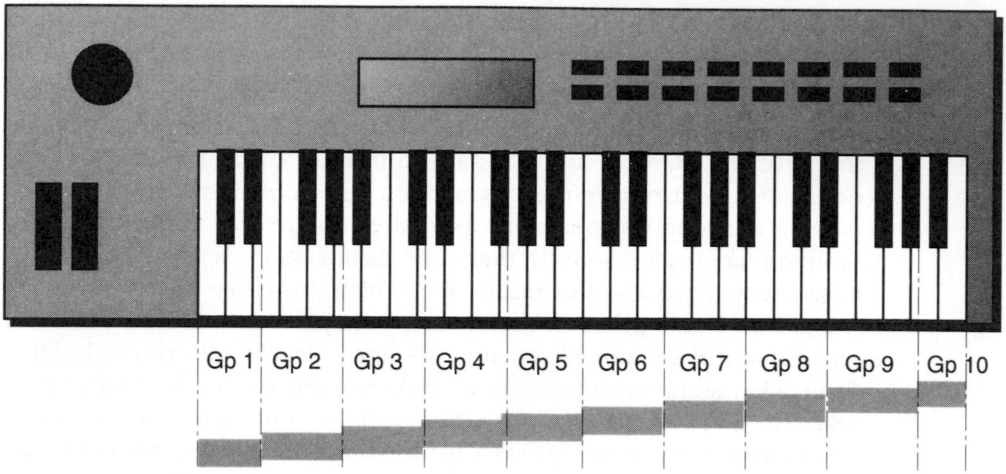

Keyboard divided into groups, in this case with five semitones per group. One sample is used to cover each group, which means no sample ever has to play much over one tone away from its original pitch. This results in a more natural sound than using just one or two samples to cover the whole keyrange. The number of multisamples required depends to a large extent on the characteristics of the instrument being sampled

Figure 7.2: Creating a keygroup

is to take several samples of the original instrument at different pitches and use each sample over a limited part of the keyboard. This is what we mean by multisampling, and the zones of the keyboard covered by each sample are known as keygroups. The more keygroups you have, the more accurate the sound will be but the more memory you'll need to hold all the samples. Pianos tend to be close to the top of the list of critical instruments while strings, flutes and brass can be stretched a little further before they start to sound artificial. Figure 7.2 shows how a keygroup may be built up.

Related to keygroups is the idea of velocity switching or crossfading, which simply means that you take two samples, a loud one and a quiet one, and then use key velocity to control which one plays. Velocity switching is the most efficient option as it doesn't affect your overall polyphony. Crossfading to a louder sample as you play harder sounds more convincing as you get a more gentle transition, but it also halves your polyphony as two samples are playing at the same time.

samplers as recorders

When samplers first came on the scene, the main aim was to sample individual notes or sounds so that you could play them in much the same way as you'd play any other keyboard instrument. Now that we have longer sampling times available, it has become popular to sample whole musical phrases which can be played back from a single key. Probably the first application of this type was to sample whole sections of vocals allowing the engineer to copy a good chorus from one part of a song and then 'fire' it into the mix at the appropriate point when the next chorus came around. However, it was quickly realised that there was enormous creative potential in working this way, and that if you sampled several complete drum rhythms at the same tempo, then assigned each one to a different key on the keyboard, you could effectively play your whole drum part just by holding down the appropriate keys.

looping drums

Samplers usually allow you to loop your drum parts so they play continuously, but when you're working with a sequencer, there's a strong likelihood that the drum loop's timing will drift away from the tempo of the sequencer over a period of time. A far better option is not to loop your drum rhythm at all but simply to retrigger it every bar or however long the pattern is by using a note from the sequencer, quantised to the first beat of the bar. You can match up the sequencer tempo to the drum beat tempo pretty easily, and if there is a tiny discrepancy, it doesn't really matter because every time the drum rhythm is retriggered, it's brought back into perfect sync. The same is true of other rhythmic elements such as guitar riffs, and even with long vocal sections, it can be better to break them down into shorter phrases, then trigger each phrase independently. Figure 7.3 shows how timing errors can occur if you don't trigger your rhythmic sample loops from the sequencer.

You really should experiment with sampling your own sounds – even the most innocent everyday objects can yield interesting results when played back at different speeds. Once you've got past the obvious blown bottles, sewer pipe didgeridoos and pinged kitchenware, you start to find that steel garage doors make great snare drums, bouncing balls can be tuned down into monster kick drums and innocent wooden banister rails can sometimes blossom into very organic marimbas.

sampling levels

An important point to note about sampling is that because it is a digital process, you need to sample the signals at the highest possible level to get the best signal quality and the lowest noise. However, if you go too far and clip the signal, the chances are it will sound pretty dreadful – digital has no margin of safety like an analogue recorder. If the sound you're trying to sample isn't repeatable, it may be better to record it to tape first, then

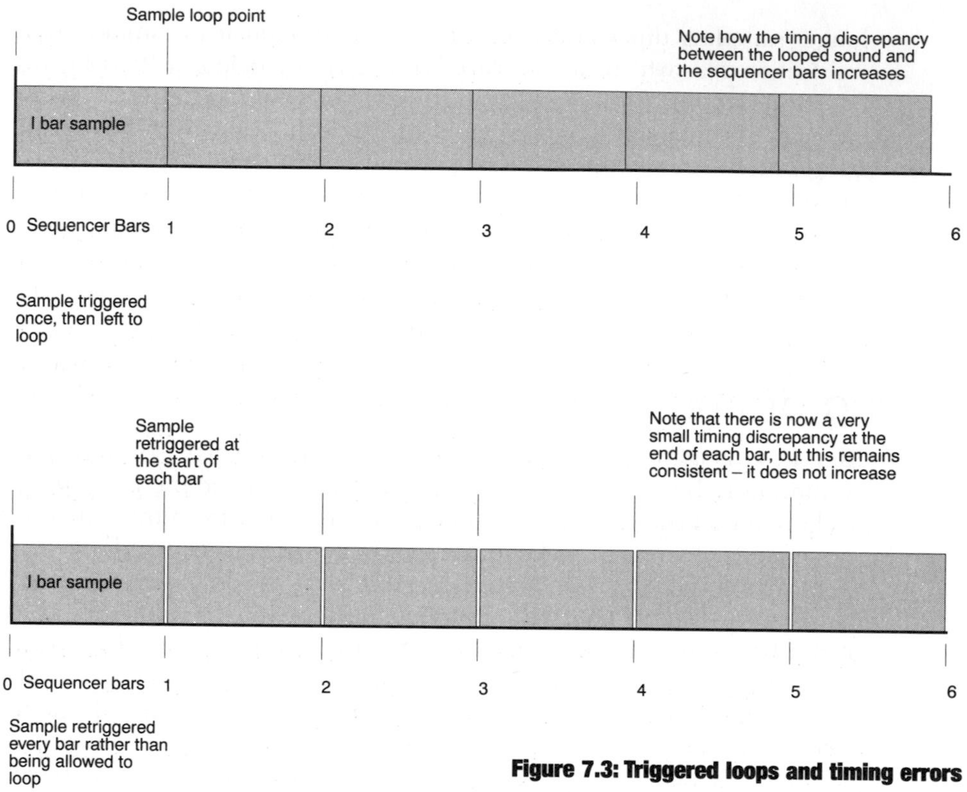

Figure 7.3: Triggered loops and timing errors

sample it so you'll have the chance to try again if it doesn't work out first time.

sample libraries

So far, I've covered just the essentials of sampling, and once you get into it, you'll discover a lot of things for yourself. One thing you soon discover is that life is too short to make your own grand piano samples, so standard orchestral and instrumental sounds are best obtained from a sound library. If you have a sampler that can read CD-ROMs, this makes life much easier – virtually all modern samplers can be connected to a CD-ROM drive or have one built in.

Samples provided on CD-ROM are already set up in programs containing looping information, key mapping, envelope settings and so on, so you really just need to load them and play. The majority of CD-ROMs are supplied in a format for Akai samplers, but because of the popularity of these machines, most of their major competitors also make it possible to load Akai format disks. If you're after stock sounds, well produced drum loops or exotic ethnic bits and pieces, it's far easier to buy the sounds than it is to sample your own. Creating your own samples is fun and it's a central part of what sampling is all about, but there are few people with the time and skill to produce something like a perfectly multisampled grand piano.

Sample CDs are a useful source of new sounds and have the benefit of being significantly cheaper than CD-ROM sample libraries, and you can play them directly into the analogue inputs of your sampler using a domestic CD player. All you have to do is set the record levels, and if you're lucky enough to have a sampler with a digital input and a CD player with a digital output, you can pipe the data in digitally. If you go via the analogue ins, it is well to remind yourself that the sampler is really a digital recorder, and that overloading the input will result in very unpleasant distortion. Even so, always get as much level in as you can without clipping – this will produce the best signal-to-noise ratio.

organising samples

The hard work starts after you've sampled the sounds from CD because you now have to name your samples, create loops where appropriate, sort out crossfades, and put the samples into keygroups so that you get a smooth transition from one sample to the other as you go up the keyboard. You may also have to create keyboard zones so that sounds can be velocity crossfaded or cross-switched. I don't know what you consider 'fun', but as far as I'm concerned, unless the sample is marvellous beyond belief, life is simply too short for this kind of thing. Loading drum loops from CD is fine, but multisamples take a long time.

A far easier alternative is to use CD-ROMs, but first, you have to confirm that your sampler can work with a CD-ROM drive. Most CD-ROMs cost as much if not more than the drive you slot them into, but I have to say that when you actually get around to using CD-ROMs, it's a real luxury, because the samples load up into neatly named programs, ready looped and key-grouped, complete with the appropriate envelope settings so that all you have to do is load them and play them. I can't, however, guarantee that you'll find all the samples on any particular disk as exciting as your credit card statement!

compatibility

At least three of the major sampler manufacturers, Akai, E-mu and Roland, are supported by a vast library of both in-house and third-party CD-ROMs so it comes as no surprise that each has developed an operating system allowing CD-ROMs made for one of their competitors' machines to be used as well their own. However, because every sampler has slightly different parameters, facilities and characteristics, the degree of translation isn't always perfect. Sometimes the only difference is a change in tonal quality, but there are occasions when you need to edit the programs to make them fully usable.

sample storage

If a basic memory provision of 2Mbytes is inadequate, you might well ask what use is the integral 1.44Mbytes floppy drive for storing samples, especially as many machines don't have the provision to save longer samples over multiple disks? What you need is an SCSI hard drive or, better still, removable media drive – providing your sampler is fitted with a SCSI interface. When it comes to choosing a specific model of drive, I think I would put quietness of operation at the top of my 'needs' list rather than speed of data transfer. Any hard drive is going to load up a typical set of samples fairly quickly, but some are intrusively noisy. If you're going to buy any type of removable drive though, it might be as well to check with any other musicians or local studios with whom you are likely to collaborate with a view to settling on the same model. Not only does this guarantee compatibility, it also provides the opportunity for you to order blank media in bulk which can result in very significant savings.

sample editing software

Even with all the bolt-ons and a selection of sample CDs at your disposal, you're still going to want to do some sampling of your own, and it soon becomes clear that working from the front panel of a typical sampler isn't the easiest way to do things. Looping samples and setting them into keygroups is more easily managed from a screen environment, and unless you have one of the very few samplers that supports a computer monitor, you might be tempted to check out the software sample editors on the market. Powerful sample editors are available for both Mac and PC platforms as well as some of the less prevalent machines.

MIDI can be used to transfer samples from a sampler to a computer and back again, but this is very slow. A far better and faster option is to use a system that can communicate over SCSI.

creative sampling

While only a real sampling diehard would dream of attempting to multisample an entire grand piano, what often really makes a recording stand out is the use of something that's a little out of the ordinary. In the early days of sampling, we'd blow over a milk bottle, sample the result and then play it back over the whole keyboard span. It didn't matter that it sounded like a penny whistle at the top end of the scale and a demonic fog horn at the bottom, that was part of the magic of the sound, and for me, part of the magic of sampling.

With rhythm playing more of an important part than ever in contemporary pop music, the sampler provides the perfect opportunity to capture unusual sounds for use in a rhythmic context. The great advantage here is that the sounds don't need multisampling, fine tuning or looping, so aside from a little topping and tailing, they're ready to use as soon as you've saved them to disk and put them into a program.

Before you can record your own samples, you're going to need a mic, and if your sampler doesn't have a mic input, then you'll need to use a mixer or something similar as a mic preamp. Having said that, almost any decent dynamic vocal mic will do for most basic sampling jobs, especially when the result is to be used as a percussive element. You'll only benefit from using a studio capacitor mic when sampling really high pitched sounds such as triangles.

improvise

The most exciting thing about sampling is that you don't need any real instruments at all to create some really powerful sounds. There's a multitude of natural sounds that can be captured and then manipulated, and usually all you need to do is adjust the pitch, sharpen up the attack by truncating the leading edge of the sample if need be, and adjust the decay rate. Here are some examples of things that can be turned into great percussion sounds. If you have a DAT machine or a good cassette recorder, it's best to record a series of samples to tape first, then you only need sample the ones that seem as though they're going to work.

- Slamming an up-and-over garage door: this produces a powerful sound that reverberates around inside the garage so you get a different result depending on whether you are miking from inside or outside. You'll probably want to trim the sound so you only use the bang at the end, and you might find the decay time is too long in which case you can reduce the decay time using the sampler's envelope controls. Try the sound at different pitches for kick or snare drum substitutes.

- Door slam: an ordinary interior door can produce a gratifying bang if closed with sufficient vigour. Leaving a window or other door open may help as it prevents air pressure in the room from cushioning the slam.

- Bouncing a plastic football on a hard surface: this is the UK version of miking a bouncing basketball. Tuned down it makes a wonderful kick drum, especially with the addition of gated reverb.

- Suitcases: we've all heard of drums that sound like suitcases, but if you get the right suitcase, you can make it sound just like drums. Try hitting it with different things including rolled up newspaper or a wooden mallet. Keep the mic fairly close and watch the record levels to make sure you don't go into clipping.

- Soggy paper: for this you'll need a lump of soaked newspaper pressed into a ball. Hurl it at various surfaces and record the results. It can be surprisingly effective, but isn't recommended indoors. Again makes a passable kick drum.

- Baking foil: hold up a sheet of baking foil and then hit it flat-on using a wooden spoon or similar implement. You'll probably tear it so try to get this one right first time. If you get the mic close enough and pitch shift the result downwards, it should sound like an old reverb plate being shot!

- Snapping wood: a simple length of wooden beading can be snapped in half to provide a satisfying substitute for a techno snare sound. You'll probably have to drop the pitch quite a bit unless you're strong enough to break logs!

- Bits of wood: hitting a couple of offcuts together should produce a nice resonant thunk which can be shifted up to give you claves or down to create marimbas or log drums. You can play the resulting sound over a couple of octaves, and if you're lucky, you might have captured enough of the pitch to tune it.

- Domestic radiators: most radiators ring if you knock them, and by hitting them with a felt beater of even a rolled up newspaper, you can capture a useful sample which, when pitch shifted down, sounds like a weird gong. Pitch shift the sound up and you have an alternative cow bell. The same applies to most metal containers so check the house and see what's around.

- Speaker cone: tap any speaker cone (gently) and you'll hear a noise, but on larger speakers such as those used in studio monitors or instrument amplifiers, the chances are that the noise will be a deep thud, not unlike a kick drum. Mic at close range, drop the pitch further if need be and you have another kick drum.

- Vacuum cleaner: okay, so it's not really percussive, but if you sample anything that uses an electric motor and then drop the pitch, you'll find you have something that sounds like a monstrous generator. If you can tune the pitch to match the song, you can trigger short bursts of sounds to produce a techno/rave, gated bass line feel.

- Spanners: large spanners suspended on cotton or fishing line produce excellent bell-tree sounds, though to really capture these at their best, you'll need a capacitor mic. The spanners can be tapped with any metal object or banged together, and if you want to try dropping the pitch, you can end up with some quite moody tibetan gongs or bells.

Once you have your sound, you may need to add some effects to make it sound more impressive, and virtually any percussive sounds will benefit from reverb. If your sampler doesn't have internal effects, a low cost outboard effects unit can be used in conjunction with your mixer.

recording samples

By now you should have some ideas for things to sample, but you may be unsure as to how to mic up the sounds or how to treat them afterwards. As intimated earlier, you don't need a fancy mic unless you want to make high quality recordings of bright sounds, but positioning the mic is fairly important. My usual approach when producing this kind of sample is to set the mic up around a foot from the object being struck, and then change the mic position if this initial setting doesn't produce the desired result. As a rule, you'll only need to use longer mic distances if you're miking up something large such as a garage door or radiator, and because you're not after a natural sound, the only criterion is whether the sound works or not – not how good the recording is.

By recording to tape first, you can experiment with recording levels and sort the good sounds from the bad before you get down to sampling. If the sound has too slow an attack, it can either be truncated so that the first few milliseconds of the sample are thrown away, or you could consider adding another sound. For example, if you create a sample of a bouncing ball and then decide it doesn't have enough bite, you could trigger the sample at the same time as a short percussive sound from a drum machine (or another sample) and mix the two together. The mixed sound can then be recorded onto tape and subsequently resampled. Sounds that work well alongside kick samples are things like finger snaps, claps, rim shots and other short sounds, and the trick is to mix them low enough so that they merge with the sample to create a new sound.

Once you start, the list is endless, and because you can amplify the sound to any level you like, the most insignificant event can form the basis of a huge-sounding sample. A snapping twig could become a monster snare drum, a kitchen cleaver slammed into a cabbage gives you yet another kick drum, a length of scaffolding provides the basis for tuned industrial percussion and so on.

chapter 8

alternative MIDI controllers

MIDI and keyboards are a match made in heaven – electronic circuitry likes the certainly of switches, and a MIDI keyboard is really just a row of switches. However, not every musician plays a keyboard, so what alternatives are available for everyone else out there? In fact various instruments have been manufactured or adapted to generate MIDI information, including – but not limited to – guitar, violin, wind instruments, drums and even accordions. The electric guitar is still the most popular contemporary instrument, so I'll tackle that one first.

guitars and midi

Guitars don't lend themselves naturally to MIDI because, unlike the electronic keyboard, the notes are created by vibrating strings, not by turning oscillators on or off with switches. In order to generate MIDI information, there has to be some means of measuring the pitch of each string, but the signal from a conventional guitar pickup is too complex to analyse when more than one string is sounding at a time. The most common solution is to use a split pickup – in effect one pickup per string – so that each string can be monitored independently of the others. Once a note is picked, a specially designed circuit measures the frequency of the string and passes it onto a small processor that generates the required MIDI data. Unfortunately, the first part of a plucked note comprises mainly unpitched pick noise, then, when the string does start to vibrate, there's a short time delay before the circuitry can figure out the pitch. Modern circuits track the pitch pretty quickly, but tracking is always slower on the lower strings, leading some players to complain that the delay on the bottom couple of strings puts them off.

A further problem is that guitar sounds are harmonically complex, and if you happen to play a harmonic, the circuitry may lock onto its frequency rather than onto the fundamental pitch of the string. In fact accidental mistracking occasionally plagues even the best systems. To compound the difficulties, there's no 'key up' event to tell the note when to end, so if the player doesn't terminate the note by damping or lifting a finger off, there's no telling when the note will stop – it all depends on the sustain of the guitar. A related problem is that the very action of lifting a finger off a string can cause the open string to vibrate just enough to cause an accidental retrigger. It all sounds horrendously fraught, but used with a sequencer where you have the opportunity to fix mistakes afterwards, it can be a practical way of recording MIDI information.

pitch bend

One way modern MIDI guitar designers have found to improve note-tracking is to use MIDI pitch bend controller information to continually correct the pitch of the tracked note. Hammer-ons tend to be implemented entirely by pitch bend information, so if you are working with a sequencer, the notes you see on the edit page may be a little different from what you actually played. For example, a hammer-on trill will be shown as a single picked note followed by pitch bend data.

midi mono mode

To enable each string of a guitar to be used for independent note bends over MIDI, each string must be handled by a different MIDI channel. The most guitar-like results are achieved using a synth that can work in MIDI Mode 4; in effect, this puts each guitar string in control of its own part of a multitimbral module and allows each part to play only monophonically. After all, a guitar string can only play one note at a time.

Even when there is no intention to bend notes, it is essential to stick with the one-channel, one-string approach if hammer-ons and slides are to be tracked accurately. There are occasions when it can be advantageous to simply plug the guitar synth into a module set to Poly mode. Though bends, hammers and slides can't be used, this mode does provide a reasonably reliable way of triggering simple parts such as block chords or straight melody lines.

guitar setup

It is important that any guitar you intend using with a MIDI guitar synth system is properly set up. This means the split pickup should be mounted as close to the bridge of the guitar as possible, and the spacing between the pickup and the strings should be around 1mm when the string is fretted on the highest fret. This may differ slightly from model to model, so consult your handbook carefully. It is important that the strings pass over the centre of each section of the divided pickup, so as to avoid crosstalk between adjacent strings. Fret buzz causes tracking problems – very low actions and guitar synths don't mix.

Having established that guitar synths prefer to track cleanly vibrating strings, here are a few playing tips:

● Avoid playing harmonics, and play as cleanly as possible using even picking strokes.

● Conventional fast strumming doesn't work well as the notes are too short for the synth to lock onto reliably. Try an arpeggio or a simple finger-picking pattern instead.

Instruments like the piano have a rigidly fixed pitch. Don't bend the notes or use the vibrato arm, and if your MIDI guitar system has a Bend Off option (sometimes called Chromatic mode), this might produce better results.

● Don't think like a guitar player, think as though you are playing the instrument you're imitating. For example, if you're playing a solo flute patch, don't play chords – flutes are monophonic. If the sound you're using has a slow attack, then play slow, uncomplicated parts to let the sound develop. If the slow attack throws your timing, then listen to the sound of your pick on the guitar and take your timing cues from that.

● If your guitar synth has a noticeable delay on the bottom strings, try playing the part one or two octaves higher and then use your sequencer's Transpose function to bring the pitch of the synthesized sound back to where you want it.

● Because you never know exactly how long a plucked note will sustain, use the Hold pedal for long chords.

● Don't sit too close to the computer monitor as most MIDI guitar pickups react to the interference from the screen, resulting in erratic note tracking and triggering.

tips

The following tips and guidelines might be useful to anyone using a

MIDI guitar in conjunction with a sequencer or with external expander modules.

● Always ensure that your guitar synth and any expander modules are set to the same MIDI pitch bend range – usually twelve semitones (as opposed to the more normal two used by keyboard players).

● To record a guitar part using complex string bends, the sequencer must be set to record on all six MIDI channels simultaneously. Consult your sequencer manual to see how to do this. Less sophisticated sequencers may not have this option.

Double-triggered or very low velocity notes can often be removed automatically by your sequencer. Check the handbook to see what labour saving functions are available to you.

Make full use of any sustain or hold pedal functions available to help when playing sustained chords. Such functions as 'note length quantise' and 'force legato' can also be used to good effect to create certain musical styles.

mental approach

Getting to grips with different sounds is something electronic keyboard players have always had to do, but guitar players are conditioned to expect every sound they play to have an instant, percussive attack. Give a rock guitar player a brass patch with a slow attack and he'll probably complain that the synth can't keep up with him. What he really should be saying is that the attack time of the instrument is too long to allow the notes to develop at the speed he's trying to play. A tuba player isn't likely to attempt double-time triplets, so why expect a tuba synth patch to be able to?

midi violins

MIDI violins usually work on a similar principle to MIDI guitars insomuch as they have a separate pickup for each string, but as violins don't use metal strings, the pickups are more likely to be piezo electric devices. Because of the possible interference that bow noise can cause to the tracking process, ingenious multiple pickup systems are sometimes employed in an attempt to cancel the bow noise, and elaborate electronic filtering is used to strip away harmonics so that the fundamental frequency is less difficult to detect.

wind controllers

Various wind controllers have been built at one time or another, most relying on switches or touch sensors to duplicate the functions of the keys on a clarinet or similar instrument. These switches provide the note information in much the same way as the keys on a regular keyboard, but a special mouthpiece capable of measuring breath pressure and lip pressure provides additional controller information so as to add more life to the sound. The instruments may also be fitted with sliders, modulation wheels or ribbon controller that the player can operate with his thumb. Other refinements include octave switches.

Played well, the wind controller is a most impressive instrument, and used in combination with one of the newer physical modelling synths, the results have a stunning realism about them. Like real wind instruments, these controllers are monophonic, though you can still set your synth to play parallel intervals, such as 4ths, 5ths and octaves.

drum controllers

MIDI drum systems have been around for many years because they're not too difficult to design compared to other controller systems. Usually, a synthetic rubber pad is used instead of a real drum head, and this is fitted with a special pickup that monitors how hard the pad has been struck. Each hit is converted by a processor into a MIDI Note On and Off message of differing velocities depending on how hard the pad has been struck.

A separate floor mounting pad is often used in conjunction with a conventional bass drum pedal for producing bass drum sounds, and a regular footswitch often serves as a simple hi-hat open/close switch. Cymbals and hi-hat sounds are usually triggered by the same type of pads as the drum sounds, though some more sophisticated systems use pads with position sensors that allow two MIDI controlled sounds to be crossfaded as the player plays across the surface of the pad. For example, a cymbal might have a cymbal bell sound near the centre and a ride cymbal sound near the edge.

drum pads

Drum pads are available on full size pads to replace the conventional drum kit, or they may be presented as a number of smaller pads fitted to the surface of a briefcase-sized unit. This latter type is more practical in the home MIDI studio, and most have inputs to accept pedals and bass drum pads.

The most advanced pad systems allow the user to send out sequences of notes from specific pads, either in programmed or random order, and if these are assigned to, for example, slightly different cymbal sounds, the sound will change every hit making for a more natural sound. The same trick can be used to make snare drum rolls sound more natural.

chapter 9

practical sequencing

So far you've read a lot about MIDI and sequencing, and you may even have tried a couple of MIDI experiments just to convince yourself that it really does work, but now it's time to try a few moves on the sequencer to see what it can do. However, the first thing you should do is make sure you have a comfortable working position. Sitting at a badly positioned computer for any length of time soon results in back ache, neck ache and wrist ache, none of which helps the creative process of writing music. Even though you may think you do most of your work using the mouse, put the keyboard in a position where it feels comfortable to type on. You also need to be able to get at your music keyboard – and of course you need to be comfortably placed relative to that too,

Even a high resolution computer monitor can cause eyestrain so try to position the screen so that it's at least two feet from your eyes. You should also use adequate ambient lighting so that you don't get dazzled by the screen. An anti-glare filter might help, but providing you follow the above guidelines and don't set the screen brightness to high, you shouldn't have any problems. If you do find your eyes getting sore, consider buying a pair of VDU operator's spectacles to filter out any glare and UV that may be coming from your monitor screen. These have the same effect as an anti-glare screen but work out rather cheaper, especially if you work with a large monitor.

Always use a mouse mat, not the table top or the back of a book. Apart from making the mouse run more smoothly, it will also extend its life by reducing the amount of dust that accumulates on the ball and internal rollers. If you're really short of desk space, consider a trackball; some people really like working with these while others hate them. At least you don't keep running out of mouse mat!

sequencer familiarisation

MIDI sequencing starts at the keyboard, which is connected via its MIDI Out to the MIDI In of your MIDI interface or soundcard. (If you have an Atari ST, the interface is built into the computer.) If your keyboard includes a synth

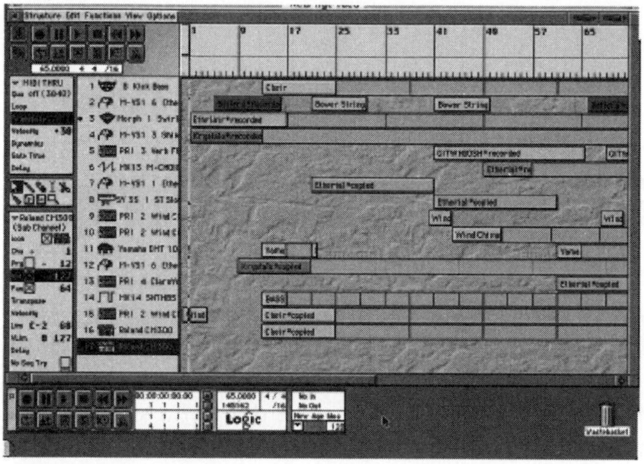

Figure 9.1: Arrange page of a typical software sequencer

section (rather than just being a dumb master keyboard), then turn Local Off and plug a MIDI cable from the sequencer's MIDI Out to the keyboard's MIDI In. If you have other MIDI modules in the system, you can daisy chain them in any order by feeding the MIDI Thru of one piece of gear to the MIDI In of the next module along.

If you haven't done it already, plug everything in, check all the connections, check that your synthesizer is plugged into a suitable amplification system, switch on, and ensure that the volume is turned up loud enough for you to hear properly. When you're satisfied everything is okay, load the sequencing software. If you haven't used a computer before, take some time to read the manual, then try a few exercises to get used to the mouse. Ensure that you know how to start the machine, and how to shut it down – you don't just pull the mains plug out when you're done. You'll need to know how to format and use floppy disks, how to open and close files, and in the case of Macs and PCs, you'll need to know how to open, close and move windows. Only once you're happy with the basic computer operations should you attempt to do any sequencing.

the arrange page

Though every sequencer package on the market has a slightly different user interface, most of the successful ones bear more than a passing resemblance to Steinberg's Cubase – where the main page shows the sequencer tracks running from left to right across the screen. Hardware sequencers tend to be a little less consistent, but the basic principles of selecting tracks, recording tracks, playing back sequences and editing are roughly comparable. The arrange page of a typical sequencer is shown in Figure 9.1.

Each track can be set to record on any MIDI channel – you don't have to use track 1 for MIDI channel 1, but to start with, it might be less confusing to set up track 1 to channel 1, track 2 to channel 2 and so on. If you have a system which comprises both an external MIDI module and a soundcard, you'll find that you also have a choice of sound source for each track. For example, on a PC system with a simple SoundBlaster card, this is likely to show up in the form of a choice between the on-board AWE32 Synth and MIDI, where MIDI is the external MIDI connection to your sound module.

Mac users don't usually have access to internal MIDI soundcards, so the normal choice will only be between MIDI channels, unless a multiport MIDI interface is fitted. If a multiport interface is fitted, then you'll get a choice of 16 channels on, for example, MIDI ports A, B, C and so on, probably prefixed with an M or P to denote whether the interface is plugged into the modem or printer port sockets. If you have a really big MIDI system, you might have an interface plugged into each port. The maximum number of ports on an external multiport MIDI interface is usually eight with a full 16 MIDI channels per port, though some top end interfaces offer almost double this number.

program selection

Having set your tracks to the MIDI channels you wish to use, you should enter a MIDI Program Change number in each track – this will force your synth module or soundcard to play the sound program of your choice. Most GM soundcards can have their patch names displayed within the sequencer arrange page, which makes choosing sounds a little easier. If not, you'll need your synth's manual open on the patch chart page so you can see what number corresponds to what sound unless you have one of the sequencer packages that allows you to type in the patch names of all your synths. This may be tedious first time around, but you'll be thankful of it later when you can call every synth patch up by name rather than by number. If you have to work using program numbers, it helps to have a photocopy of the General MIDI patch list pinned to the wall.

tempo

Now adjust the tempo to suit the music you wish to record. You can always change the tempo after recording, so if you're not a great player, you may want to set this slightly slow to make recording easier – you can always speed it up again once you're finished. Once you start recording, the computer will play a simple metronome click, either via the speaker in the monitor, or via your MIDI drum sounds. After a count in of one or two bars (depending on what you've set up in the preferences section of your sequencer), the currently selected track will record everything you play into it.

Personally, I find click tracks very limiting to play to – I'd rather play to a drum rhythm, so if you find your timing wandering, record a simple drum pattern first and use this as your metronome. If you're using a General MIDI sound module, the drums will be on channel 10, and switching to different program numbers may give you a choice of different sounding drum sets, depending on the module or soundcard you're using. Something simple with bass drum, snare drum and hi-hats is usually fine, and don't worry if it's not exactly what you want for the final version, because you can always replace it or edit it later. However, unless your timing is really good, you should quantise it so as to force all the beats to line up with the nearest 16th note (for a 4/4 time signature). Different time signatures may require a different quantise value, and most sequencers offer a pull down menu of different quantisation values from which to choose.

Important: The better sequencers have fully undo-able quantise, so that at any time you can unquantise your work or apply a different quantise value. However, some of the cheaper systems don't let you fully undo quantising, even when they claim to allow it. If you have such a machine, save a backup of your song file to disk before quantising, just in case you don't like the result!

drumming made easy

If you find playing drum parts difficult, here's a tip. Create three or four sequencer tracks, all set to the channel of your drum sounds (usually channel 10), and record your drum part in layers. First put the bass drum part on one track, then when this is okay, record the snare drum part in isolation on the next drum track. When these are both working together okay, play in a hi-hat part. It sometimes helps if you actually drum on the keys with the forefingers of your two hands rather than trying to play the drum rhythms 'piano style'. If you don't know which drums are on which keys, refer to the drum map in your sequencer manual, and consider sticking labels on the keys corresponding to the drum sounds you use.

Most sequencers have a facility for merging the data on different tracks – Cubase and similarly styled programs use a 'tube of glue' icon in the tool palette. The usual system is to select the tracks to be joined by holding down the shift key, clicking on the desired tracks until they are all high-lighted, then clicking on any one of them with the glue tool. If you want to tidy up your drum tracks after you're sure they're okay, simply merge them all to one track. This way, all the drum data will be combined into a single track, leaving the arrange page looking less cluttered.

copy and loop

Obviously you don't want to have to tap in the drum rhythm for the whole five minutes of the song you plan to write, so the best bet is to create just one or two bars – then copy that part as many times as is needed. Some sequencers, such as Logic, allow you to loop sections so that they play indefinitely, while other programs, Cubase being one, have a copy menu into which you enter the number of copies you want. These copy and looping functions are immensely useful, especially in pop music where there tends to be a lot of repetition.

the next track

Once your guide drum part is tapping away happily, choose a new track and play whichever keyboard part is most appropriate. Now you have a drum part, you can turn the original metronome click down or off if it's distracting you. A chord part is a good choice to put down second as it serves as a good guide for subsequent parts. If you're doing dance music, you might find a bass part more helpful at this point – it's up to you.

timing

Once you've played in two or three tracks, listen to your performance to see how the timing feels. If you're a good player, you'll almost certainly get more feel in your performance by not quantising it, but if you're a bit on the sloppy side, you may feel it needs tightening up. Before you dive straight for the quantise button, check to see if your sequencer supports percentage quantise. Most good sequencer have this facility, and the idea is that if you set, say 50% quantise, the note you've played will be shifted so that it falls half way between where you played it and where the computer thinks it ought to have been. The higher the percentage you set, the further the note moves towards the rigid quantise value. By choosing the right percentage, you can tighten up your performance, but still leave a degree of human feel in it.

moving your music

Another very powerful feature of sequencers is that you can move data around. For example, you may have put together a composition, but now you decide the synth solo should start a couple of bars later. This is no problem if you're using Cubase or one of the packages with a similar interface, because all you have to do is use the mouse to drag the sequence to a new position. What's more, if you want to copy it to a new position without changing the original, there's usually a keyboard short cut, whereby you hold down a key, then drag a copy to its new location. Once again, the key commands vary from package to package, so check your manual to see how your system works. This technique is invaluable for copying repeated sections such as verses or choruses – you only have to record each section once, then you can drag copies around to experiment with alternative arrangements.

divide and conquer

Before leaving this section, I should mention the Knife or Scissors tool usually found in the tool palette. This is provided so that you can cut up a recorded sequence into two or more parts. You may simply want to divide an eight-bar section into two four-bar sections so that you can copy or move the individual parts, but you can also use it, for example, to chop up an improvised solo into good bits and reject bits. The reject bits can be deleted, then you can arrange the remaining good sections in any order you like to form a new and technically perfect solo!

Though there is a lot of similarity between leading sequencer software packages, the tool palettes tend to differ slightly. Ensure that you know what all the tools are for and practise using them.

more on editing

At this stage in the proceedings, the idea is to gain familiarisation with the sequencer, not to record a hit single, so rather than trying to perfect that solo synth part, let's move on to explore some of the editing tricks that can be performed on the data you've just recorded.

Find the Transpose option and move the melody part up or down an octave and see how that sounds. Transpose is very handy if you want to create a part that's outside the range of your keyboard, but you might also find that the part you've recorded simply sounds better when played back an octave higher or lower. A useful trick is to copy the data from one track to an empty track set to a different MIDI channel, set it to a different sound, then raise it

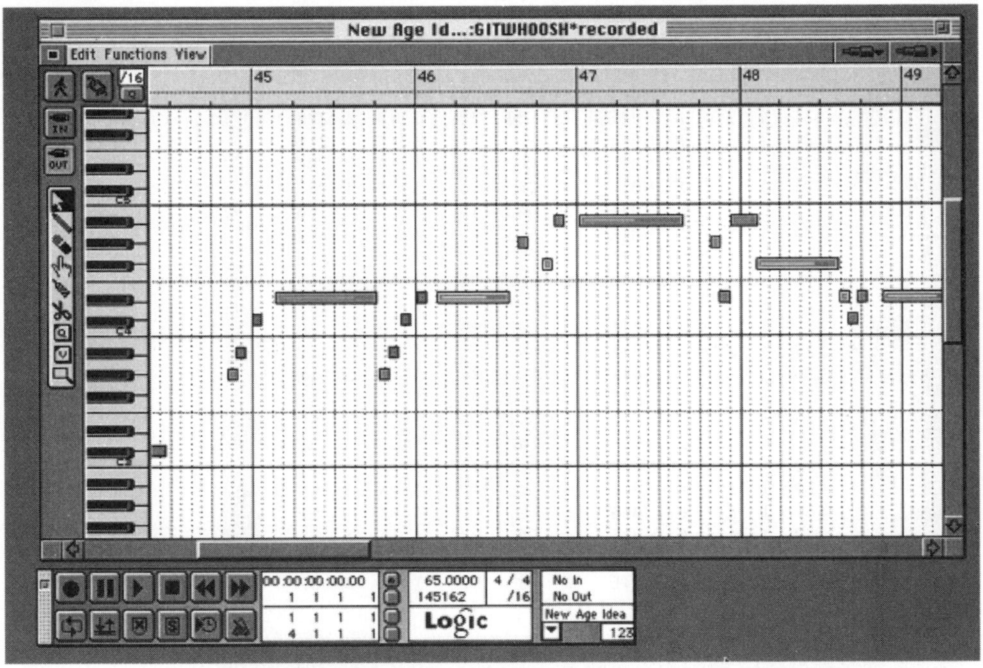

Figure 9.2: Grid edit page from a popular sequencing package

or drop it by an octave. Now you have two different instruments playing back the same part, but an octave apart.

grid edit

The other editing process with which you should familiarise yourself, is the fixing of wrong notes. Once again, most sequencer packages have a 'grid edit' window of some kind where the notes are represented as bars on a grid depicting time (in beats and bars), in one direction and pitch in semitones, in the other. This is sometimes called a piano roll editor where a piano keyboard graphic is used to depict the pitch axis of the grid. Figure 9.2 shows the grid edit page from a popular sequencing package. To correct wrong notes, it is necessary only to drag them using the mouse (click, hold and move the mouse), until they at the right pitch or the right timing position.

midi event list

If you're not comfortable with grid editing, you should also have a MIDI event list which represents your composition as a long list of MIDI events, each marked with its beat and bar location. Values in this list may be changed either by typing in new values or by using the mouse to scroll up and down

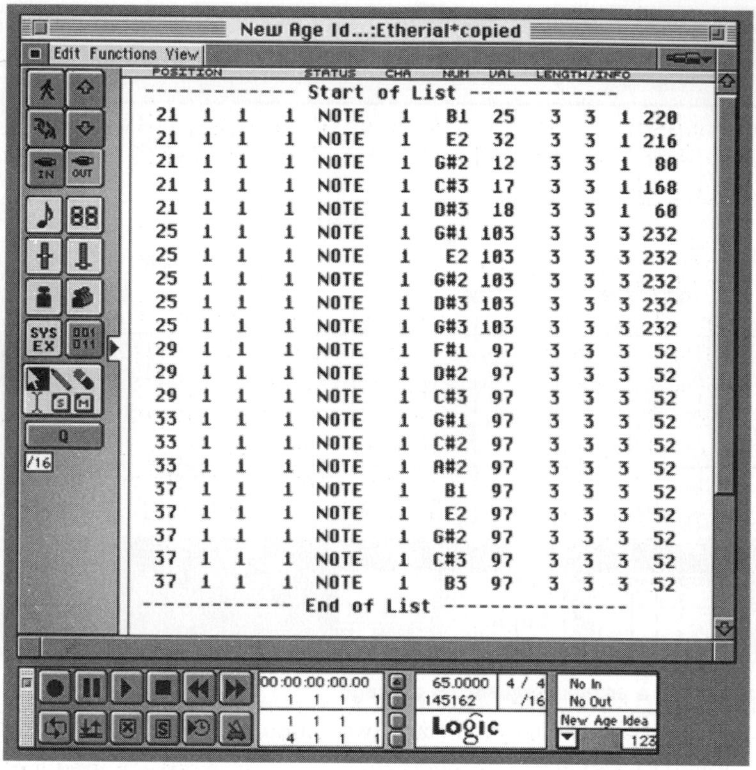

Figure 9.3: MIDI edit list

through the available values. As different packages adopt slightly different methods, it is important to refer to your manual when trying out any of the editing techniques discussed here. Figure 9.3 shows the edit list from a typical sequencing package.

score edit

Finally, the musically literate may prefer to edit notes on the stave, and the majority of serious sequencer software allows this. Notes may be physically dragged to new pitches, notes may be deleted or inserted, and the more advanced packages allow you to prepare a full multi-part score, ready for printing. Figure 9.4 shows the score edit window from a typical sequencing package.

Once you've finished your song and done any editing that needs to be done, don't forget to save your song before switching the computer off, otherwise all your work will be lost.

bad news and good news

The bad news is that what has been described so far represents only a small proportion of what a powerful sequencer package can do. The good news is that once you've mastered the basic recording and editing skills that have been discussed so far, you'll know enough to start making serious use of your sequencer. The majority of the time, you only need to use a fraction of your sequencer's features; you can explore the more sophisticated features as and when you feel you need them. However, you're bound to come up against the occasional difficulty, so I've listed some of the more common problems and their solutions.

troubleshooting

- Two or three modules can usually be daisy chained without any problem, but any more than three and you may suffer stuck or missed notes. If this happens, use a MIDI Thru box on the output of your sequencer and feed each module from a separate output on the Thru box.

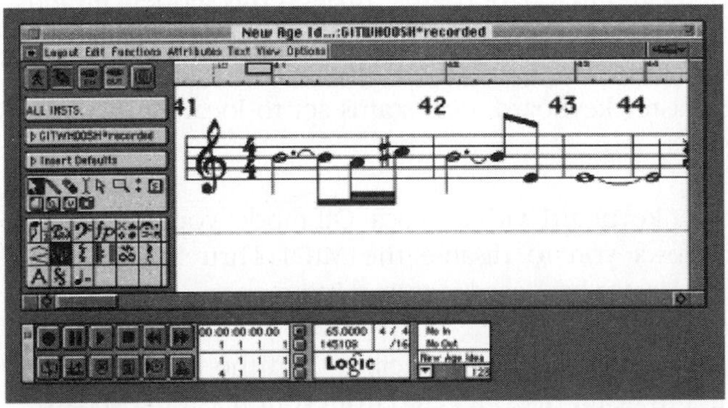

Figure 9.4: Score edit window

Let's assume you've wired your system up properly, but no sound comes out. Here are a few things to check – some obvious, some less so.

● Sounds obvious, but check everything is switched on. If you're using modules that have both multi and single modes, make sure multi is selected for multitimbral operation. Also, make sure the volume controls are turned up on your synths and on the amplification system you're using for listening.

● Double check your MIDI cable connections – you may have a faulty MIDI lead or you may be plugged into a MIDI Out when you meant to connect a MIDI In. Most sequencers have an on-screen indication that they're receiving MIDI data while many modules have a MIDI LED or other indicator that lets you know data is being received.

● If two or more instruments try to play the same part, the chances are you've either got more than one module set to the same MIDI channel or something's been left set to Omni.

● If your master keyboard plays its own sounds when you're trying to record using the sound of another module, make sure that Local Off is really set to Off. On some instruments, Local status defaults to Local On every time you switch the machine on.

● If playing a single note results in a burst of sound, rather like machine-gun fire, or if you get stuck notes or apparently limited polyphony, suspect a MIDI loop. In a MIDI loop, MIDI data passes through the sequencer and somehow gets back to the input of the master keyboard where it starts its round trip all over again, rather like acoustic feedback. Once again, the most common cause is the master keyboard local status set to local On when it should be Off.

Note: If you have an older keyboard with no Local Off mode, you'll probably find your sequencer allows you to disable the MIDI Thru function on whichever channel your master keyboard is transmitting on.

If you are unlucky enough to have neither facility, then the best bet is to record with the MIDI In physically disconnected from your master keyboard. In other words, you just use the sounds generated by your external modules. When you've finished recording, you can then reconnect the master keyboard's MIDI In and use it to play back one or more of the recorded parts. Fortunately, few people buying a new system will come across these limitations.

- The sequencer records okay, but the wrong sound plays back. This can happen when you forget to enter a MIDI Program Change number into your sequencer track.

saving your songs

If you're using a computer without a hard drive, you'll need to have a formatted floppy disk on hand to save your work, but on a machine with a hard drive, you can save your song file to that in exactly the same way as you save any other kind of file. It also makes sense to save every few minutes, just in case there's a crash, but if you regularly use a computer for other tasks, you won't need to be reminded of this. Each sequencer has its own file format, so you can't normally change song files from one sequencer platform to another. There are some exceptions however, where software manufacturers have built in the ability to import song files from other manufacturers.

standard midi file

However, most sequencers will allow you the option of saving your work in Standard MIDI file format, and these can be freely swapped between platforms. Commercially available song files are invariably in Standard MIDI file format, usually on PC format disks. Atari ST computers can read Standard MIDI files from PC disks, while Apple Macs need to have either System 7.5 running, or use a PC to Mac utility program such as AccessPC.

automating midi

This next section is just a little more advanced, so if you don't feel like trying it out yet, that's okay. However, it's easier to do than to read about, and I'm sure you'll find it opens up many interesting possibilities.

As you've learned already, MIDI Controllers can be used to adjust many different parameters relating to a musical instrument, the most useful in a mix situation being Main Volume (Controller 7) and Pan (Controller 10), but you aren't limited to automating volume and pan during a mix – you can, in theory, change any parameter of an instrument that is assignable to a MIDI Controller including portamento rate (Controller 5), Sustain pedal (Controller 64) and, where supported, things like filter frequency or resonance. These latter parameters aren't defined Controllers so it's up to individual manufacturers if and how these are implemented, so it's a case of looking in the back of the instrument manual to see exactly what you can access via MIDI; so it really is worth looking into those apparently tedious back pages once in a while.

automating patch changes

The other fundamental of MIDI mix automation is the Program Change command. If you have a limited number of MIDI instruments, it can be very useful to be able to change sounds mid song. Most sequencers will let you enter a new program change command directly from within the event list so that you can decide at exactly which bar and beat the change should take place. Sometimes you need to be careful where you put the command in order to get a graceful changeover of sounds, but the vast majority of synths help you out by retaining the old patch sound for any sustained notes – these don't change until they are released, even if newly played notes have switched to the sound of the new patch.

If you have a sequencer that doesn't let you enter program changes directly, and to be honest, I can't think of anything even semi-serious off hand that doesn't allow you do this one way or another, you can instead use the Program Select buttons on your master keyboard to send a patch change command at the appropriate time. The patch change will be recorded into your sequencer just like any other MIDI event, and if it isn't in quite the right place, you can always go into the edit list and move it.

Even if you don't intend to change patches during a song, you can still put Program Change commands at the start of each track, ideally during the count-in period, so that all your instruments are automatically set to the appropriate patches before playing commences. Some sequencers automatically set up the tracks to appropriate instruments, in which case you won't need to do this, but it's useful to be aware of the possibility.

It also pays to be aware that if you copy a track so that you can use it with a different MIDI instrument, any embedded patch change information will also be copied, so don't omit to update these Program Change numbers before continuing work, otherwise you might find totally inappropriate patches being called up. I've fallen for this one more times than I'd like to admit!

practical midi automation

When it comes to using Controller information to set up volume and pan effects, you first have to make sure that your instruments respond to these messages. This may sound obvious, but there are a few older instruments out there that are totally oblivious to master volume, Controller 7. The only way to fade one of these is to either pull down the fader by hand or doctor the MIDI note velocity data in your sequencer's MIDI event list so that the notes actually become quieter.

Thanks to modern sequencer design, there are now lots of ways to enter Controller information. In the early days, you had to add Controller numbers and values to the MIDI event list or record them in real time, but now there are often more intuitive graphic methods. If you have a keyboard with assignable data sliders or wheels, then you have an even more convenient way of sending Controller data in real time without having to edit it afterwards.

level tricks

Even if you don't need traditional fade-outs or fade-ins, Controller 7 is a useful way of tailing off a long sound that otherwise ends too abruptly – especially useful at the end of a song. You could achieve this by editing your synth patch, but the Controller 7 workaround is generally a lot easier and arguably more precise. Equally usefully, Controller 7 lets you vary levels during the course of a song, just as you would with an automated mixing console, and the easiest way to enter data in this case (if you don't have a hardware MIDI fader unit or a bank of assignable faders on your master keyboard), is to create an on-screen fader assigned to the appropriate Controller and MIDI channel (or use your keyboard's assignable faders if you have them).

Most of the current computer-based sequencers allow you to create faders which can be moved via the mouse, and if there are functions you want to use regularly, it's best to save these as part of your default song to save you having to re-invent the wheel every time you start to write a new tune.

When automating things like level and pan using controller data, you have to remember that if you fade out at the end of a song, the next time you run the song, those instruments will still remain turned down until new Controller information is sent. That being the case, don't just use Controller data to fade the last few seconds of your song but also put Controller data at the beginning during the count-in bar to set your starting levels. The same is true of pan: if everything goes out stage left, it will stay there until either the instrument is reset or new Controller information is registered. Putting Controller information at the start of a song is a good habit to get into, and once again, you can do this in your default song so you only have to do it once. You can always make any required changes once the song is loaded.

Pan effects can work very nicely when synced to the tempo of the song, and an easy way to do this is to create a short section of pan information and then either copy or loop it. You could save a few examples as part of your default song, then you can either use them or dump them when the song is loaded up.

Because it's so easy to automate instruments in a MIDI mix, you'll probably find that you're able to do things never before possible, and though you may go over the top at first, don't be reluctant to experiment – it's only because users have constantly pushed at the boundaries of MIDI's capabilities that we have such a powerful MIDI specification available to us today. What's more, all your automation data is saved with your song, so you can recreate the same mix exactly any time.

advanced uses of controller 7

Controller 7 acts exactly like a conventional volume control, enabling you to turn the level up or down during a single sustained note – something you can't do simply by changing the note's velocity data. In practice, this means that if you have the patience, you can actually create envelopes for sounds using Controller 7 data, and one neat trick is to emulate a keyed 'gating' effect by using Controller 7 values of 0 and 127 to create a full-on or full-off effect. In other words, you can use Controller 7 to switch your sound on and off rhythmically to create a contemporary 'chopped' effect. For example, if you take a four-beat bar where each beat is one eighth of a bar in duration, set Controller 7 to 127 at the start of each beat and to 0 at the end of each beat, your synth patch will pulse four to the bar. With a little imagination, you can design your Controller data to create interesting rhythmic effects, and you can, of course, use intermediate Controller values if you want the level to pulse rather than switch hard on and off.

transferring sequencer files

Standard MIDI song files have already been introduced as a means of transferring data from one sequencer to another, and within their limitations, they can work extremely well. In fact there are three different types of MIDI file: Format 0, where the entire song is saved as a single sequencer track, Format 1, where the sequencer tracks are kept separate, and Format 2, which saves the song as a series of patterns. Format 1 is probably the most useful, and is the most commonly encountered. However, when you load up a Format 1 MIDI file, you may find the tracks don't come up with their original MIDI channel numbers, and sometimes they lose their names too. This all depends on how the sequencer on which the sequencer that created the data stores its information, and restoring order is usually fairly straightforward. It must be noted however that standard MIDI files don't convey MIDI port information – they can only be used to store a maximum of 16 different MIDI channels.

If you need to transfer a file to or from a hardware sequencer of from a non-standard computer platform, you may find the disk formats completely incompatible, in which case it may be possible to transfer files by playing them out of one sequencer and recording them into another. However, there is slightly more to this than meets the eye, and to get it to work properly, you should proceed as follows.

- Connect the two sequencers together with MIDI leads such that the MIDI Out of each machine feeds the MIDI In of the other. This two-way connection is necessary to ensure accurate timing of the transferred information.

- Set the sequencer containing the song you want to copy to external sync mode. It must be clocked by the receiving device to ensure optimum timing accuracy. The receiving sequencer is left in internal sync mode. If the receiving device has a so-called soft MIDI Thru function, switch this off to minimise the amount of data sharing the MIDI Out with the timing clock.

- Set the receiving sequencer to record MIDI data, but choose a slow temp, again to maintain optimum timing accuracy. The reason we're so concerned with timing accuracy is that all the data for all the tracks is being recorded at once, and sequencers are better at outputting lots of tracks than they are at receiving them. A tempo of around 50bpm should be okay. You can set this to the correct value once you've captured the data.

- Start the receiving sequencer recording and the transmitting sequencer will automatically start and run in sync with it.

- If you still find that the timing is insufficiently accurate, repeat the procedure with all the source sequencer tracks muted except for one. This way you can send one track at a time. When the recording is complete, select a new source track, a new destination track, and repeat the procedure until all the tracks have been recorded. This is a trifle slow and tedious, but if it's an important song, the effort may be worth it.

tidying up

Finally, if you did manage to transfer all the data in one go, you'll find your whole song occupies a single track in the destination sequencer. Most modern sequencers have a 'demerge by MIDI channel' function, and this will automatically sort the data out into separate tracks based on MIDI channel number. You will probably still need to identify what instrument is supposed to be playing each part, but if the original file contained program information, this should have come over too. If you don't have a 'demerge by MIDI channel' function, you can look forward to picking through the data manually, which is time consuming. One way to do this would be to copy the

Figure 9.5: Sequencer to Sequencer transfer

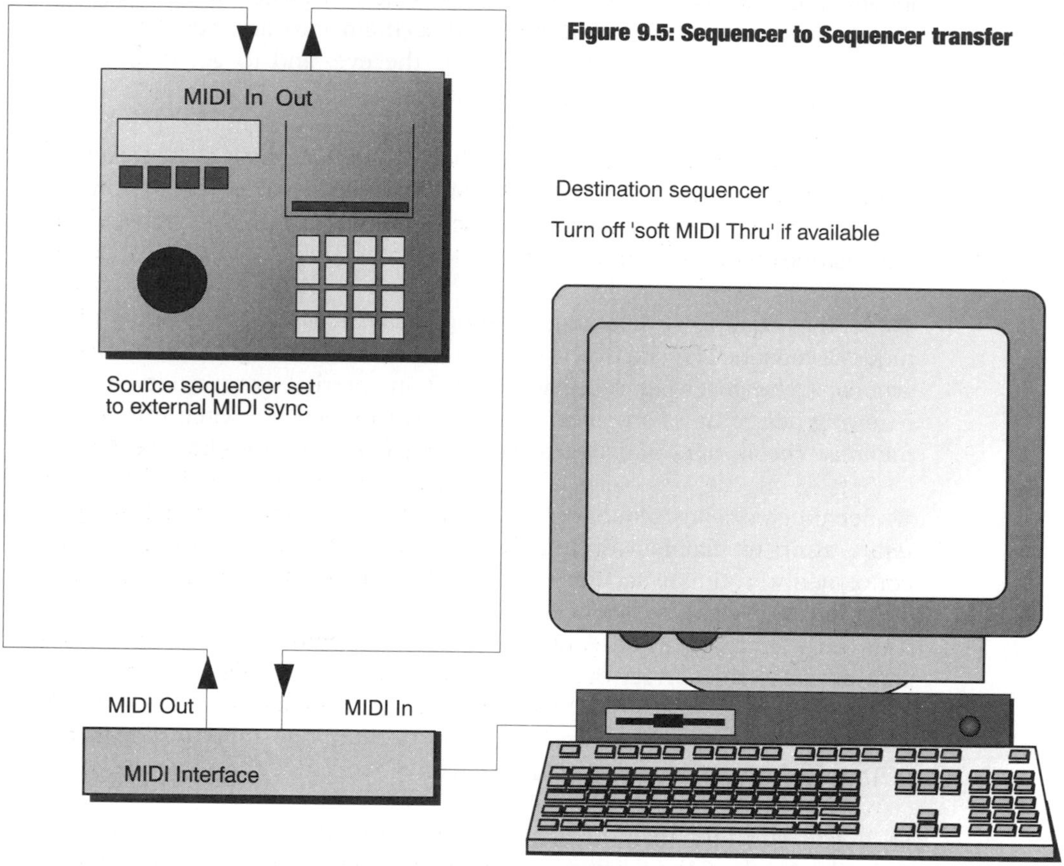

song track to all 16 tracks, then edit one track at a time so as to discard any data not on the MIDI channel appropriate to that track. This way, you'll end up with all MIDI channel 1 data on track 1, channel 2 data on track 2 and so on. Figure 9.5 shows how two sequencers are connected for data transfer as described here.

more user tips

● Create a default song, an 'empty' song file that has your instruments already set up and ready to go. Store a copy on a locked floppy or as a locked file on your hard drive so that it can't be overwritten by accident. A typical default song contains the MIDI channel and track assignment for your different instruments, suitable 'vanilla' starting patches, any user options the software might provide and various MIDI status functions such as MIDI

Thru, MIDI click and so on. To set this manually every time you start a new song is obviously a chore you can do without.

● Create your own metronome: rather than use the default metronome when recording, program a simple drum part to work to. As well as providing you with a better feel, you'll also find it easier to keep time to. Most modern rhythms are based on four beats to the bar so if you're using a conventional metronome, you're playing directly over the top of it which, in turn, makes it difficult to hear. By adding a suitable hi-hat pattern, you're much more likely to stay in time. Rather than re-invent the wheel every time you start work, it pays to save your guide percussion parts, either in a separate song or as a part of your default. That way, they'll always be available whenever you start a new song.

● Use your computer keyboard: just because most jobs can be tackled using the mouse, some things are faster and easier from the keyboard – if you can remember the commands. A useful trick is to print out all the main keyboard commands and put the printout under a transparent-topped mouse mat. Failing that, take the low-tech approach and pin it to the wall.

● Copy important documentation: the trouble with most MIDI systems is that you end up with a stack of manuals a foot thick. It helps enormously to photocopy the preset patch lists for all your instruments and also to type out the names and descriptions of your user patches and memory card contents. These sheets may then be put into plastic sleeves and clipped into a single 'Voices' binder or pinned to the wall.

● Use Custom Screens: some programs, such as Notator Logic, have a built-in system for saving and accessing various screen layouts. In a program where several windows might need to be open at once, this can be a real time saver because a single key can bring up a screen layout you have previously specified with all the windows properly sized and exactly in the right place. The smaller your monitor, the more you'll appreciate this function; without it, you spend most of your time opening and closing windows, dragging them about the screen and resizing them so you can see everything you need to.

● Don't over-quantise: those who criticise electronic music for its robotic feel have probably heard the result of too much quantisation. It's true that some forms of music demand a rigid, robotic approach to timing, but if you want to keep the feel of the original performance, it may be better not to quantise at all – just use the sequencer as you would a tape recorder. If you feel your playing needs tightening up, but you don't want it to sound lifeless, try the percentage quantise function if your sequencer has one. This will bring your playing closer to the nearest tick but will still leave some of the original feel intact. On a more practical point, it also helps if you don't rigidly quantise everything because doing so makes the sequencer attempt to play lots of notes at the same time. This creates a MIDI bottleneck and may lead to MIDI timing errors in a busy mix.

● Playing 'free': if you have a part that needs to be played 'free' (without any specific tempo reference), simply turn down the click track, turn off all quantisation and record the part just as if you were using a tape recorder. If you have to make this part match up to a more rigidly quantised section that follows, you can either move the whole free section backwards or forwards in time until it matches the start of the first bar of the next section, or you could insert a couple of radical tempo changes between the point where the first section ends and the next section starts. Putting in a fraction of a bar of very low tempo will create a longer gap while speeding up the tempo for a while will reduce the amount of time between the two sections.

● Back up your work: be paranoid about backing up – computers have a habit of crashing or locking up when you least expect it so save every few minutes. If you're using an Apple Mac, you'll probably develop a nervous twitch which makes your left hand press 'Command S' automatically. When working with a hard drive, back up important work to floppies at the end of each session. Modern drives are reliable, but they're not infallible, and besides, computers occasionally get stolen!

● Keep a notebook: paper may be low tech, but when you come across a six month old disk filled with MIDI files named something like Ideas 1-99, a few notes are worth their weight in gold.

● Don't re-invent the wheel: if you create your own MIDI control data for cyclic panning, or if you have an assortment of killer drum fills, hoard it. You can create your own MIDI equivalent of clip art, so that instead of always working from scratch, you can copy and paste various useful odds and ends from a library song. Other things worth keeping are MIDI messages used to reset bender range after patch changes (Roland's CM32P, for example, always defaults to 12 semitones after a patch change), or major and minor chord arpeggios which can be transposed and copied. The list is endless – the only rule is not to waste time repeating the same action.

chapter 10

sequencing with audio

For several years MIDI sequencing and hard disk recording existed side by side as two quite separate disciplines. However, both use computers and hard disk drives, and it became evident from quite early on that the way forward for the desktop music studio would involve the integration of MIDI sequencing and digital direct-to-disk audio within a single operating environment. With the introduction of cheap audio soundcards (or in some cases, external audio hardware), low cost, high capacity hard disk drives and integrated 'MIDI plus audio' sequencing software, it's now possible to store sound digitally and manipulate it from within the sequencer program. Instead of having all MIDI tracks, the sequencer program now provides both MIDI tracks and audio tracks, each of which can be chopped up, moved and copied in similar ways. Not all MIDI sequencers can run with audio, but an increasing number now include some basic provision for audio recording and playback as standard, with more sophisticated options available at an additional cost.

The majority of serious MIDI plus audio software is designed to run on either the Apple Macintosh computer or the Pentium/MMX PC. At the time of writing, the Apple Mac platform is the choice of most professionals and seems least problematic, though the relatively low cost and widespread ownership of PCs has prompted software designers to work very hard to bring their PC programs up to the same level of sophistication as their Mac versions.

audio capabilities

A Pentium PC fitted with a basic consumer soundcard will typically allow the recording of up to two tracks of audio at a time and the simultaneous playback of up to eight tracks. More sophisticated hardware may provide considerably more tracks. Budget soundcards mix all the audio tracks to a single stereo output, but a number of affordable cards with multiple outputs are also available for those who demand the ability to mix the audio sounds externally. The majority of general purpose consumer soundcards are designed primarily for the

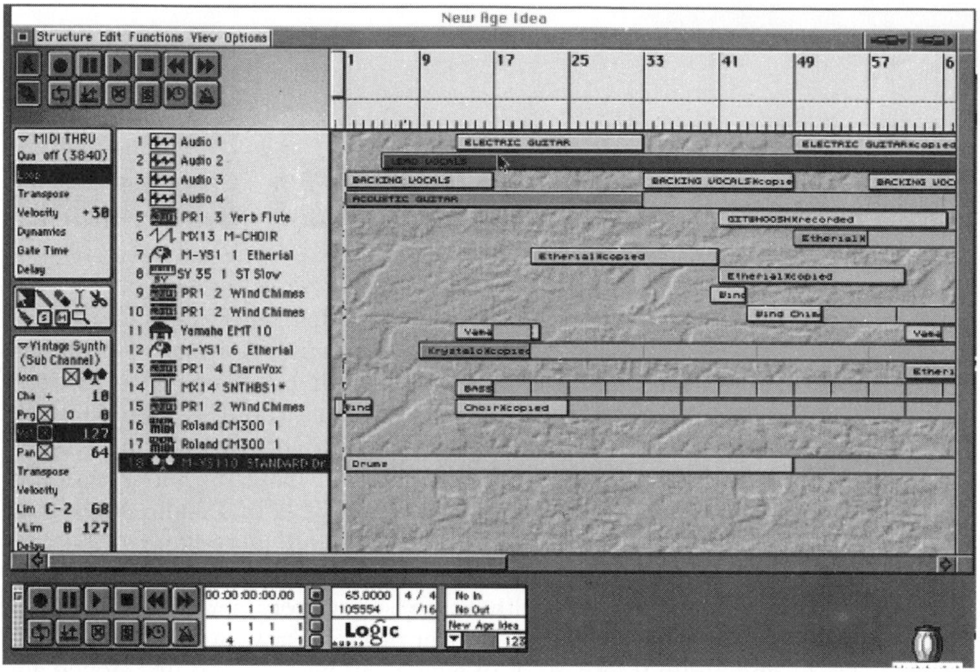

Figure 10.1 shows the arrange window of a typical audio plus MIDI sequencer

computer games and multimedia market, but most include an on-board MIDI sequencer, stereo audio in and out, and a MIDI interface.

Once you've recorded your audio tracks, which are stored on hard disk the same as any other computer data, they can be moved, copied and pasted in much the same way as MIDI tracks, though there are obviously some things you can do to MIDI data which are either immensely difficult or impossible to do to audio. For example you can't just click a button and directly transpose your audio or quantise it as you can with MIDI notes – both these processes are trivial in the MIDI domain, but involve complicated signal processing in order to achieve the same effect with audio signals. Even so, many of these seemingly impossible tasks can be done (to some extent), using the better packages, though side effects of over ambitious processing are often audible. For example, audio can be pitch shifted or changed in length, and even quantised to a degree, providing the degree of change is modest. As a rule, small pitch shifts or time stretches can be handled quite adequately, but larger ones show up side effects caused by the processing. Figure 10.1 shows the arrange window of a typical audio plus MIDI sequencer where the audio and MIDI tracks can be clearly seen.

magic of dsp

Because of the increasing power of computers, and the digital signal processors (or DSPs), used on the more advanced soundcards (and external audio hardware systems), it is possible to use software to emulate functions that traditionally required recording studio hardware. For example, an audio sequencing package may not only allow you to control the level and pan positions of the various tracks as they are mixed internally, it may also provide equalisation (studio type tone controls), effects such as reverb and delay, dynamics processing such as gates and compressors, and spatial enhancement techniques to make the mix appear to move outside the confines of the loudspeakers. Many of these functions can be handled using just the processing power of the computer itself, though professional systems tend to involve multiple powerful internal cards carrying the DSP chips, plus external hardware containing the digital to analogue and analogue to digital converters. Though such systems tend to be very expensive compared to consumer soundcard-based systems, they have the power to run a great many mixing, processing and effect functions at the same time.

Because computers get more powerful with every generation, and because of the commercial pressures of the games and multimedia markets, it is envisaged that relatively inexpensive systems using only the computer's own processing power will soon rival the performance of current high-end hardware assisted systems. It is also becoming more common to see audio with MIDI packages that can also integrate with on-screen video. These more advanced areas are outside of the brief of this book, but it may be of interest to you to know that such things exist.

benefits of integration

Being able to record and manipulate audio alongside MIDI is very powerful, because you can use techniques like copying the best vocal chorus to every chorus position in the song, or you can apply a little pitch shifting to a flat note to bring it back into pitch. You can also import sound samples in .WAV or AIFF audio file format from the numerous CD-ROMs available, giving you access to drum rhythms, voices and instrumental phrases that can be worked into your own compositions. Virtually all modern dance and techno music is composed in this way, but the process is just as applicable to conventional pop music, TV commercials, New Age music and so on.

Another significant benefit is, as well as saving on the cost of buying a multitrack tape recorder, using a sequencer with integrated audio avoids the need to provide a means of synchronisation between the tape machine and the sequencer.

Multitrack audio recording requires approximately 5Mbytes of disk space per track for every minute recorded – assuming you're recording 16-bit audio at a 44.1kHz sampling rate – the professional audio standard format. If you're not familiar with these terms, suffice it to say that this is the audio format used to record CDs, and should be used whenever you want to produce a recording that is equal to or better than what you might expect when recording to a conventional tape recorder. For multitrack work, a fast AV (Audio Visual) drive is a good idea, otherwise there may be problems such as glitching or tracks refusing to play.

Accepting that you need 5Mbytes of disk space for every minute of every track you record, using audio within a MIDI sequence may take up less space than you imagine, simply because data is only recorded where it is needed. For example, if you have a pause in the vocals for the guitar solo, you don't need to record the pause, whereas with tape recording, tape is always used whether anything is recorded on it or not. In addition, because you can use the same data more than once, you might find that a single 30 second audio file containing the backing vocals for a chorus is all you need to provide backing vocals for a whole five minute song. Similarly, if the guitar solo is only one minute long, then you only use one minute of disk space. If much of your musical backing is provided by conventional MIDI instruments, you might find that the audio parts of your song only add up to three or four track-minutes in total, which means you may end up using only 15 or 20Mbytes of disk space. Given the low cost of 1, 2 or even 4Gbyte hard drives (a Gbyte is 1,000Mbytes), this is quite acceptable.

the soundcard

To get audio into and out of your computer, you need either a soundcard equipped with A to D and D to A converters, or external hardware that does the same job. These essential bits of hardware digitise the sound from your microphone or instrument when you record, and when you play back, they convert the digital data back into an audio signal that can be played through your hi-fi, desktop multimedia speakers or mixing console.

Budget soundcards tend to have relatively poor audio quality, but providing the signal path is 16-bit, the quality should still be adequate for writing demos or composing. For more serious work, either more sophisticated soundcards or external hardware is recommended, and if there is a need to mix the audio tracks externally, hardware with multiple outputs is required.

choosing a soundcard

When choosing a soundcard to work with your MIDI/Audio sequencer, it is advisable to check with the software distributor's product specialist to see which cards work okay and which have known compatibility problems. PCs in particular throw up more than their fair share of compatibility problems, and though Microsoft's 'plug and play' has made things easier, it isn't a complete solution. You also need to be sure the audio side of the card supports full duplex operation – in practical terms, this means that you can listen to previously recorded material at the same time as recording a new part. If the hardware doesn't support full duplex operation, you won't be able to listen to your existing audio recordings at the same time as recording new parts, though for some applications, it may be enough to hear the MIDI tracks while recording.

The majority of affordable soundcards will support up to eight tracks of audio, where you can record up to two tracks at a time, but the system performance also depends on the type and speed of computer you're using. If you choose the PC platform, then a Pentium or MMX machine should be considered the minimum requirement for audio work, and you should buy the fastest model you can afford. Also check with the software and soundcard suppliers that they are compatible with each other and with your make and model of computer. Because PCs are built by so many different companies, and because not all use the same ICs on the main circuit board, you can end up in a situation where certain combinations of hardware and software either run incorrectly, or fail to run at all. A little good advice at this stage can save a lot of expensive disappointment later on, and there is much to be said for buying the computer, hardware and software from a single supplier, ready configured. This may cost slightly more, but at least you have some comeback if things don't work properly. If you buy all the parts from different suppliers, then find the system doesn't work, you may find it difficult or impossible to get anyone to agree to take responsibility, and you may not be able to get your money back either!

Realistically, a Pentium 90 with 16Mbytes of RAM, a large hard drive and Win95 should be considered the minimum configuration for any serious work, and if you're not confident about installing hardware in your PC, it's well worth spending a little money to get it done for you. However, don't expect to be able to use a computer-based MIDI plus audio system without learning something about computers. In an ideal world, a system such as this would be just a tool to do a job, but you'll soon discover that learning to operate and maintain the tool is quite an involved business.

Soundcards vary enormously in the sound quality of which they are capable. The audio path should ideally be 16-bit, 44.1kHz (usually switchable to 48kHz as well), and the signal-to-noise ratio should be 90dB or better. This is a measure of how much background hiss the system produces – the higher the ratio, the less the hiss. The synthesizer sections that are available on most general purpose soundcards can also differ wildly. The amount of wavetable ROM can give you some idea of the sound quality of the synthesizer (4Mbytes is a minimum for high quality sounds), but the only way to judge the artistic quality of the sounds is to listen to them. For this reason, arranging a demo before you buy is very important.

the growing system

As pointed out earlier, a typical budget soundcard will mix its on-board MIDI synth sounds with any recorded audio and pipe them through a single stereo output, and for composing or making basic demos, this is fine. However, if you get more serious about recording, you may end up with two or more soundcards in your computer and possibly an external MIDI synth module or two as well. When you get to this stage, you really need a mixer. In any event, using an external mixer will allow you to produce better audio quality recordings, and will provide you with a greater degree of control over individual sounds, or groups of sounds.

Sometimes you can avoid having to use an external mixer in a multiple soundcard system by feeding the audio out of the first soundcard through the second card and so on. However, in my experience, the audio quality usually suffers noticeably, and you have little control over the individual sounds. If you're on a tight budget, by all means record this way, because when you do eventually add a mixer, you'll be able to go back and remix your songs to a higher standard. See the next chapter for more detail on soundcards.

the separate mixer

By using a small mixer, you gain separate control over the level, tone and pan position of each input to the mixer, and you should also notice a significant improvement in sound quality with more clarity and less hiss. You still won't have independent control over sounds that come out of the same soundcard output jack (other than any software control that may be provided), but you will be able to balance the outputs of the different soundcards and external MIDI modules relative to each other. It's unlikely that you'll want every MIDI instrument you own playing all possible parts all the time, so by distributing parts between your cards and modules in a logical way, you can divide your sounds into manageable groups. For example, you might want to get all your string sounds from the same card or synth so that when you're mixing, you can can control the level of the whole string section from a single fader. Similarly, you may use one of your soundcards purely for audio with a separate module providing MIDI drum and bass sounds. With just a little thought, you can gain a surprising amount of control over your work, and if your budget will stretch to it, you might even want to buy a separate effects unit so you can add more professional sounding reverb, echo and suchlike to your mixes.

Another benefit of a separate mixer is that you can plug in a good quality microphone and use the mixer to convert the mic signal to line level before you feed it into your soundcard. Most budget soundcards have atrocious mic inputs, so by using a mixer, you can get professional quality sound into your computer. Figure 10.2 shows a simple MIDI/audio studio linked to a small mixer.

audio drives

Recording and playing back multiple tracks of audio to or from a hard drive makes the drive work very hard, so it helps enormously if you can use a completely separate drive for audio. AV drives are recommended for multitrack work, because unlike regular hard drives, AV drives are designed to produce an uninterrupted flow of data. A regular drive may occasionally pause for an instant to recalibrate itself, and this can lead to breaks or glitches in the sound being recorded or played back.

Another reason for having a separate drive is that audio files need to, where possible, be contiguous. If they are broken into fragments, the drive has to spend time looking for the various bits, and again, this can cause glitching. The more you save and delete files on disk, the more fragmented the available free space becomes, so new files may be recorded in shorter segments to fit the available spaces. To get around this, you should run a defragmentation program before any serious recording session. Such programs move the files around, joins up

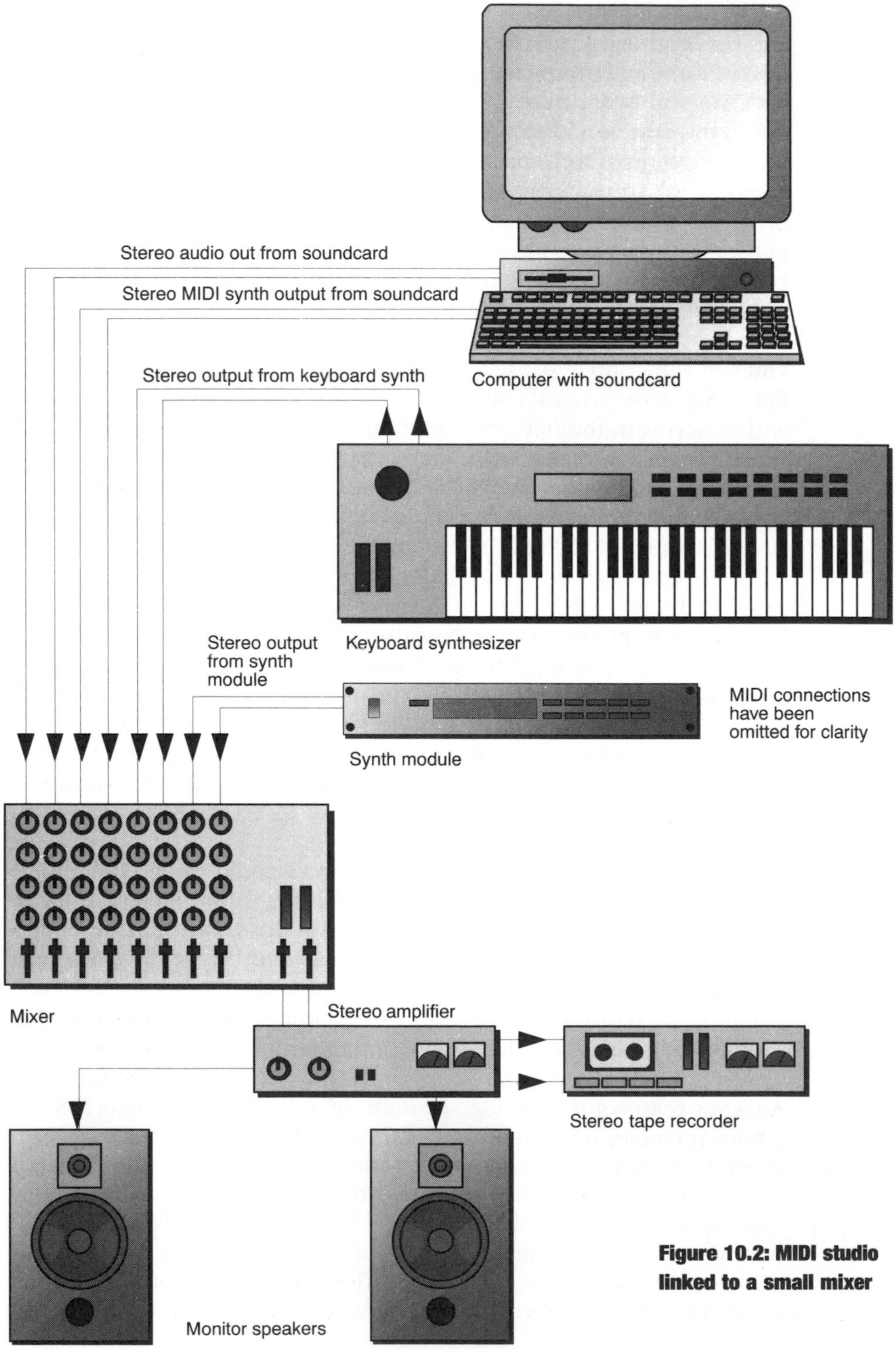

Figure 10.2: MIDI studio linked to a small mixer

unconnected file segments, and ensure that all the free space on the disk is in one continuous chunk.

backup

What do you do with your data once the hard disk is full? A MIDI file takes up only a few tens of kilobytes, but a CD quality audio track takes up around 5Mbytes of disk space for each minute you want to record. Obviously you don't want to leave your hard drive full of audio data, but at the same time, you probably don't want to wipe the data either – what if a record company hears your demo and wants you to do a remix?

One answer is to use a removable drive, but some are too slow to work with real-time audio, and if this is the case, you'll have to work on your fixed hard drive, then transfer your backup files to the removable drive for archiving. However, there's a growing number of high capacity, removable drives that are fast enough to replay a minimum of eight tracks simultaneously.

Data DAT systems are also available for backing up data, and they have the overriding advantage of cheap media, but the save and load times are very long. Most systems will save stereo data in real time, four-track data in double real time and eight-track data in four times real time. In practice, this means that a half hour, eight-track recording on your fixed drive will take around two hours to back up, and a further two hours to reload when you next want to work on it.

An option that is becoming increasingly less costly is to store data on a recordable CD using a CD-R drive. CD-R disks can only be recorded once, but they hold over 600Mbytes of data and cost about the same as a couple of videotapes.

At the time of writing, fast removable drives are the obvious way forward – the price is falling to meet that of professional multitrack recording tape, and you don't have to keep transferring the data from one place to another whenever you want to change projects. So far, HDVD (High Density Video Disk) appears to be the great low cost, high capacity hope of the future.

mastering

One point I haven't touched on yet is how do you record the end result of your labours? The cheap and cheerful way is to use a cassette deck, and providing the deck is cleaned fairly regularly, and used with good quality cassettes, the results can be surprisingly good. However, if you want to release your own cassette or CD album of your work, you'll need to mix onto something capable of rather better sound quality. The professional standard is DAT – Digital Audio Tape – but DAT machines are quite expensive. A cheaper option is to buy a Sony MiniDisc, or even use your hi-fi video recorder. High Density Video Disk (HDVD) is also likely to provide an affordable and reliable mastering option in the near future.

chapter 11

soundcards

In the previous chapter, both audio and MIDI soundcards were mentioned. As it becomes possible to put more sophisticated synthesizers, and even samplers onto computer cards, the cost of setting up a serious MIDI desktop studio will fall even further, and less space will be needed for conventional hardware.

Until very recently, soundcards had a reputation for producing second class sound quality, but the chip that turns up in this year's premium priced keyboard synth is quite likely to reappear fitted to a low cost soundcard within a year or so. The basic SoundBlaster compatible PC card offers a lot of possibilities, considering its very low price, but if you're prepared to spend a little more on a better wavetable-based synth card, you can expect quality that rivals that of a stand-alone synth. What's more, because PC cards are purely software driven, you often find a surprising amount of useful support software bundled with the card, including sequencers, editor librarians, MIDI song files, mixer maps for the most commonly used sequencers, and even sampling.

what is a soundcard?

A typical multimedia soundcard will have one stereo audio input and one stereo audio output, allowing analogue audio to be recorded and played back. These inputs and outputs interface with analogue to digital and digital to analogue converters so that recordings can be made in a digital format. A dedicated synth only card will normally just have an output, usually stereo, though some models have inputs to allow external sounds to make use of their on-board effects. Also on the card may be a wavetable (sample and synthesis) synthesizer chip providing GM sounds with effects, a joystick port that can double as MIDI In and Out ports, and possibly a sample player that can play .WAV sounds (the standard PC format for sound files). Both the sounds and effects can normally be edited via software. All cards should come with a software driver, a small program which enables other programs, such as sequencers, to communicate with them.

Many soundcards have RAM sockets on the board so that the sample RAM can be increased if desired. This simply enables longer samples (or more samples at once) to be used. There will most likely be audio input connections for a CD-ROM drive, on-board amplifiers for driving headphones or small desktop speakers, and a bundle of support software to make use of the various facilities offered by the card. This bundle will also include software drivers where appropriate. Other facilities that may be found on more upmarket cards include digital input and output connectors (for interfacing with DAT machine or a suitable CD player), and multiple audio inputs and/or outputs.

Future cards are likely to provide improved audio performance as well as greater synthesis power, and we're already seeing low cost audio-only cards with eight or more physical output connectors. Expect to see far more professional synth cards using techniques such as physical modelling, wavetable synthesis, conventional sampling and even analogue synthesizer emulation.

daughterboards

Many budget soundcards have connectors for a so-called daughterboard, a piggy back circuit board that provides enhanced functionality. For example, there are several high quality synthesizer daughterboards that can be used to upgrade the instrument sounds a budget card can provide. Usually, the output from the daughterboard is mixed with the stereo output of the host soundcard, but it's sometimes possible to have daughterboards modified to provide a separate stereo output. If this can be done, it usually results in increased audio quality, and more flexibility when it comes to mixing.

installing cards

Because PCs have a number of expansion slots, it's sometimes possible to use two or more soundcards in the same machine, though installing hardware isn't always the painless procedure it ought to be. If you're using Windows 95 or later, then choosing a 'plug and play' compatible card should help simplify things, even though plug and play isn't entirely foolproof. However, unlike typical all-in-one 'audio plus MIDI' multimedia cards, some dedicated synth cards install without taking up any of your valuable IRQs (Interrupt Requests) or DMAs (Direct Memory Access) (see glossary). If you're non-technical, these numbers, in effect, relate to 'virtual' connections which must match up between the cards and the computer in order for the card to work with the computer. Earlier non-plug and play compatible hardware did this by means of little jumper switches on the circuit board, but modern p&p compatible cards handle everything in software. The 'plug and play' part of Windows 95 and later is designed to look after hardware installation for you so that you don't need to get too involved in such matters, but what you should know is that the number of available IRQs and DMAs is limited, and once they're all taken, you can't add any more cards without first taking out one of your existing cards. Again, the in depth workings of specific computers is not within the remit of this book, but it does serve to warn that you need to discuss your needs with a technically competent supplier before parting with any money.

There are also two main types of card slot in modern PC machines – ISA and PCI. Before buying a card, you need to confirm that your machine has at least one of the necessary slot types free. New Macintosh computers currently use exclusively PCI slots, though who knows what changes the future might bring?

audio connections

While a cheap soundcard plugged into a pair of nasty little powered AV monitors isn't going to threaten the conventional studio, for very little additional expense it's possible to build a desktop studio system capable of professional results. What's more, it's often possible to mix and process the sounds in a far more comprehensive way than you might imagine, as hinted at in the last chapter. For example, there may be several separate stereo outputs coming from different soundcards and daughterboards that can be conventionally mixed. While there's often an option to daisy chain the audio ins and outs of various soundcards to enable you to mix everything to stereo before it leaves the computer, the quality penalty is significant. By keeping your outputs as separate as possible, you can connect each one to a different channel of an external mixer, which is quite obviously far more flexible.

pan and separate

Even if you only have two sets of stereo outputs to play with, a separate mixer will allow you to create up to four separate groups of sounds (by using MIDI panning to move sounds hard left or right within each stereo output). This will leave you with, in effect, four mono groups of sounds, though any effects that were applied will still be present on both the left and right channels. If you want to add external effects, turn the effect levels on your soundcard synths right down using the appropriate controller information or the included software.

Once the sounds are separated into groups, you can independently EQ and effect each group as required using your mixer and an outboard effect processor. Furthermore, you can monitor your work via a good hi-fi system

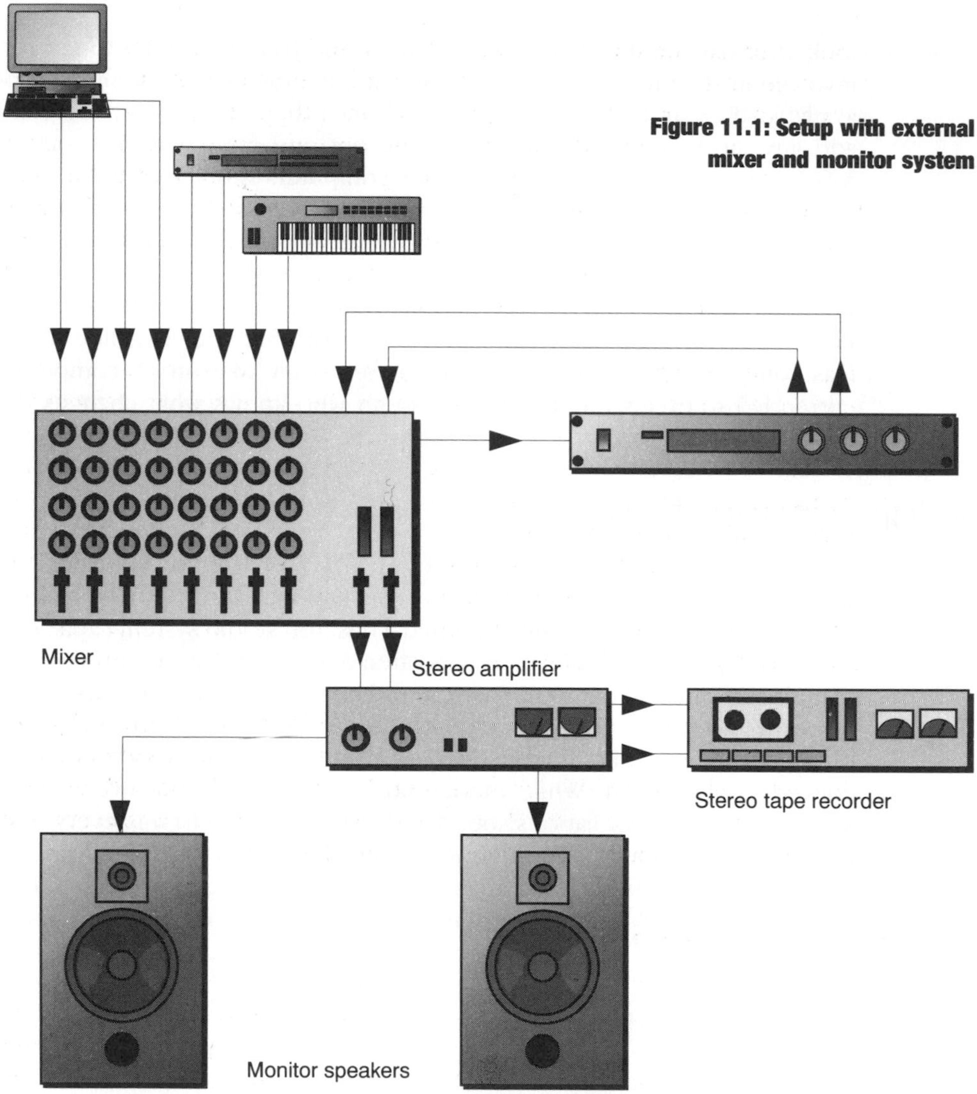

Figure 11.1: Setup with external mixer and monitor system

or via a pair of small studio monitor speakers and an amplifier, which will give you a far better idea of what your work really sounds like than the powered AV monitors that come bundled with most computer system. Figure 11.1 shows a small mixer and monitor system.

recording via a mixer

While budget soundcards often come with mic or line inputs that allow you to record your own .WAV audio files, the signal path through these is usually pretty poor (as are the mics that interface with them). What's more, as well as being built to a price, budget soundcards have to work inside the PC where there's potential for high gain mic inputs to pick up lots of interference from the various data busses inside the computer. A far better option is to use an external mixer to bring the output from a decent mic up to line level, then feed this into the soundcard's line level input. Not only does this give you a chance to use a studio quality mic, it will also improve the signal-to-noise ratio of the recording by amplifying the signal within the mixer rather than within the soundcard.

Even using a budget general purpose mixer, you can use one channel as an independent mic preamp simply by turning the channel fader right down and using the channel insert send or pre-fade foldback send to feed your soundcard. The mic gain is set using the mixer's channel gain trim. See the manual that comes with your mixer for the types of connectors needed to interface with the channel insert send or pre-fade aux send connectors. Working this way means that you can both record and mix at the same time using an external mixer. Why would you want to record and mix at the same time? The main reason is so that you can hear a mix of what you've already done while you're recording a new part.

To use the pre-fade aux send output, you could feed your mic into channel 1, then route this to the aux 1 output by turning up the aux 1 send knob on channel 1 only. The level fader on channel 1 would be fully off and the level sent to the soundcard controlled by both the mic input gain trim and the aux 1 master output level knob as shown in Figure 11.2.

outboard effects

Outboard effects may be connected to your external mixer via the mixer's post-fade aux sends and effects return channels – more of that in the next chapter. The input to the effects unit is connected to the post-fade aux send output on the mixer, and the outputs of the effects unit (they are invariably stereo), are connected back to a stereo effect input on the mixer. The post-fade aux send knob on each channel then varies how much of that channel's signal is sent to the effects unit, and hence how much effect is applied to the signal being fed through that channel. Any mixer handbook will provide full details of how to do this.

and there's midi

A basic PC MIDI music system will generally make use of the MIDI interface provided by the soundcard, and a common way of working is to use a MIDI adaptor cable that plugs into the card's joystick port. Alternatively, you can

Figure 11.2: Recording via a mixer

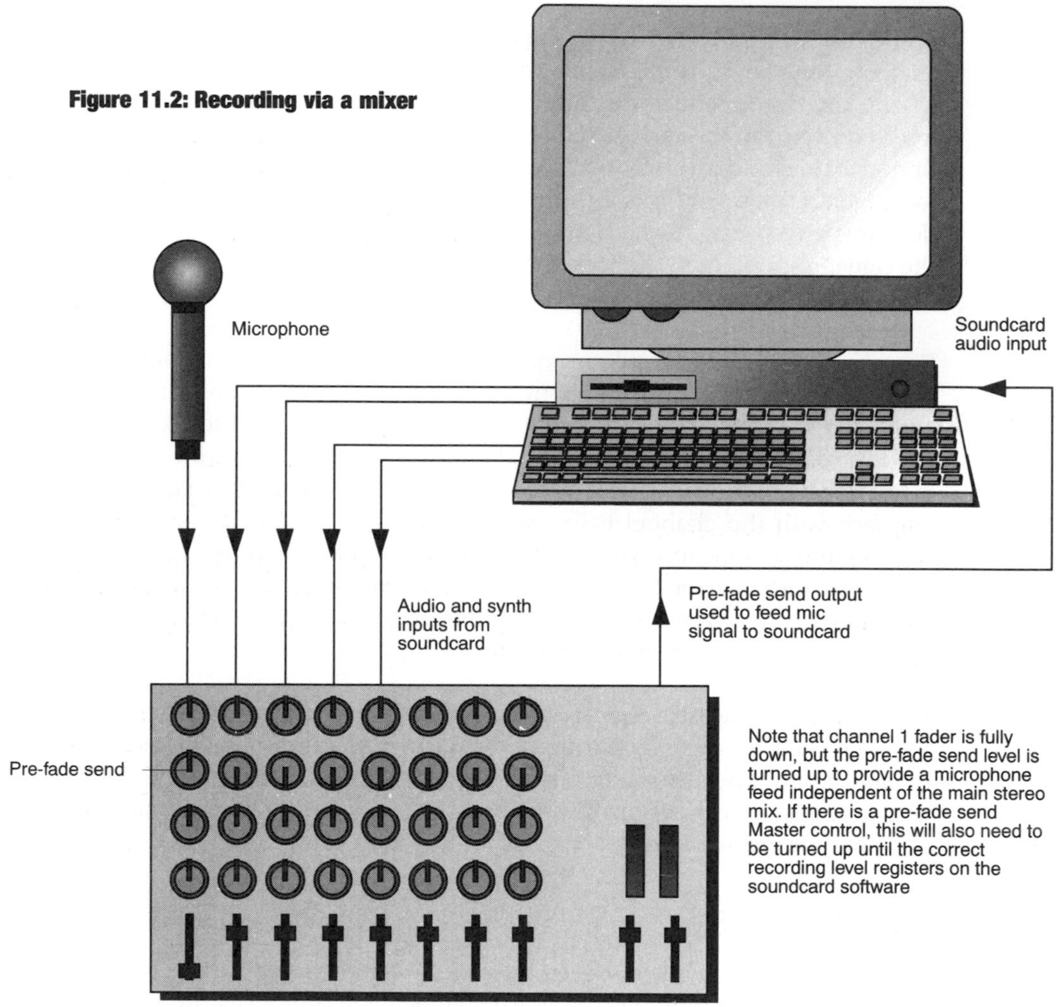
Microphone
Soundcard audio input
Audio and synth inputs from soundcard
Pre-fade send output used to feed mic signal to soundcard
Pre-fade send
Note that channel 1 fader is fully down, but the pre-fade send level is turned up to provide a microphone feed independent of the main stereo mix. If there is a pre-fade send Master control, this will also need to be turned up until the correct recording level registers on the soundcard software

buy a hardware adaptor that looks like a long multipin plug with MIDI sockets built into it. These often allow you to leave your joystick connected via a joystick thru socket, but I'm informed that some MIDI programs get upset if a joystick is left connected, so if in doubt, unplug it.

The limitation of a simple 'one-in, one-out' MIDI interface is that you can only drive 16 external MIDI channels. With today's synth modules, that usually means a single multitimbral instrument, but remember that the internal soundcards, other than possibly the daughterboard, use virtual MIDI ports. This is obviously good news if you're on a budget, as you can use your internal soundcard sounds at the same time as your external MIDI module and still only need one MIDI port.

If you need more ports to handle additional external synths, then you'll need a multi-port MIDI interface offering two, four or eight sets of MIDI outputs. These are discussed in more detail in the chapter on sequencing. A 'dumb' MIDI master keyboard can simply be connected to the MIDI In while a MIDI synth would need to be set to Local Off so that the synth section could be driven from the MIDI Out port of the computer. The implications of MIDI Local On and Off are explained in the chapter Introducing MIDI.

desktop versus studio

The PC-based MIDI/.WAV audio studio has the advantages of being inexpensive, compact and (once set up) convenient. With the addition of a mixer, a monitoring system, and possibly some outboard signal processing, you have the basis of a serious desktop music recording system, and as soundcards continue to become more powerful and better specified, you can upgrade your system a piece at a time without having to sell up and start from scratch.

Undoubtedly the more traditional MIDI studio, comprising racks of modules, sampler and drum machines, will be with us for very many years to come, but as the capabilities of PC-based systems continue to increase, the boundaries are bound to become blurred. By choosing your cards carefully, and by incorporating a small mixer plus a modest amount of external signal processing, you can build a serious desktop studio for less than you might once have paid for a stereo sampler.

software synthesis

Though not entirely at home in a chapter on soundcards, I'd like to introduce the concept of software-based synthesis (that uses the computer's own processing power rather than hardware, to create sounds). Once the domain of high powered university computers, software synthesis is becoming more practical as computers continue to increase in power. Obviously these packages use up some of the computer's processing power and memory, and depending on how sophisticated (and how well written), the software is, this can be anything from just a few per cent up to nearly the entire processing power of the system.

At the budget end of the market, software synthesis can rival budget soundcards for sound quality, and they tend to be GM compatible, but their main application is in the games market. They are very cheap, and may seem tempting, but with decent soundcards now being so affordable, it's probably better to pay the little extra for the real thing – this way you'll maximise your processing power and probably enjoy better sounds. However, there are advanced software synthesis systems that are more than mere emulations of cheap GM modules, and some of these are potentially very interesting. Check these out only once you've mastered your basic system.

chapter 12

mixers, monitors & effects

In any music system where two or more signals have to be blended together to form a single stereo signal, a mixer is required. In a computer-based system, internally generated sounds can be mixed internally using MIDI controller information to set things like level and pan, but if you have multiple soundcards or a combination of soundcards, external synth modules, and perhaps even a multitrack tape machine running in sync, there's no option but to use a mixer.

There's more to a mixer than simply mixing signals together – you can use it to change the level, pan position or tone control settings of individual inputs, and with the aid of an external effects processing box, you can add varying amounts of effects, such as reverb, to the various inputs. In fact mixing is where all your efforts are turned into a final artistic event, and for me, mixing is a very creative part of the music making process.

In principle, a mixing console is pretty straightforward. Mixers comprise several identical 'building blocks' known as channels, and the purpose of a channel is to change the level of the signal fed into it, to enable the signal to be EQed, and to provide variable feeds to external effect units. EQ or equalisation is just another way of describing a tone control. The output of the channel then passes through a pan control onto what is known as a stereo mix buss, a sort of two-lane audio highway, where the signals coming in from all the different channels are combined.

mic and line levels

Internally, mixers are designed to work within a particular range of signal levels – if you put in a signal level that's too high, the sound will be distorted, but if the level is too low, the sound will be too quiet, and very probably hissy as well. Microphones produce very small signals, so these have to be beefed up or amplified right at the start of the mixer channel. On more elaborate mixers, the mic amplifier might also be fitted with phantom power circuitry enabling it to be used with capacitor microphones. This might sound

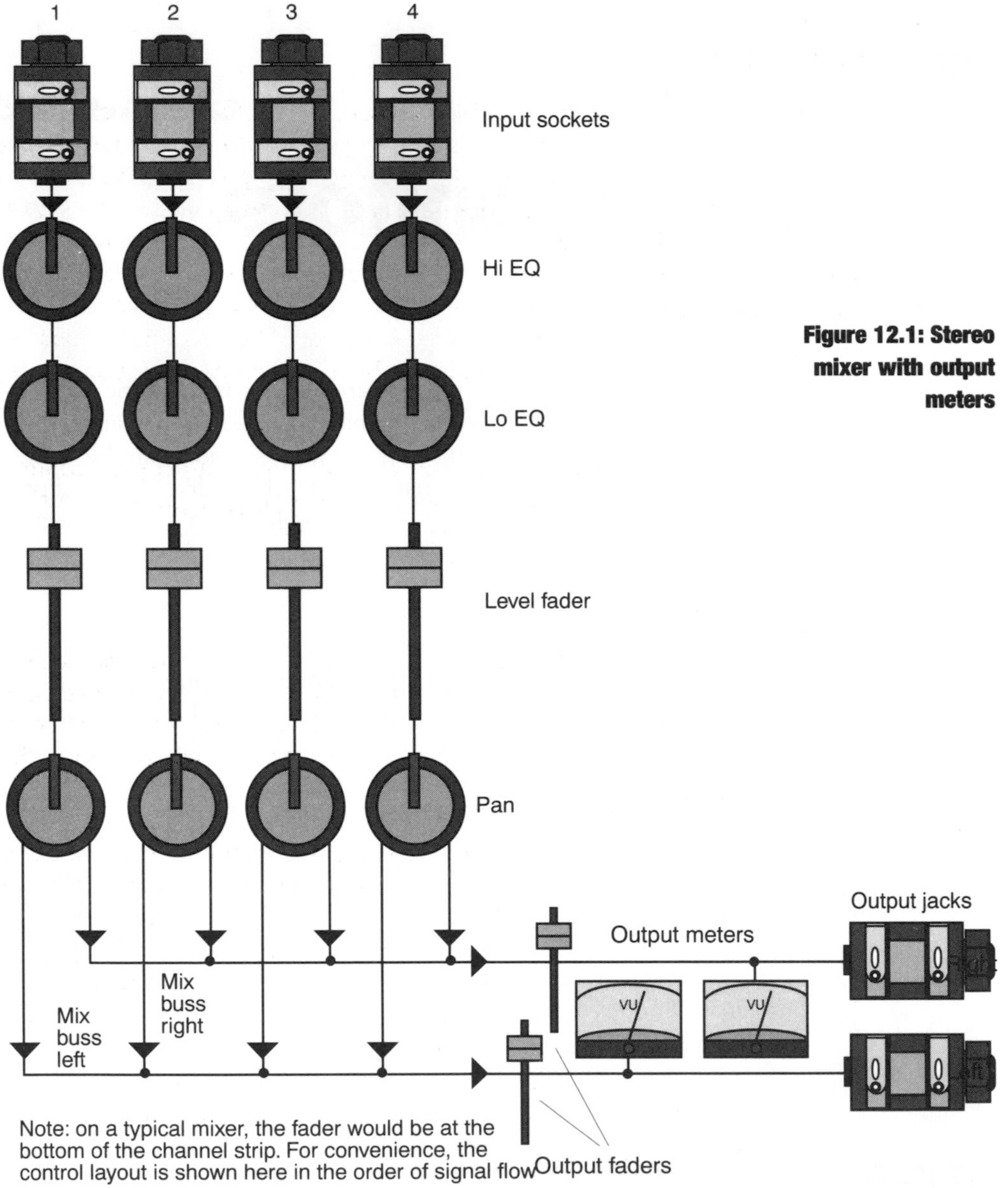

Figure 12.1: Stereo mixer with output meters

complicated, but all it means is that some types of studio microphone require power to operate, and a mixer with a phantom power facility provides it. Phantom power is not compatible with non-professional 'unbalanced' microphones, so if you don't need phantom power, ensure it is switched off before you plug in any microphones.

channel gain

Because not all microphones produce the same level of output, and because the output level also depends on how close and how loud the sound being recorded is, the microphone amplifier is invariably equipped with a gain control which determines the amount of amplification applied to the signal. In other words, the setting of the gain control relates to how much bigger the signal will be made. Line level signals (from electronic keyboards, modules, soundcard audio outputs, tape machines, CD players and so on) don't need to pass through the microphone amplifier, so mixer channels also have a line input. Normally only the channel's line or mic input may be used, not both at once.

The line input on a typical mixer will also be fitted with a gain control, because even line level signals vary, though on most basic mixers, a common control is used for both mic and line gain adjustment.

mixer channels

Figure 12.1 shows a simplified schematic of a four-channel mixer with simple bass and treble equalisation. Separate mic and line gain controls have been shown to aid clarity, but in practice, a single, shared control is more likely on a mixer of this type. Separate input sockets are shown for both the microphone and line input signals.

After the input gain stage comes the equalisation section which can be as simple as the bass/treble (also known as Hi\Lo) arrangement shown here, or there may be additional controls to adjust the mid-range of frequencies. Finally the signal level is controlled by a knob or fader before it passes to the stereo mix buss via the pan control, and sometimes an 'on' or mute switch. Leaving the pan control in the centre routes equal amounts of signal to the left and right busses, making the resulting sound (when reproduced over a stereo speaker system) appear to originate from midway between the speakers. Note that all four input channels are identical, and a larger mixer would have more input channels.

The combined signal on the mix busses passes through further amplification stages (known as mix amplifiers) controlled by the master level faders or knobs. These set the output level of the mixer, allowing it to send the correct signal level to the tape recorder on which you're recording your finished composition. The master fader may also be used to make controlled fade-outs at the end of songs. The diagram shows the controls arranged so as to make the signal flow easy to follow, but in practice, the channel fader is usually at the bottom of the strip for convenience of use.

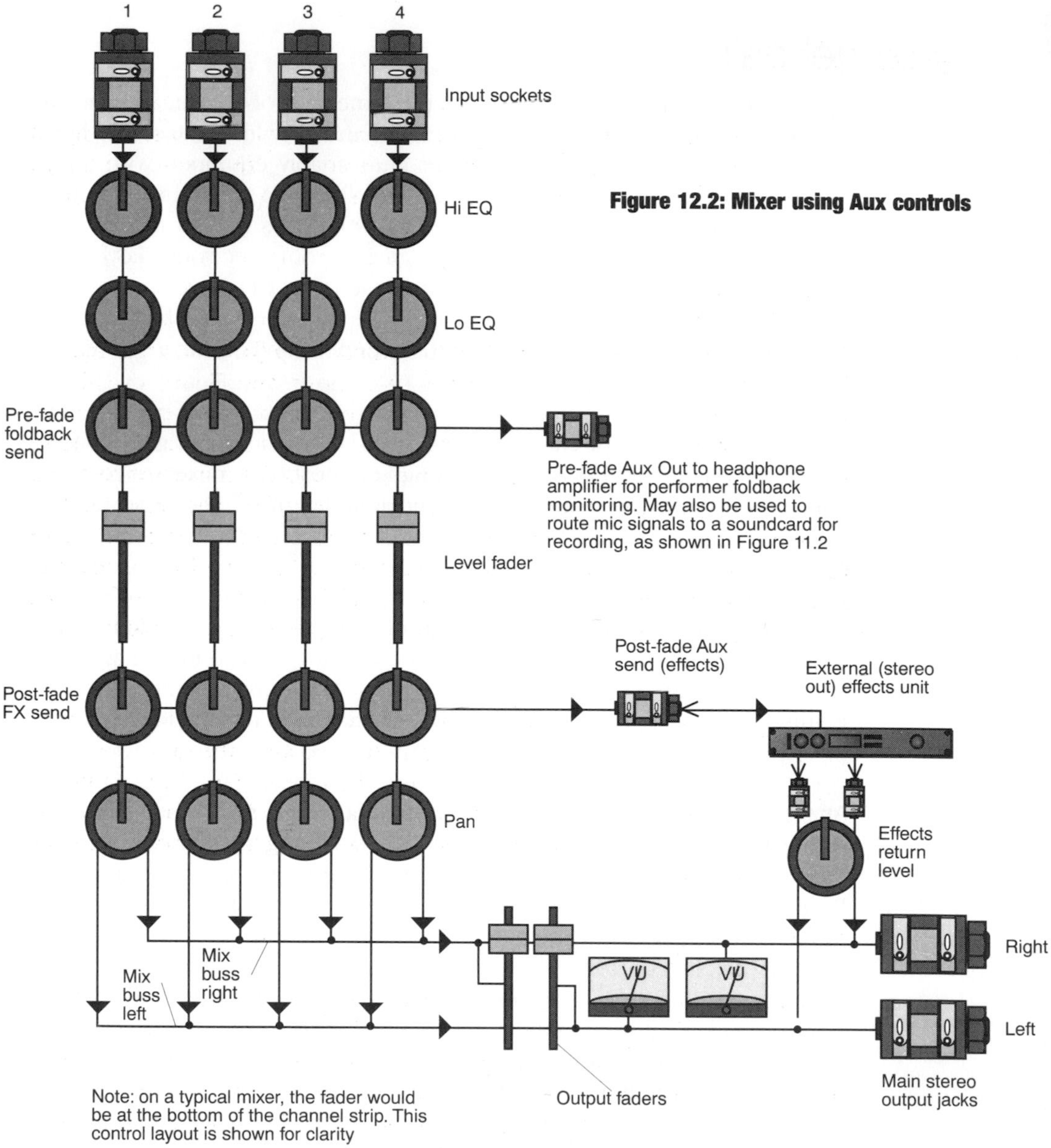

Figure 12.2: Mixer using Aux controls

Most mixers have an output level meter, which could take the form of a moving-coil meter with a physical pointer or it could be a row of LEDs (Light Emitting Diodes) arranged in the form of a ladder. A stereo mixer of this type is usually described in the form of 'something' into two; for example, a twelve into two (12:2) mixer has twelve input channels and two (left and right) outputs.

auxiliaries

So far then, we have the tools to change the levels of individual inputs, we can change the tonality using the EQ controls, and we can pan the signal anywhere from left to right in the mix. However, we also need to do things like add effects, and in a more sophisticated setup, we may wish to send a mix to the performer's headphones.

pre-fade send

Both effects and the performer's foldback monitoring (headphone mix), can be handled using the auxiliary controls on a mixer, and Figure 12.2 shows how these fit into the channel strip. Here you can see two new controls: Aux 1 and Aux 2, where aux is short for auxiliary. Aux 1 is simply another level control feeding a mono mix buss which runs across the mixer to the Aux 1 master level control and then to the Aux 1 output socket. The signal feeding the Aux 1 control is picked up from a point in the circuit before the channel fader, and so is known as a pre-fade send. The implication of this is that the Aux 1 signal level doesn't change if the channel fader is adjusted, so any mix set up using the pre-fade aux send will be completely independent of the channel faders.

Using a pre-fade send, the engineer can provide the musician with a monitor mix that is exactly to his or her liking rather than sending the same mix that's coming over the main monitor speakers. The overall Aux 1 mix is under control of the Aux 1 master level control, and the Aux 1 output would normally feed a headphone amplifier. You can't plug headphones directly into an Aux output.

post-fade send

For adding effects to the mix, we need to use the second aux control, Aux 2. This takes its feed from after the channel fader (post-fader), so its level is affected by changes in the channel fader setting. This way, when the channel signal level is turned up or down, the amount of signal sent to the external effects unit varies by a corresponding amount. In other words, regardless of the fader setting, the ratio of original sound and added effect remains the same.

By using different settings of the Aux 2 control on each channel, it is possible to send different amounts of each channel's signal to the same effects unit. When the output from this effect unit is added to the main stereo mix, this has the advantage that different amounts of the same effect can be added to different sounds in a mix. For example, one reverberation unit might be used to provide a rich reverb for the vocals, less reverb for the drums and little or none for the guitars and bass. Note: An effects unit used in conjunction with a channel aux send should be set up so that it produces only the effected sound and none of the original. This is usually accomplished by means of a mix control or mix parameters accessed from the front panel controls. In either case, the mix should be set to 100% effect, 0% dry.

effects returns

The output of the effect unit may be fed back into the mixer via spare input channels or via dedicated effects return inputs, also known as aux returns. Aux returns are electrically similar to input channels but have more basic facilities. Normally these are provided as a stereo pair of sockets and feed straight into the main stereo mix, usually via a level control.

A spare input channel (or pair panned hard left and right for stereo) may be used as an effect return, but you must ensure that the corresponding aux send (in this case Aux 2) is turned down on the return channel, otherwise the effect signal will 'feed back', building up to a howl.

monitor speakers

If you're interested in producing high quality mixes of your compositions, you need an accurate pair of monitor speakers, otherwise you won't really know how your music sounds. A theoretically perfect speaker would reproduce the entire audio spectrum with no distortion or coloration, but because of the limitations of both physics and cost, there are inevitably compromises.

So-called nearfield monitors have become popular, both in professional studios and in home music studios. These are small, but nominally accurate, loudspeakers that can be used close to the listening position, thus helping to cut out any undesirable effects from the acoustics of the room. The closer you are to the speakers, the greater proportion of direct sound is heard compared with the sound reflected from the room. Furthermore, the closer you sit to a speaker, the less power you need to produce an adequate monitoring level.

Small hi-fi speakers are often suitable, providing they are selected for honesty rather than an ability to flatter the music, but don't expect to get deep bass from small speakers. In reality, a very deep bass response is undesirable, because unless the room is acoustically designed to handle it, the results will be unpredictable, leading to inaccurate mixes that don't sound right on other audio systems.

A good two-way loudspeaker system with a bass driver of between five and eight inches in diameter is usually more than adequate for home studio use, especially when used in the near field. This may be powered from a hi-fi amplifier, but don't stint on the power, otherwise your system might not be able to handle peaks, such as drum beats, cleanly. Around 50 watts per channel should be considered a realistic minimum, even if you tend to monitor at moderate levels. Use proper heavy duty speaker cable, not bell wire, but don't be conned into buying anything too esoteric – it won't make any significant difference.

where to mix

Domestic living rooms and bedrooms tend to absorb quite a lot of sound, because of the amount of carpeting, curtains and soft furnishings, but because we're used to listening to music under these conditions, a studio with a similar acoustic characteristic makes a perfectly workable alternative to a purpose built studio. However, because no monitoring systems or rooms sound exactly alike, it's important to compare your own mixes with commercial music played back over the same system in the same room. Bedrooms or domestic rooms with carpets and soft furnishings are perfectly adequate for mixing music demos, and even some commercial projects. If your room seems too lively or reverberant, hanging rugs or heavy curtains on the rear wall, and at either side of the mixing position, often helps.

speaker positions

Speakers should be arranged so that they form two points of an equilateral triangle with the listener at the apex. The speakers should be angled inwards so that they point directly at the head of listener, and they should be at around head height. Consult the instructions that come with the speakers to see whether they work best close to or a little further away, and if at all possible, avoid putting speakers in or close to corners as this has an unpredictable effect on the way the bass end will sound. You may seem to get more bass by doing this, but in reality, you'll probably EQ your mix to compensate for it, so when you play your songs back on anybody else's system, they'll sound bass light. Figure 12.3 shows the position of the monitor speakers relative to the listener.

using effects

Whereas conventional instruments are usually played in real acoustic spaces to give them character, electronic instruments, or indeed 'acoustic' sounds recorded in an acoustically 'dead' studio, have to rely on electronic effects

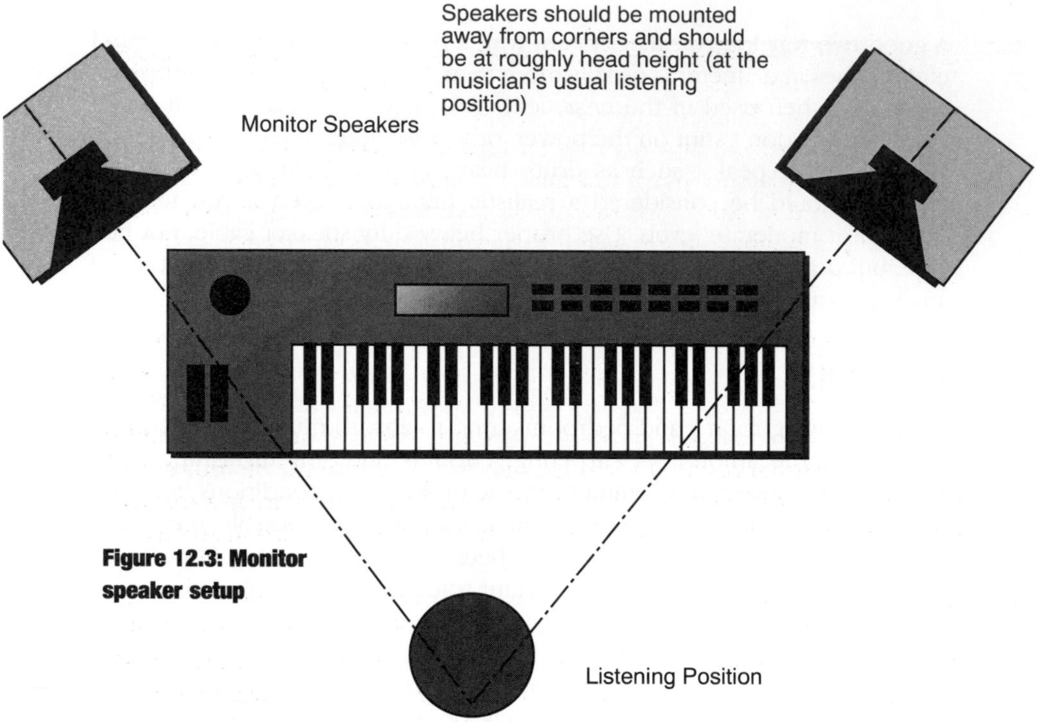
Speakers should be mounted away from corners and should be at roughly head height (at the musician's usual listening position)
Monitor Speakers
Listening Position

Figure 12.3: Monitor speaker setup

to give them interest and realism. In today's MIDI studio, many instruments, modules and soundcards come with their own effects, though if these are inadequate in any way, external effects may also be connected via a mixer. Wherever your effects come from, the basic principle is the same, and the purpose of this section is to describe the more common effects and their applications. If you don't want to get involved with these just yet, simply use your instrument or soundcard default settings. Most default settings tend to be slightly heavy on the effects, but they are fine for demo work, or for just getting to know your system.

reverberation

Western music is invariably performed indoors where a degree of room reverberation is part of the sound. Conversely, most pop music is recorded in a relatively small, dry-sounding studio, so artificial reverberation has to be added to create a sense of space and reality.

Reverberation is created naturally when a sound is reflected and re-reflected from the surfaces within a room, hall or other large structure. Clap your hands in a large hall or church and you'll hear reverberation. Digital reverberation units simulate this natural occurrence by creating thousands of random echoes every second, and most provide a choice of treatments, from small rooms to great echoing caverns. Though long reverb times are initially impressive, most musical applications require a relatively short reverb time of between 1.5 and 4 seconds. A popular reverb setting is the 'plate', a patch designed to simulate the mechanical plates that were used in studios before digital reverb was developed. The plate setting has a bright, diffuse sound that works well on virtually anything, from drums to vocals.

Electronic reverb devices produce a stereo output – that's how they create the illusion of spaciousness, even though the sound you're treating may be mono. The reverb unit's outputs should be panned hard left and right, regardless of whereabouts in the mix the original, dry signal is panned if you want a natural result. If the effects are plugged into the stereo returns of a mixer, this will happen automatically, and if the effects are internal to a soundcard or module, the added effects will be also be heard in stereo.

On an artistic level, busy music works best with shorter reverb settings, while slower, less complicated music can benefit from longer settings. It also helps to avoid putting much, if any, reverb on bass sounds as this can make your mix sound muddy. Listen to your records and see how reverb has been used there. You'll probably be surprised at how little is required to achieve the necessary result.

echo

Echo was extensively used on both guitars and vocals in the 60s and 70s, though at the time it was created using a tape loop rather than digital electronics, as it is today. Unlike reverb, echo (sometimes called Delay), produces distinct, evenly spaced repeats, and if you can set the delay time to a multiple of the tempo of the song, some very interesting rhythmic effects can be created. Try echo on vocals, guitars and keyboard sounds.

chorus and flanging

Chorus is based on a short delay combined with pitch modulation to create the effect of two or more instruments playing the same part. In effect, the original part is accompanied by a slightly delayed part that varies slightly in pitch, thus creating the ensemble illusion.

Flanging is also a modulated delay effect, but the delay time is very short and feedback is used to create a much stronger effect, not unlike the old tape 'phasing'. Both these treatments work well on synth pad sounds such as strings and are best used in stereo where they create a sense of movement as well as width. Because flanging is quite a dramatic effect, it may be best used sparingly.

pitch shifters

Pitch shifters are to be found in almost all external multieffects units, though they tend not to be included in soundcards. Furthermore, when you're working purely with MIDI sounds, you can change pitch simply by transposing a part.

As the name implies, pitch shifters can change the pitch of an original audio signal, usually by up to one octave in either direction. Small pitch shifts are useful for creating detuning or doubling effects – a nice alternative to chorus – while shifts of whole semitones can be used to create octaves or parallel harmonies.

glossary of terms

ADSR:

Envelope generator with Attack, Sustain, Decay and Release parameters. This is a simple type of envelope generator and was first used on early analogue synthesizers. This form of envelope generator continues to be popular on modern instruments. See Decay for more details.

active sensing:

A system used to verify that a MIDI connection is working, that involves the sending device sending frequent short messages to the receiving device to reassure it that all is well. If these active sensing messages stop for any reason,the receiving device will recognise a fault condition and switch off all notes. Not all MIDI devices support active sensing.

aftertouch:

A means of generating a control signal based on how much pressure is applied to the keys of a MIDI keyboard. Most instruments that support this do not have independent pressure sensing for all keys, but rather detect the overall pressure by means of a sensing strip running beneath the keys. Aftertouch may be used to control such functions as vibrato depth, filter brightness, loudness and so on.

analogue:

Circuitry that uses a continually changing voltage or current to represent a signal. The origin of the term is that the electrical signal can be thought of as being 'analogous' to the original signal.

amplitude:

The actual level of a signal, usually measured in volts.

attenuate:

To make lower in level.

audio frequency:

Signals in the human audio range: nominally 20Hz to 20kHz.

band pass filter (bpf):

Filter that removes or attenuates frequencies above and below the frequency at which it is set. Frequencies within the band are emphasised. Bandpass filters are often used in synthesizers as tone shaping elements.

CV:

Control Voltage used to control the pitch of an oscillator or filter frequency in an analogue synthesizer. Most analogue synthesizers follow a one volt per octave convention, though there are exceptions. To use a pre-MIDI analogue synthesizer under MIDI control, a MIDI to CV converter is required.

channel:

In the context of MIDI, channel refers to one of 16 possible data channels over which MIDI data may be sent. The organisation of data by channels means that up to 16 different MIDI instruments or parts may be addressed using a single cable.

In the context of mixing consoles, a channel is a single strip of controls relating to one input.

chase:

Term describing the process whereby a slave device attempts to synchronise itself with a master device. In the context of a MIDI sequence, 'chase' may also involve chasing events – looking back to earlier positions in the song to see if there are any program changes or other events that need to be acted upon.

cutoff frequency:

The frequency above or below which attenuation begins in a filter circuit.

cycle:

One complete vibration of a sound source or its electrical equivalent. One cycle per second is expressed as 1Hertz (Hz).

decay:

The progressive reduction in amplitude of a sound or electrical signal over time. In the context of an ADSR envelope shaper, the Decay phase starts as soon as the Attack phase has reached its maximum level. In the Decay phase, the signal level drops until it reaches the Sustain level set by the user. The signal then remains at this level until the key is released, at which point the Release phase is entered.

digital:

Electronic system which represents data and signals in the form of codes comprising 1s and 0s.

dma:

Direct Memory Access: part of a computer operating system that allows peripheral devices to communicate directly with the computer memory without going via the central processor or CPU.

envelope:

The way in which the level of a sound or signal varies over time.

envelope generator:

A circuit capable of generating a control signal which represents the envelope of the sound you want to recreate. This may then be used to control the level of an oscillator or other sound source, though envelopes may also be used to control filter or modulation settings. The most common example is the ADSR generator.

event:

In MIDI terms, an event is a single unit of MIDI data, such as a note being turned on or off, a piece of controller information, a program change, and so on.

file:

A meaningful list of data stored in digital form. A Standard MIDI File is a specific type of file designed to allow sequence information to be interchanged between different types of sequencer.

filter:

A type of powerful tone shaping network used in synthesizers to create tonal sweeps and wah effects. The term Filter may also be found in some MIDI sequencers where there is provision to exclude or filter out certain types of MIDI data, for example, Aftertouch.

gate:

An electrical signal that is generated whenever a key is depressed on an electronic keyboard. This is used to trigger envelope generators and other events that need to be synchronised to key action.

general midi:

An addition to the basic MIDI spec to assure a minimum level of compatibility when playing back GM format song files. The specification covers type and program number of sounds, minimum levels of polyphony and multitimbrality, response to controller information and so on.

gm reset:

A universal Sysex command which activates the General MIDI mode on a GM instrument. The same command also sets all controllers to their default values and switches off any notes still playing by means of an All Notes Off message.

gs:

Roland's own extension to the General MIDI protocol.

high pass filter (hpf):

A filter which attenuates frequencies below its cutoff frequency.

irq:

Interrupt Request. Part of the operating system of a computer that allows a connected device to request attention from the processor in order to transfer data to it or from it.

lsb:

Least Significant Byte. If a piece of data has to be conveyed as two bytes, one byte represents high value numbers and the other low value numbers, much in the same way as tens and units function in the decimal system. The high value, or most significant part of the message, is called the Most Significant Byte or MSB.

local on/off:

A function to allow the keyboard and sound generating section of a keyboard synthesizer to be used independently of each other.

low frequency oscillator (lfo):

An oscillator used as a modulation source, usually below 20Hz. The most common LFO waveshape is the sine wave, though there is often a choice of sine, square, triangular and sawtooth waveforms.

low pass filter (lpf):

A filter which attenuates frequencies above its cutoff frequency.

midi:

Musical Instrument Digital Interface.

midi bank change:

A type of controller message used to select alternate banks of MIDI Programs where access to more than 128 programs is required.

midi controller:

A term used to describe the physical interface by means of which the musician plays the MIDI synthesizer or other sound generator. Examples of controllers are keyboards, drum pads, wind synths and so on.

midi control change:

Also knows as MIDI Controllers or Controller Data, these messages convey positional information relating to performance controls such as wheels, pedals, switches and other devices. This information can be used to control functions such as vibrato depth, brightness, portamento, effects levels, and many other parameters.

midi file:

A standard file format for storing song data recorded on a MIDI sequencer in such a way as to allow it to be read by other makes or models of MIDI sequencer.

midi implementation chart:

A chart, usually found in MIDI product manuals, which provides information as to which MIDI features are supported. Supported features are marked with a 0 while unsupported features are marked with an X. Additional information may be provided, such as the exact form of the Bank Change message.

midi merge:

A device or sequencer function that enables two or more streams of MIDI data to be combined.

midi module:

Sound generating device with no integral keyboard.

multitimbral module:

MIDI Sound Source capable of producing several different sounds at the same time and controlled on different MIDI channels.

midi mode:

MIDI information can be interpreted by the receiving MIDI instrument in a number of ways, the most common being polyphonically on a single MIDI channel (Poly-Omni Off mode). Omni mode enables a MIDI Instrument to play all incoming data regardless of channel.

midi note number:

Every key on a MIDI keyboard has its own note number ranging from 0 to 127, where 60 represents middle C. Some systems use C3 as middle C while others use C4.

midi note on:

MIDI message sent when note is played (key pressed).

midi note off:

Message sent when key is released.

midi out:

The MIDI connector used to send data from a master device to the MIDI In of a connected slave device.

midi port:

The MIDI connections of a MIDI compatible device. A Multiport, in the context of a MIDI interface, is a device with multiple MIDI output sockets, each capable of carrying data relating to a different set of 16 MIDI channels. Multiports are the only means of exceeding the limitations imposed by 16 MIDI channels.

midi program change:

Type of MIDI message used to change sound patches on a remote module or the effects patch on a MIDI effects unit.

midi splitter:

Alternative term for MIDI Thru box.

midi thru box:

Device which splits the MIDI Out signal of a master instrument or sequencer to avoid daisy chaining. Powered circuitry is used to 'buffer' the outputs so as to prevent problems when many pieces of equipment are driven from a single MIDI output.

midi in:

The socket used to receive information from a master controller or from the MIDI Thru socket of a slave unit.

midi out:

The socket on a master controller or sequencer used to send MIDI information to the slave units.

midi sync:

A description of the synchronisation systems available to MIDI users – MIDI Clock and MIDI Time Code.

midi thru:

The socket on a slave unit used to feed the MIDI In socket of the next unit in line.

non-registered parameter number:

An addition to the basic MIDI spec that allows Controllers 98 and 99 to be used to control non-standard parameters relating to particular models of synthesizer. This is an alternative to using System Exclusive data to achieve the same ends, though NRPNs tend to be used mainly by Yamaha and Roland instruments.

oscillator:

Circuit designed to generate a periodic electrical waveform.

patch:

Alternative term for Program, referring to a single programmed sound within a synthesizer that can be called up using Program Change commands. MIDI effects units and samplers also have patches.

pitch bend:

A special control message specifically designed to produce a change in pitch in response to the movement of a pitch bend wheel or lever. Pitch bend data can be recorded and edited, just like any other MIDI controller data, even though it isn't part of the Controller message group.

polyphony:

The ability of an instrument to play two or more notes simultaneously. An instrument which can only play one note at a time is described as monophonic.

portamento:

A gliding effect that allows a sound to change pitch at a gradual rate, rather than abruptly, when a new key is pressed or MIDI note sent.

pressure:

Alternative term for Aftertouch.

pulse wave:

Similar to a square wave but non-symmetrical. Pulse waves sound brighter and thinner than square waves, making them useful in the synthesis of reed instruments. The timbre changes according to the mark/space ratio of the waveform.

pulse width modulation:

A means of modulating the duty cycle (mark/space ratio) of a pulse wave. This changes the timbre of the basic tone; LFO modulation of pulse width can be used to produce a pseudo-chorus effect.

q:

A measure of the resonant properties of a filter. The higher the Q, the more resonant the filter and the narrower the range of frequencies that are allowed to pass. This will be explained in more detail when we talk about filters later in the series.

quantise:

A means of moving notes recorded in a MIDI sequencer so that they line up with user defined subdivisions of a musical bar, for example, 16s. The facility may be used to correct timing errors, but over-quantisation can remove the human feel from a performance.

ram:

Abbreviation for Random Access Memory. This is a type of memory used by computers for the temporary storage of programs and data, and all data is lost when the power is turned off. For that reason, work needs to be saved to disk if it is not to be lost.

rom:

Abbreviation for Read Only Memory. This is a permanent or non-volatile type of memory containing data that can't be changed. Operating systems are often stored on ROM as the memory remains intact when the power is removed.

e-prom:

Similar to ROM, but the information on the chip can be erased and replaced using special equipment.

release:

The rate at which a signal amplitude decays once a key has been released.

resonance:

The characteristic of a filter that allows it to selectively pass a narrow range of frequencies. See Q.

ring modulator:

A device that accepts and processes two input signals in a particular way. The output signal does not contain any of the original input signal but instead comprises new frequencies based on the sum and difference of the input signals' frequency components. Ring Modulators will be covered in depth later in the series. The best known application of Ring Modulation is the creation of Dalek voices but it may also be used to create dramatic instrumental textures. Depending on the relationships between the input signals, the results may either be musical or extremely dissonant – for example, ring modulation can be used to create bell-like tones. (The term 'Ring' is used because the original circuit which produced the effect used a ring of diodes.)

sample and hold:

Usually refers to a feature whereby random values are generated at regular intervals and then used to control another function such as pitch or filter frequency. Sample and hold circuits were also used in old analogue synthesizers to 'remember' the note being played after a key had been released.

scsi:

Small Computer System Interface (pronounced SKUZZI). An interfacing system for using hard drives, scanners, CD-ROM drives and similar peripherals with a computer. Each SCSI device has its own ID number and no two SCSI devices in the same chain must be set to the same number. The last SCSI device in the chain should be terminated, either via an internal terminator, where provided, or via a plug-in terminator fitted to a free SCSI socket.

sequencer:

Device for recording and replaying MIDI data, usually in a multitrack format, allowing complex compositions to be built up a part at a time.

sine wave:

The waveform of a pure tone with no harmonics.

slave:

A MIDI device under the control of a master device, such as a sequencer or master keyboard.

square wave:

A symmetrical rectangular waveform. Square waves contain a series of odd harmonics.

sawtooth wave:

So called because it resembles the teeth of a saw, this waveform contains only even harmonics.

subtractive synthesis:

The process of creating a new sound by filtering and shaping a raw, harmonically complex waveform.

timbre:

The tonal 'colour' of a sound.

tremolo:

Modulation of the amplitude of a sound using an LFO.

triangle wave:

Symmetrical triangular shaped wave containing odd harmonics only, but with a lower harmonic content than the square wave.

velocity:

The rate at which a key is depressed. This may be used to control loudness (to simulate the response of instruments such as pianos) or other parameters on later synthesizers.

voice:

The capacity of a synthesizer to play a single musical note. An instrument capable of playing 16 simultaneous notes is said to be a 16-voice instrument.

vibrato:

Pitch modulation using an LFO to modulate a VCO.

waveform:

A graphic representation of the way in which a sound wave or electrical wave varies with time.

xg:

Yamaha's alternative to Roland's GS system for enhancing the General MIDI protocol so as to provide additional banks of patches and further editing facilities.

ALSO AVAILABLE FROM SANCTUARY TECHNIQUES

RECORDING & PRODUCTION TECHNIQUES

by Paul White

ISBN 1 86074 188 6

£11.95/$17.95

This book takes a practical approach to demystifying the various techniques used to record and produce contemporary music. Aimed at the recording musician, the techniques described in this book are equally applicable to the home studio environment or the professional studio. In plain English, clearly illustrated with copious diagrams, **Recording & Production Techniques** takes the reader through planning a recording session, getting the best performances from the artists and producing the best possible mix making creative use of effects and processors.

The book concludes with an invaluable section on master tape formats and an overview of the various processes involved in duplicating CDs, cassettes and vinyl records. Features traditional analogue equipment as well as digital machines, including tapeless recording, plus a full glossary.
Clearly illustrated with comprehensive diagrams.

HOME RECORDING MADE EASY

by Paul White

ISBN 1 86074 199 1

£11.95/$14.95

When Paul White started recording, the most sophisticated equipment he could afford was a four-track tape deck and a very simple mixer. Yet that basic system taught him virtually all he needed to know about recording, and he learned a lot from having to think his way around its limitations. Nowadays professional recording studios are full of stupendously expensive equipment. Studio time adds to the cost. However, by choosing home recording equipment carefully, and by using it properly, you can create professional demos or even independent release quality recordings for very little outlay.

All you need to know to make your own recordings is presented here in clear terms with the minimum of jargon. Using the information in this book, you'll be able to make your own professional sounding recordings, no matter how tight your budget.
Clearly illustrated with comprehensive diagrams.

MUSIC TECHNOLOGY – A SURVIVOR'S GUIDE

by Paul White

ISBN 1 86074 209 2

£11.95/$14.95

Written in Paul White's jargon-free, thoroughly comprehensive style, this book highlights common problems in recording and mixing music, addresses equipment dilemmas and does some troubleshooting. Most importantly it provides answers. It discusses the debate on MIDI recording versus conventional multitracking, the basics of soundproofing, how to rescue an unsatisfactory mix, how to put together an accurate monitoring system and how to organise a recording session to get the best results with the fewest problems.

It also provides an overview of equipment types: for example, the pros and cons of hard disk recording compared to analogue and the difference between the various types of studio outboard equipment including compressors and reverb units. Finally Paul covers the hype and reality of vintage equipment.

Clearly illustrated with comprehensive diagrams.

RHYTHM

A STEP BY STEP GUIDE TO UNDERSTANDING RHYTHM FOR GUITAR

by David Mead

ISBN 1 86074 198 3

£19.99/$17.95

Most guitarists don't read music. Fact. They prefer to take the easier route of reading tablature. But tablature, unlike standard notation, includes no rhythmic information. Unless you read music you won't understand a piece's rhythmic content, which makes it almost impossible for the non-reading guitar student to learn anything he has either never heard, or is in any way unfamiliar with. Imagine a book which lays out all you need to know to develop a razor sharp sense of timing with progressive exercises. One which even teaches you to read rhythmic notation painlessly. This is that book.

Rhythm drastically simplifies the task of reading rhythm: dividing it into reading pitch and rhythmic notation. Although designed to teach rhythm from scratch, the book includes several examples far more complex than anything the majority of players would ever come across in the field – that way the player is prepared for anything he or she might be asked to play in any environment. Also included are regular assignments where the reader is tested on what he or she has learned so far.

Includes one hour CD, full notation, chord boxes and tab.

HOT COUNTRY

A COMPREHENSIVE GUIDE TO LEAD AND RHYTHM COUNTRY GUITAR PLAYING

by Lee Hodgson

ISBN 1 86074 138 X

£19.99/$17.95

Whether you're a pro eager to add to your stylistic and technical abilities, or a newcomer who's drawn to that clean, twangy country sound, **Hot Country** offers more than any other package: more than 150 licks, solos plus backing tracks, practical advice and CD demos of lead and rhythm guitar including a large chord vocabulary section and much more.

You don't need a hat, just your guitar and a passion to play some hot country. It also includes a foreword by Albert Lee, leading country picker and former guitarist for Eric Clapton.
Includes one hour CD, full notation, chord boxes and tab.

THE JAZZ STANDARD

by Frank Evans

ISBN 1 86074 163 0

£19.99/$19.95

The Jazz Standard contains more than twenty classic pieces by many of the greatest composers ever, from Richard Rodgers to Duke Ellington, George Gershwin to Cole Porter, arranged for solo guitar. Among the pieces included are 'Georgia On My Mind', 'My Funny Valentine', 'But Not For Me', 'Ev'ry Time We Say Goodbye', 'Tangerine', 'Prelude To A Kiss', 'Misty', 'Manhattan', 'Here's That Rainy Day', 'Sweet Lorraine' and 'Like Someone In Love'.
Includes one hour CD, full notation and tab.

PHIL HILBORNE'S A-Z OF GREAT GUITAR RIFFS – VOLUMES I & II

by Phil Hilborne

ISBN 1 86074 153 3 (Vol I)/1 86074 207 6 (Vol II)

£19.99/$19.95 (each volume)

The two books in this series form the most comprehensive collection yet of classic intros, rock riffs and signature guitar parts. Aerosmith, Bon Jovi, Cream, Dixie Dregs, Eagles, Vince Furnier, Rory Gallagher, Jimi Hendrix, Tony Iommi, Eric Johnson, Lenny Kravitz, Led Zeppelin and Metallica are covered in Volume I and Nirvana, Ozzy Osbourne, The Police, Queen, Randy Rhoads, Michael Schenker, Thin Lizzy, U2, Van Halen, The Who, King's X, Angus and Malcolm Young and ZZ Top in Volume II. With up to ten examples from each artist **A-Z** is an invaluable encyclopaedia of great playing and presents an excellent way for any guitarist to expand and develop their own repertoire. Available Spring 1998.
Includes one hour CD, full notation, chord boxes and tab.

LEGENDS

HOW TO PLAY LIKE THE WORLD'S GREATEST GUITARISTS

by Adrian Clark

ISBN 1 86074 220 3

£19.99/$17.95

If you've ever wondered what it is that your guitar heroes can do that sets them apart from other players, then here is the answer. In **Legends** Adrian Clark reveals the playing secrets of the guitar greats, from Jeff Beck to Ritchie Blackmore, Charlie Christian to Jimi Hendrix, Django Reinhardt to Joe Satriani. Each guitarist's trademark licks and tricks of the trade are written out in standard notation and tab for you to learn, with each example played on the accompanying CD for easy reference. Working through each player, the reader will be offered hints on technique in a way that encourages further experimentation away from the book. Using the detailed examples given, you'll soon build up your own musical vocabulary and be able to not only play, but compose in the style of your heroes.

Each chapter also features a biography of the player, plus a breakdown of what gear he uses and recommended further listening tips. Other artists include Eddie Van Halen, Brian May, Pete Townshend, Chuck Berry, Kurt Cobain, Jimmy Page, Johnny Marr, Stevie Ray Vaughan, Albert Lee and many, many more.
Includes one hour CD, full notation, chord boxes and tab.

GIANTS OF BLUES

LEARN TO PLAY BLUES GUITAR LIKE THE ALL-TIME GREATS, FROM ROBERT JOHNSON TO ERIC CLAPTON

by Neville Marten

ISBN 1 86074 211 4

£19.99/$17.95

Blues guitar is the most passionate and emotional style there is, and therefore one of the hardest to teach. But there are lessons to be learned from the world's greatest players, which can not only make you appreciate their talent, but can give an insight into how you too can achieve their results. Tracing the history of blues guitar from Robert Johnson through to Eric Clapton – via John Lee Hooker, Stevie Ray Vaughan, Jimi Hendrix, Peter Green and many more – Neville Marten explains each player's definitive techniques, teaching how to emulate their solos, for example, and how to develop their tricks to expand your own musical vocabulary. Lessons on playing styles, personal trademarks and characteristics are written clearly in notation and tab, as well as played in full on the CD. By following the examples in the book, the reader should then be ready to test his learning by playing along to each artist's backing track on the CD. Biographical information assesses each artist historically in the genre's development, while the musical traditions from generation to generation are examined.
Includes one hour CD, full notation, chord boxes and tab.

LIVE & KICKING

A HISTORY OF THE ROCK CONCERT INDUSTRY

by Mark Cunningham with Andy Wood

ISBN 1 86074 217 3

£9.99/$14.95

Following the best selling **Good Vibrations – A History Of Record Production**,this book tells how today's concert industry became a complex business and a balance of artistry and economics. From the pre-war era of the Music Hall, it follows developments in primitive amplification and loudspeaker technology, through the dawn of psychedelic and progressive rock in the late 1960s, to the contemporary science of concert sound and multi-media stage and set designs.

A fly on the wall insight into life on the road, the book offers interviews with leading sound and lighting designers, road crew personnel, production managers, promoters and artists and focuses on classic tours and shows, including exclusive material from U2's 1997 Pop Mart tour. **Live & Kicking** is illustrated by more than one hundred colour rare photographs and pieces of tour memorabilia and features a foreword by leading concert promoter, Harvey Goldsmith CBE.

SEVENTEEN WATTS?

THE FIRST 20 YEARS OF BRITISH ROCK GUITAR, THE MUSICIANS AND THEIR STORIES

by Mo Foster

ISBN 1 86074 182 7

£19.99/$29.95

In the early sixties Mo Foster's school band, The Tradewinds, played with primitive amplifiers – little Selmers and converted radiograms, five watts each at the most. Bracing themselves for fame, the band discussed upgrading to the wedge-shaped blue and white, seventeen-watt Watkins Dominator amplifier which, at £38 10/-, they could afford between them. But the band was divided: did they really need seventeen watts? Twenty years on, touring with Jeff Beck, Mo's bass rig alone was 1,500 watts.

Seventeen Watts? chronicles the rise to pre-eminence of rock guitar in Britain, featuring contributions from scores of players – Jeff Beck, Ritchie Blackmore, Eric Clapton, Lonnie Donegan, Roger Glover, George Harrison, Mark Knopfler, Hank Marvin, Gary Moore, Pino Palladino, Rick Parfitt, John Paul Jones, Gerry Rafferty, Francis Rossi, Mike Rutherford, Andy Summers, Bert Weedon, Bruce Welch, Muff Winwood... Semi-autobiographical and illustrated by period advertisements, memorabilia and rare photographs, many from the artists' private collections, **Seventeen Watts?** is idiosyncratic, charming, naive, optimistic, but above all very funny.

MIND OVER MATTER

IMAGES OF PINK FLOYD

by Storm Thorgerson

ISBN 1 86074 206 8

£30.00/$39.95

Mind Over Matter is a book of images used by Pink Floyd throughout their history, starting with the *Saucerful Of Secrets* LP in 1968, through *Dark Side Of The Moon* in 1973 up until *The Division Bell* in 1994 and *Pulse* in 1995.

Primarily the work of one man – Storm Thorgerson – it comprises ninety per cent of Pink Floyd's total output. Focusing on design and photography, it is a showcase for approximately one hundred artworks, including never before seen roughs, rejects and variations with text which deals with method and technique, relevance and meaning, passion and business. But this book is also about the music industry, about developing a particular and successful kind of profile, and finding a way of dealing with the difficult issue of packaging. At its core the crucial debate: art versus commerce.